APPOINTED TIMES SERIES

חג פסח
KHAG PESAKH
PASSOVER

Rabbi Jim Appel

חַג פֶּסַח KHAG PESAKH, PASSOVER
Appointed Times Series - Passover
Copyright © 2019 by Rabbi James Appel

All rights reserved. No part of this book may be reproduced, stored in a retrieval system or transmitted in any way by any means—electronic, mechanical, photocopy, recording or otherwise—without the prior permission of the copyright holder, except for short excerpts acredited to the author, per the USA copyright laws.

Printed in the USA
ISBN 978-1-941173-36-7

1. Jewish Holidays 2. Messianic Judaism 3. Spiritual Growth

Published by

Olive Press Messianic and Christian Publisher
www.olivepresspublisher.com
olivepressbooks@gmail.com

Messianic & Christian Publisher

    Our prayer at Olive Press is that we may help make the Word of Adonai fully known, that it spread rapidly and be glorified everywhere. We hope our books help open people's eyes so they will turn from darkness to Light and from the power of the adversary to God and to trust in יֵשׁוּעַ Yeshua (Jesus). (From II Thess. 3:1; Col. 1:25; Acts 26:18,15 NRSV *New Revised Standard Version* and CJB) May this book in particular reveal more deep meaning in the Jewish roots of our faith.

Front cover ancient Egypt painting is by William Margetson, public domain.

[To honor Him, all pronouns referring to Adonai are capitalized, satan's names are not. Scripture quotes are left as they are because of copyright laws.]

All New Covenant (Testament) Scripture, unless otherwise indicated, and those elsewhere marked CJB, are taken from the *Complete Jewish Bible*. Copyright © 1998 by David H. Stern. Published by Jewish New Testament Publications, Inc. All rights reserved.

All Tanakh (Old Testament) Scripture, unless otherwise indicated, and those elsewhere marked TLV, are taken from the *Tree of Life* Translation of the Bible. Copyright © 2015 by The Messianic Jewish Family Bible Society.

Scriptures marked:

NASB are taken from the *New American Standard Bible* Copyright © 1960, 1962, 1968, 1971, 1972, 1973, 1975, 1977, 1995 by The Lockman Foundation, La Habra, California. All rights reserved.

NIV are taken from the Holy Bible, *New International Version*. Copyright © 1973, 1978, 1984 by International Bible Society. All rights reserved.

NKJV are taken from the *New King James Version*. Copyright © 1982 by Thomas Nelson, Inc. All rights reserved.

NLT are taken from the Holy Bible, New Living Translation, copyright ©1996, 2004, 2007 by Tyndale House Foundation. Used by permission of Tyndale House Publishers, Inc., Carol Stream, Illinois 60188. All rights reserved.

Other books by Rabbi Jim Appel:

Messianic Judaism Class Teacher Book, Student Book, and five *Answer Books*.

Rosh Hashanah, Yom Teruah, The Day of Sounding the Shofar

Yom Kippur, The Day of Atonement

CONTENTS

1. What is a Passover Seder? — 9
2. Plague of the Firstborn — 26
3. Mixed Multitude — 39
4. The Servant and The Son — 55
5. Removing Khametz — 73
6. Two Seders — 104
7. Must Be Ritually Pure — 109
8. Yeshua's Purity Paradigm Shift — 124
9. Shabbat HaGadol — 142
10. The Unblemished Lamb — 164
11. Yeshua, The Passover Lamb: Parallels and Tradition — 177
12. Costly and Spotless — 190
13. Silent as a Lamb — 204
14. Even Intentional Sin — 223
15. Footwashing, Servanthood — 242
16. Washing Feet in Ministry, Finding Felt Needs — 252
17. Covenant Meal, Renewing Old, Establishing New — 272
18. Renewing the New: Promises and Conditions — 285
19. The Cups of the Covenant — 304
20. Children and Passover — 323

Bibliography — 336
Appendix A: Passover Seder Notes — 340
Appendix B: Yeshua's Last Seder Scriptural Outline — 369

CONTENTS IN DETAIL

1. WHAT IS A PASSOVER SEDER? ... 9
    - Everlasting Ordinance ... 9
    - The Exodus Story ... 11
    - The Seder in Yeshua's Day Compared to Today ... 15
    - The Significance of the Seder ... 16
    - Unleavened Bread ... 17
    - My Experience ... 18
    - Dayenu ... 21
    - Messiah ... 22
    - The New Covenant ... 23
2. PLAGUE OF THE FIRSTBORN ... 26
    - God's Lamb ... 30
    - Passover Vigil ... 31
3. MIXED MULTITUDE ... 39
    - Question About Prayer ... 45
    - The Mystery of Why We Pray ... 48
4. THE SERVANT AND THE SON ... 55
    - Moses' Difficulties. ... 56
    - The Fruit Moses Produced ... 58
    - How Moses was able to Overcome ... 58
    - Yeshua's Difficulties ... 63
    - Yeshua's Fruit ... 63
    - How Yeshua Overcame ... 64
    - Our Difficulties ... 66
    - Our Fruit ... 66
    - How We Overcome Difficulties ... 66
5. REMOVING KHAMETZ ... 73
    - How Does the Appointed Time of Passover Point to Yeshua Being the Messiah? ... 78
    - How did Yeshua Use the Traditions Around This Moad in His Teachings? ... 79
    - Tzfoon Ceremony ... 79
    - Get Rid of Khametz ... 81
        1. Khametz of Asking for a Sign ... 83
        2. Khametz of Hypocrisy ... 87
        3. Khametz of Personal Legalism ... 88
        4. Khametz of Self Exaltation ... 89
        5. Khametz of Institutional Legalism ... 90
        6. Khametz of Intellectualism ... 91
        7. Khametz of False Teachings ... 92
        8. Do What I Say, Not What I Do ... 96
        9. Fear of Man Rather Than Fear of God ... 96
        10. Covetousness, laying up treasure on earth ... 96
    - Spiritual Bread - The Word ... 97
    - How Did Yeshua fulfill this Moad? ... 98
    - Matzah of Life ... 99

6. TWO SEDERS ... 104
    Two Passover Days Tradition ... 105
    The Significance of Two Seders ... 107
7. MUST BE RITUALLY PURE ... 109
    Running Water - Mikveh ... 113
    Cut Off From the People ... 114
    Passover Grace ... 114
    The Red Heifer ... 115
    Seven Days of Cleansing ... 117
    Staying Cleansed ... 118
    Spiritual Cleansing ... 120
    Three Spiritual Cleansing Agents ... 121
8. YESHUA'S PURITY PARADIGM SHIFT ... 124
    Fence Around the Law ... 125
    Interpretation Is Needed ... 125
    Go to God to Get the Interpretation ... 126
    Contradict Scripture ... 127
    Manmade Laws Cause Barriers ... 129
    Yeshua's Halachic Judgment ... 130
    Paradigm Shifts ... 130
    Yeshua's Major Paradigm Shift ... 131
    Yeshua Touched the Defiled ... 132
    Insiders With Yeshua ... 133
    Yeshua Was Not Defiled by Touching the Unclean ... 134
    Is This For Us Today? ... 136
    Authority Over Four Things ... 137
    Power With the Authority ... 138
    My Personal Testimony ... 139
    Our Feet Get Contaminated ... 140
9. SHABBAT HaGADOL ... 142
    The Name of the Month ... 142
    Foreigners/Gerim Can Keep Pesakh ... 143
    Passover Parasha ... 143
    Yeshua Fulfilled the Haftarah Reading ... 145
    Were Verses Removed from the Haftarah? ... 150
    Yeshua Fulfilled Shabbat HaGadol ... 151
    Cross Examined ... 153
    Two Words For Freedom ... 157
    How Does This Apply to Us? ... 160
10. THE UNBLEMISHED LAMB ... 164
    The Mystery ... 165
    Born Under the Law ... 168
    Application ... 170
11. YESHUA, THE PASSOVER LAMB,
    PARALLELS AND TRADITION ... 177
    Parallels ... 178
    Traditions ... 182

12. COSTLY AND SPOTLESS	190
Why Were Unblemished Sacrifices Required?	191
Costly	195
Yeshua's Sacrifice Had to be Powerful Enough to Enable the Promises	196
13. SILENT AS A LAMB	204
14. EVEN INTENTIONAL SIN	223
15. WASHING FEET, SERVING	242
16. WASHING FEET IN MINISTRY: FINDING FELT NEEDS	252
My Experience in Leadership	256
17. COVENANT MEAL, RENEWING THE OLD ESTABLISHING THE NEW	272
18. RENEWING THE NEW: PROMISES AND CONDITIONS	285
Taking Communion	302
19. THE CUPS OF THE COVENANT	304
The First Cup	305
The Second Cup	307
The Third Cup	310
Baggage	314
The Fourth Cup	315
The Fifth Cup	316
The Sixth Cup	317
Get Rid of the Khametz Crumbs	318
20. CHILDREN AND PASSOVER	323
Parenting Children	324
BIBLIOGRAPHY	336

Appendix A
PASSOVER SEDER NOTES   338

Appendix B
YESHUA'S LAST SEDER, SCRIPTURE CHART   367

GLOSSARY

פסח Pesakh (also spelled Pesach) *pay'-sock* [ending with a softened k (kh), a guttural sound in the back of your throat] - **Passover**

חג Khag (also spelled Chag) *khahg* (The a is an ah sound. Again the kh is a guttural sound. There is no ch sound in Hebrew.) holiday, festival, feast

סדר Seder *say'-der* - order, the Passover ceremonial meal

הגדה Haggadah - Seder booklet that gives the Seder order along with Bible verses, traditional blessings, explanations, notes, teachings, etc. There are traditional Haggadahs in existence today that are hundreds of years old.

ישוע Yeshua *Yeh-shoo'-ah* - Jesus' original Hebrew Name, which basically means Salvation and is pronounced almost exactly the same as the Hebrew word for salvation ישועה.

מועד Moad *moh'-odd* - Appointed Time, Biblical Holiday

מועדים Moadim *moh-ah-deem'* - plural of Moad

ברית חדשה Brit Khadashah (also spelled B'rit Hadasha or Chadasha) *B'reet Khah-d'-shah* (Again the kh is a gutteral sound.) - **New Covenant** (sometimes referring just to the Covenant itself, sometimes to the whole New Testament.)

CE - common era (same as AD)

BCE - before the common era (same as BC)

CHAPTER 1
WHAT IS A PASSOVER SEDER?

Everlasting Ordinance

Passover is *Pesakh* פסח in Hebrew and Yiddish. [The kh is a guttural sound in the back of your throat.] It is a feast designed by the Lord and commanded by Him to be kept throughout our generations. When the Lord commands us to keep a certain day, I find that it is usually for our good and not just for His sake. Take Shabbat, for example. We would burn ourselves out if we ran seven days a week. The Lord tells us we need that day of rest for refreshment.

How about Passover—*Pesakh*—is it for our good? Well, we get to eat good stuff; we get to gather together with our extended families; and we get a day off of work or school. Also, God calls us to a commitment—to obey something, and if we obey it, we get to grow and be blessed.

> Exodus 12:14a *This day is to be a memorial for you.*

---

* Painting: An ancient Israeli family Seder. Unable to find original or artist.

The word *memorial* in the Hebrew is the word *zikaron*. You have to use your high school English here. When we say we have a memorial, it is a day that causes us to remember. It comes from the same root word as remember.

> Exodus 12:14b *You are to keep it* [Passover] *as a feast to ADONAI* (the LORD). *Throughout your generations you are to keep it as an eternal ordinance.*

What is it we remember? We remember the incredible story of the grace and power of God in the Exodus in delivering the children of Israel out of Egypt. When you think about what was accomplished in the Exodus, it is astounding. These people were slaves and it was impossible for them to free themselves from the mighty Egyptian empire. God's grace and power was there. He delivered His people from slavery and then entered into a Covenant with them on Mt. Sinai. All this is remembered at our Passover celebrations.

How do we remember it? Hannukah has a dreidel that you spin. Purim has the noise makers. Passover has a Seder, which is a celebratory meal. *Seder* is Hebrew for *order*. The different parts of the commemoration are done in order.

It is traditionally celebrated in the home. This is one holiday that is not normally celebrated in the synagogue (although many Messianic Synagogues hold a public Seder in addition to the one in the home.) Traditionally, everyone comes back home to the patriarch's or the matriarch's—the grandparent's—home and celebrates with the gathered family. It's a time of great joy and celebration, singing, and ceremony. When I was a kid, it was a time when my cousins and I drank too much wine, and we got a little bit rowdy. ☺ It was a great time.

The Seder is especially aimed at children because the Lord tells us to pass this down to each generation so that they won't forget. We eat symbolic foods, drink commemorative cups of wine (or grape juice), and do special, traditional activities, as a memorial, to help us remember and pass on to our children the great deliverance from Egypt. The most essential activity of the Seder is the retelling of the Exodus story.

The Exodus Story

Let me give you a short recap of the Exodus story. We give it in a lot more detail in our Seder. You can read the whole story in the book of Exodus, which I encourage you to do. It always blesses me.

So let me start from the beginning. Jacob's son, Joseph, was in Egypt as a slave and he interpreted the king of Egypt's dream of the coming seven-year famine. As a result, Egypt was able to survive that famine, as was Joseph's family, and they were given land in Egypt out of gratitude. So the family of around 74 people moved to Egypt where they were blessed by God. After a few hundred years, they had multiplied so much that there were millions of them, and the Egyptians began to fear them. So a later king of Egypt, who didn't know Joseph, enslaved them.

The Israelites continued to multiply. Finally one Pharaoh ordered them to kill all the baby boys that were born. The enemy's plan is quite obvious here. He wanted to destroy the Jewish people to keep the Messiah from coming because he knew He was coming. Moses' family, his mother, his sister, and even the Pharaoh's daughter, disobeyed the king and saved Moses. This is a significant thing because he didn't grow up as a slave, he grew up as a prince.

The Hebrews cried out for deliverance. God heard their cries, and called Moses, at the age of 80, and his brother Aaron and sent them to demand that Pharaoh release the Israelites. But Pharaoh refused. God encouraged Moses with Covenant promises which have become a big part of the Passover Seder.

Then God brought ten terrible plagues on the Egyptians to force Pharaoh to release the Israelites. Each plague was worse than the one before, but Pharaoh continued to refuse to let the people go, even though, if you read the story, his advisers were urging him to. They were telling him, let's go along with this already because Egypt is going to be ruined. But he continued to refuse.

Then we come to the time of the tenth plague, which God told Moses would be the death of the firstborn sons of Egypt. We have to understand that when God said Egypt, He didn't just mean Egyptians, He meant everybody living in the land of

Egypt. It would be the death of their firstborn sons unless the instructions were followed as to how to survive this plague.

> Exodus 12:3 *ADONAI spoke to Moses ... Tell all the congregation of Israel that on the tenth day of this month each man is to take a lamb for his family one lamb for the household.*

Each father, each head of a family is to take a lamb. Notice that this is a family thing.

> Exodus 12:5 *Your lamb is to be without blemish, a year old male. You may take it from the sheep or the goats.*

Lambs are adorable creatures.[2]

> Exodus 12:6 *You must watch over it until the fourteenth day of the same month. Then the whole assembly of the congregation of Israel is to slaughter it at twilight*

The Hebrew word there for *watch over* is *mishmeret*, which means *to observe, safeguard, watch it*. What we understand is that the people were to observe the lamb those four days for defects to make sure that it was perfect. We have to understand that during these four days the lamb would be right there amongst the family. The children would be playing with it, and it would become beloved like a pet, so this would make the sacrifice more significant to the people.

I consulted on this with our former assistant, Donita, who was actually a shepherdess at one point in her life. And she said that yes lambs are like puppies and kittens. They are lovable. So it was going to happen that the family would become attached to them.

---

* Image of a lamb, Lightstock.com. Used by permission.

> Exodus 12:7 *(after slaughtering the lamb) They are to take the blood and put it on the two doorposts and on the crossbeam of the houses where they will eat it.*

On the front cover you can see a painting of a man putting the blood on the crossbeam of his house. Notice again, that all this is going on in individual homes, not in a large gathering.

> Exodus 12:12 *For I will go through the land of Egypt on that night and strike down every firstborn, both men and animals, and I will execute judgments against all the gods of Egypt I am the ADONAI.*

So we understand that each of the plagues were for specific judgments on the many gods of Egypt. And we'll see also that the lamb was also a judgment on the gods of Egypt.

> Exodus 12:13 *The blood will be a sign for you on the houses where you are. When I see the blood, I will pass over you. So there will be no plague among you to destroy you when I strike the land of Egypt*

This is where we get the name of this holiday. The actual Hebrew word used there for *pass over* is *pesakh*. When God would see the blood on the doorposts, He would *pesakh* those houses and those firstborn would not die. Also understand that all the Egyptians were given this choice. The firstborn sons of those who didn't put blood on the doorposts of their houses died.

So after the firstborns all died, Pharaoh finally released the people and they left in haste. Actually they left so quickly that their dough that they had mixed didn't rise and they ate the flatbread—called Matzah—which is part of the tradition and the instruction for Passover.

Then Pharaoh changed his mind and came after them to bring them back. He and his army pursued them, but the Lord brought a pillar of fire between them to protect the people. They were trapped at the edge of the Red Sea, and they cried out to Moses. God told Moses to raise his staff over the water. Moses obeyed and God saved them. He parted the Red Sea, and they

crossed on dry ground.

It is hard to conceive, but there were a few million people who left Egypt. The picture above gives you a sense of the numbers. The Scripture says there were six hundred thousand men that left Egypt and each man probably had a family of at least five. So we're talking about maybe three million people.

After the Israelites got through to the other side, following the pillar of fire, God brought back the waters.

The Egyptians had pursued them into the dry sea bed. And the rushing flood of returning water destroyed the whole Egyptian army.

But that isn't the end. Passover goes all the way to Mt. Sinai. It doesn't end at the Red Sea. Passover is a remembrance of more than just getting out of Egypt. It is a remembrance of coming to Mt. Sinai, seeing the awesome sight of God on the mountain, feeling the shaking of the earth, and hearing the sound of the Shofar and the voice of God giving the Ten Commandments. The giving of the Law,

* Painting: "The Exodus," James Jacques Joseph Tissot, French, 1836-1902, The Jewish Museum, https://thejewishmuseum.org/collection/26358-the-exodus, Public domain. (Notice the huge pillar of cloud.)
* Artwork: "Red Sea Crossing," Gustave Dore, French 1832-1883. Public domain.

the giving of the instructions of the Tabernacle and the rest of the Mosaic Covenant, all of that is part of what Passover is all about. Really, this was the beginning of getting the Bible. It was the beginning of the written revelation of the Word of God.

How much grace and power was there in that story? I think it is one of the most incredible stories of God revealing Himself; of God choosing a people and carrying out His plan and exercising His power.

At Mt. Sinai the Israelites entered into a national Covenant with God—the founding Covenant of the nation of Israel.

Exodus 12:14 *This day is to be a memorial for you. You are to keep it as a feast to ADONAI. Throughout your generations you are to keep it as an eternal ordinance.*

So the Passover Seder is commanded to be a yearly celebration. During the Seder, we eat and drink things that give greater meaning to the Exodus events.

But more than remembering the story, what the Lord spoke to me a few years ago is that Passover is a Covenant Meal. It is the Covenant Meal of the Mosaic Covenant—the annual Covenant renewal meal.

So this Covenant, that we're going to be celebrating and remembering and renewing, consists of all that happened coming out of the land of Egypt and going to Mt. Sinai and receiving and sealing the Sinai Covenant:

The Seder in Yeshua's Day Compared to Today

Today Pesakh is celebrated somewhat differently from Yeshua's day in a very important way. In the time of Yeshua,

---
* Illustration from a Bible card, Providence Lithograph Company, 1907.

it was celebrated Biblically according to what was written in the Exodus 12. While the Temple still stood, the people went to Jerusalem to celebrate Passover. It was a great big gathering compared to what we have now. It started out with the selecting of a Passover Lamb on the tenth day of the month of Nissan. Those lambs were carefully selected because they were supposed to have no blemish—no defect.

Then they were watched and examined for four days to make sure there were no blemishes in them. On the 14th day of the month, the lambs were sacrificed and the blood was placed on the doorposts. That night all of the Israelites participated in a Seder, eating the symbolic foods commanded in Exodus 12, which includes eating the sacrificed lamb.

However, if you go to a traditional Seder today, you will find that the Passover lamb is no longer eaten because the Scriptures emphasize that the lambs must be sacrificed at the Temple in Jerusalem, which was destroyed in the year 70 A.D.

> Leviticus 17:8-9 *Then you are to say to them: Anyone from the house of Israel, or from the outsiders dwelling among them, who offers a burnt offering or sacrifice, 9 but does not bring it to the entrance of the Tent of Meeting to sacrifice it to ADONAI, is to be cut off from his people.*

So you can see why the traditional Ashkenazi Jewish Rabbis decided we couldn't eat lamb anymore. So they removed the lamb from the Seder and made the unleavened bread—the Matzah—the memorial for the body or flesh of the lamb. The cups of wine (or grape juice) became a memorial of the blood of the Passover lamb. (However, in the Messianic tradition, we do eat lamb.) (The Sephardic Jews also still eat lamb.)

The Significance of the Seder

Part of the reason for the Seder is also to provoke the children to ask questions like, "Why are you doing this? What is it all about?" This is because God understands the way people learn. When people are curious and ask questions, and you tell them the answer, they learn a whole lot better than when you just lecture them. So this is to provoke those questions and pass it on.

Another thing to understand is that contrary to what goes on in Seders today, in ancient Israel, the children would have seen the whole ceremony with the lamb. They would have gotten to know the lamb. Maybe they would have gone with their father to see the lamb sacrificed, and helped bring back the blood for the door and the lamb to be eaten. You can imagine the impact of that was much greater than what we have today.

And yet even without the sacrifice of the Lamb, even with the two substitutional memorials, which I believe greatly reduce the impact on children, we are 3500 years down the road from when that instruction was given. And you know what? We're still doing it! So somehow it worked! Even with that watering down, if you will, it worked!

God knew. It's just amazing to me how He understands human nature, that if He would give us something to do about remembering this thing, we would remember it better. It wasn't just to talk about it or read about it, it was to have this meal, eat these foods, drink these drinks. He knew us so well that, amazingly, it has been thousands of years and we're still doing it. We're still passing it down to our children. And they're going to pass it down to their children if the Lord doesn't return first. Absolutely amazing!

I believe this is one of the significant factors in the Jewish people being able to survive as a people. Since 70 ACE, we have been able to survive 2000 years of being totally scattered and severely persecuted, which is an incredible work of God—I wanted to say achievement, but it's really not an achievement of human beings—that we are still a distinct people after the scattering, the loss of our language, and all the persecution. This instruction helped to keep us together.

Unleavened Bread

Passover is part of the Feast of Unleavened Bread, which in Hebrew is *Khag HaMatzah*. [Remember, the kh is a guttural sound in the back of your throat.] It is a seven-day feast, sometimes referred to as the Passover Week when we can eat no leaven, which is *khametz* in Hebrew (also spelled *hametz*).

The Seder is Biblically one night, which traditionally has become two nights (more on that later), but the Feast of Unleavened Bread is seven whole days, and is commanded by God.

> Exodus 12:18 *During the first month in the evening of the fourteenth day of the month, you are to eat matzot, until the evening of the twenty-first day of the month. 19 For seven days no hametz is to be found in your houses, for whoever eats hametz, that soul will be cut off from the congregation of Israel, whether he is an outsider or one who is born in the land.*

So for seven days (eight for those who observe Passover for two nights), we eat nothing that has any kind of leaven (khametz) in it. Khametz is anything that makes things rise, which includes yeast, baking powder, baking soda, etc. So we eat no bread or donuts or pancakes or cookies or cake or bagels. No noodles, no dumplings, no pizza crust, no biscuits, no muffins, no eggrolls, no tortillas. The list goes on and on. Traditionally, through rabbinical decisions, this has grown to include no legumes of any kind, so it can be a pretty tough week.

Instead of all those things, we eat Matzah. We eat Matzah ball soup, Matzah desserts, Matzah casseroles, Matzah pizza, Matzah granola, Matzah s'mores, etc. We can get really creative. Why does God want us to deny ourselves this way for a whole week? We will answer that question and find out the spiritual significance of Khag HaMatzah in a later chapter.

My Experience

In my family, the traditional Seder lost its power through unbelief and doubt and tradition. I know many other Jewish people who would agree with that in their Seders. The Seders I attended as a child didn't really tell the story. There is a book called the Haggadah. We read through the traditional Haggadah.[6] It has a lot of the sayings of the rabbis and a lot of traditional prayers and things like that. The story was just kind

---

6 Passover Haggadah, (Compliments of the Coffees of Maxwell House), Deluxe Edition Pamphlet – 1986

of lost in all that.

My grandfather was Orthodox so we went to his house. He would chant through the Haggadah in Hebrew. Some of his children understood some Hebrew, but none of his grandchildren did. We would sit there as he would go on and on and chant, and it didn't have any power. I used to try to read the Haggadah in English.

After my grandfather died, the responsibility for the Seder went to one of my uncles. Things got a little bit better. At least they would read some of the things in English, so those of us who weren't Hebrew scholars could follow it.

After I came to know the Lord, we went to the Passover Seder that my uncle was leading. It was in a big room with about 25 people at a big table. We were going through the Haggadah in English, taking turns, each person reading a part of it.

There is an interesting thing we say about Jewish holidays. They all have this theme. "They tried to kill us. God saved us. Let's eat." In my uncle's house, that was the pattern. It was, "Let's get to the meal as fast as we can." My cousins and uncles and aunts were reading through the Haggadah very fast.

When it came to my turn, it was a passage from the Psalms. Everyone else was talking sports and business and other things. When I began to read that passage reverently, it was amazing what happened. The Spirit of God came into that room. Everyone was quiet and you could hear a pin drop. Everyone was listening. I finished my turn, handed it to the next person, and they started in just as fast as the others!

That is what has happened. The power has been lost in tradition. One time I had talked to my grandfather about it and found out he didn't even really believe the story anymore. He had scientific reasons how the Red Sea parted. "It was natural," he said. There was much unbelief. My mother actually became an atheist and totally questioned the whole thing. That is what I see happening. Perhaps you had families where it was much more Godly than that and it was wonderful, but that is not how it went in my family.

After finding out that my Grandfather didn't actually believe the Exodus story, I asked myself the question, "Can we believe today this amazing story of people being brought out? Can we grasp the magnitude of it?"

> Exodus 12:37 Then Bnei-Yisrael (the Sons of Israel) *journeyed from Rameses to Succoth, about 600,000 men on foot, as well as children.*

Can you picture 600,000 men? They had large families. They had grown enormously, so let's just say they had three kids each, which would be reasonable. As I noted earlier, that is three million people! Grasp the magnitude of this. They multiplied from 75 people to three million people in 430 years. The largest crowd I've ever seen was at a "Standing in the Gap" rally a few years ago, and there was supposed to be one million there. It was a little bit difficult to get anything done with that crowd—for instance, to get them to move from here to there. A million people is enormous. Three million people would be three times that number. They were leaving a civilized country and walking out into the desert where there's nothing! No food, no water, no shade. This was a massive amount of people. It's amazing! Just astounding! Can we believe these numbers? Did this really happen?

I found a long passage with lots of verses that really spoke to me that this really happened. This is the genealogies.

> Numbers 1:20-21 *The sons of Reuben, Israel's firstborn (their generations, their families, by their ancestral households, according to the count of their names, every male from 20 years and upward, all available for the army), 21 those counted from the tribe of Reuben were 46,500.*

It goes on and does that for every single one of those tribes. How could anyone have made up something like this where they were counted—every one—in a census, and written down. It is not round numbers. I believe it. I believe this really happened—that three million people actually came out of Egypt. When you think about it—that is awesome! It's hard to believe, but it's true! It is an amazing miracle!

Dayenu

There is a special traditional song that is sung at every Passover Seder, called Dayenu. It is sung like a little diddy while dancing to it in the traditional Jewish circle dancing. But it has great spiritual significance because what it is saying is that each thing God did would have been enough. There is a spirit of humility in this song saying "It would have been enough if He did this, but He did that, too!" There is also a spirit of thanksgiving in it—just a wonderful spirit, saying, "It was awesome that You did this, but You did more." It speaks so much to me of this day of *zikaron*.

So here's the song, Dayenu.

Ilu ho-tsi, ho-tsi-a-nu,
Ho-tsi-a-nu mi-Mitz-ra-yim,
Ho-tsi-a-nu mi-Mitz-ra-yim,
Da-ye-nu!
    CHORUS:
.. Dai, da-ye-nu,
.. Dai, da-ye-nu,
.. Dai, da-ye-nu,
.. Da-ye-nu, da-ye-nu, da-ye-nu!
.. (Repeat)

Ilu na-tan, na-tan la-nu,
Na-tan la-nu et-ha-Sha-bat,
Na-tan la-nu et-ha-Sha-bat,
Da-ye-nu!
    (CHORUS)
Ilu na-tan, na-tan la-nu,
Na-tan la-nu et-ha-To-rah,
Na-tan la-nu et-ha-To-rah,
Da-ye-nu!
    (CHORUS)
Had He brought all, brought all of us, brought all of us out from Egypt, then it would have been enough. Oh, dayenu.
    (CHORUS)
Had He given, given to us, given to us all the Sabbath,

then it would have been enough. Oh, dayenu.

(CHORUS)

Had He given, given to us, given to us all the Torah,
then it would have been enough. Oh, dayenu.

(CHORUS)

Here's what all that is saying:
It would have been enough if you had just brought us forth and not judged the Egyptians.
It would have been enough if you had just judged the Egyptians and not given us the wealth.
It would have been enough if you had just given us the wealth and not divided the Red Sea.
It would have been enough if you had just divided the Red Sea and not destroyed Pharaoh's army.
Dayenu—It would have been enough.

This captures the spirit of Passover. It would have been enough, except God kept doing more miracles. This was only the second demonstration of God's incredible grace in history, yet there was a bigger one still to come.

Messiah

Some 1500 years later, in this time of the Passover, in the month of Nissan, on the 14th day of the month, THE most remarkable demonstration of His grace occurred: the day in which the Messiah completed His work here on earth. We all know that the events of Yeshua's life were associated with the *Moadim* (pronounced moh-ah-deem). *Moadim* means *Appointed Times—Festivals—Holidays*, but the best translation of it is God's Appointed Times. All of the great events in Yeshua's life were associated with the Appointed Times.

Why did God choose this Moad—this Appointed Time for Yeshua to complete His work? I've often thought Yom Kippur would have been a more appropriate time—the Day of Atonement when atonement was made for the whole nation. Why not then? The reason is found in the Passover Seder as to why God chose this Passover, and we will get to it in a moment.

Dayenu goes on from the Red Sea to cover the events of the next month.

> It would have been enough if You had drowned the Egyptian army and not given us the Sabbath
> > but You gave us the Sabbath.
> It would have been enough if You had given us the Sabbath and not given us the Torah.
> > but You gave us the Torah.

It goes on to what happened in the desert—what happened at Mt. Sinai—the giving of the Mosaic covenant. You need to understand that the Passover Seder also commemorates the giving of the Torah at Mt. Sinai.

Why did Yeshua complete His work on Passover? I believe that God chose the Seder because it commemorates and renews the Mosaic Covenant, and He wanted to build on the Old Covenant to give us the New Covenant. If you have never seen this before, it is the most wonderful sense of continuity in the Scriptures that at the time when the people were celebrating the giving of the Old Covenant—the Mosaic Covenant—He gave us the New Covenant.

The New Covenant

Where did He give us the New Covenant? Where is it written out? It's in the story of the Last Supper.

He was having His last Passover Seder. At that last Passover Seder, He gave us the New Covenant. And He gave us the renewal ceremony of the New Covenant, which is Communion, at the same meal where the renewal ceremony of the Old Covenant was going on. We are going to cover this in great detail in a later chapter and in the Passover Seder section.

[I've seen a picture of the "Last Supper" by Salvidore Dali. Yeshua is there with His disciples with a cup in His hand and in front of Him is this nice big loaf of bread. Does that make any sense? Why not? It was a Passover Seder! They would have only had unleavened bread! That picture is indicative of lack of

knowledge within the Body of what this was all about.]
Let us establish that the Last Supper was indeed a Seder.

> Luke 22:14-15 *When the time came, Yeshua and the emissaries reclined at the table, and he 15 said to them, "I have really wanted so much to celebrate this Seder with you before I die!*

What follows is what is called in the church the Last Supper, and it includes the giving of communion. In John, this starts in chapter 13. In John 14:31, the last verse in chapter 14, it may look like the Seder is over because He says, "Get up! Let's get going!" But they don't go anywhere. If you read all the way to chapter 18:1 it says, "After Yeshua had said all this, He went out with this talmidim (disciples)" So, all of John 13-17 happened at the Seder.

That is important because that is a significant section of the Gospels. There are more verses devoted to the Seder than any other event in the Gospels. Why is there so much devoted to this? Because it is such an important event. He gives us the New Covenant at the Seder. If you want to read the New Covenant—the crux of the New Covenant—it is in John 13-17. These are some of my favorite verses in the Bible.

I would like you to say, "Dayenu" with me next as we list the things Yeshua gave us in the New Covenant. Say aloud, "Dayenu"—"It would have been enough"

> If He had only come as Messiah and taught us the ways of God. **Dayenu**
>
> If He had only given us an eternal home in heaven. **Dayenu**
>
> If He had only promised us to answer prayer in His Name. **Dayenu**
>
> If He had only given us peace in the midst of tribulation. **Dayenu**
>
> If He had only given us the fullness of joy. **Dayenu**
>
> If He had only promised to dwell within us. **Dayenu**
>
> If He had only commanded us to love one another as He loved us. **Dayenu**

If He had only given us the "Lord's Supper." **Dayenu**

If He had only shed His blood to bring us the forgiveness of sin. **Dayenu**

If He had only loved us so much that He laid down His life to save us. **Dayenu**!!!

If He had only resurrected to come back and be with us. **Dayenu**!!!

But He did, and is doing, so much more!! He promised, commanded, and gave us all these things at His last Seder, the Last Supper.

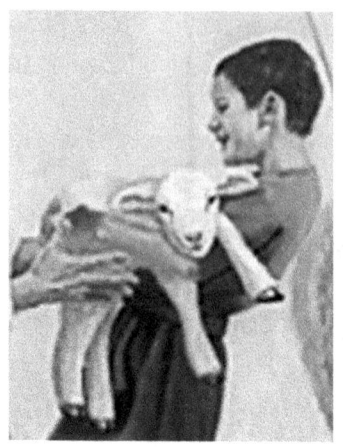

CHAPTER 2
Plague Of The Firstborn

Our God is a God of justice. He is a God who defends the weak, but He's also a God who brings judgment on the wicked. Let me give you a bit of the story again, but from a different perspective.

About 3500 years ago, the Israelite people were in Egypt. It was a sinful nation. The people worshiped many false gods. Their leader, the Pharaoh, was full of pride and considered himself to be a god. The Egyptians had enslaved the Israelite people, which was particularly wicked because the Israelites were descended from the father of Joseph (Yosef) who had saved Egypt from a terrible famine.

This new Pharaoh forgot about Yosef and what he had done for them. He and the Egyptians had come to fear the growing Israelite population, so they began to oppress them and put them into hard slave labor. For many many years they were slaves. Later, in order to keep our numbers from growing, they began to murder all of our infant sons that were born in Egypt.

---

* Painting: Bringing a lamb for sacrifice. Unable to find original or artist.

So the children of Israel began to cry out because of this and God heard them and sent Moses, an Israelite who had been raised by Pharaoh's daughter, to bring judgment on Egypt in the form of ten terrible plagues. They were meant, not to hurt the Egyptians, but to cause them to repent and turn from their wickedness. However, the king of Egypt hardened his heart through nine of these horrible plagues. Finally there came the tenth plague, which was the death of the firstborn sons of the land.

This was clearly an eye for an eye thing happening here. The Egyptians had murdered the sons of Israel, the infant children, and this was going to be the death of the firstborn sons of Egypt.

God made a way for the Israelites to be protected from this plague because the plague was going to come over the whole land. He gave instructions to Moses just before the plague was to come.

> Exodus 12:21 *Then Moses called for all the elders of Israel and said to them, "Go, select lambs for your families and slaughter the Passover lamb.*

This sacrificing was to happen on the fourteenth day of the month of Nissan.

> Exodus 12:22 *You are to take a bundle of hyssop, dip it in the blood that is in the basin, and apply it to the crossbeam and two doorposts with the blood from the basin. None of you may go out the door of his house until morning.*

I want to point out the "*none of you may go out.*" To be spared from this plague, God required faith and obedience from each individual. It wasn't enough that somebody did this and people would be saved. It required every individual.

> Exodus 12:23 *ADONAI will pass through to strike down the Egyptians, but when He sees the blood on the crossbeam and the two doorposts, ADONAI will pass over that door, and will not allow the destroyer to come into your houses to strike you down.*

This is a picture of God coming along with a destroyer and God preventing the destroyer from entering into those houses with the blood. Remember this for later, that the blood brought protection.

All the Israelites who disobeyed these commandments, their firstborn died right there in Egypt. All the Egyptians who disobeyed these commandments, their firstborn died. All the Israelites and Egyptians who obeyed the commands survived. Even Israelites who previously sinned against God and deserved punishment, if they obeyed this command, they survived.

The point I am trying to make is that the Israelites that survived this plague were not necessarily righteous or sinless, they just obeyed this particular set of commands. All the Egyptians who obeyed were also protected. So even Egyptians who had done something evil against Israel before, if they began to trust in what God was saying and they stopped worshipping these other gods and believed in the one true God, they too would have been saved.

What was happening here was that God in His mercy was giving a way, for all who would obey Him, to escape the judgment that was due upon this land. Following this plague, the Egyptians let the Israelites go and many Egyptians left with the Israelites. (Verse 38 says: *Also a mixed multitude went up with them....*)

This incident is at the heart of who we are as a people and who we are as a nation. I want to declare today that this is not a myth or a fable. This is true. This is history. There have been many archaeological studies, even recently, that have been unearthing where the Egyptian chariots crossed the Red Sea. There are broken chariot wheels and things like that.[8]

This is also an illustration for us today to help us understand our own personal need for the Messiah. We live in a world that

---

[8] Kevin Fisher, "Revealing God's Treasure - Red Sea Crossing," https://www.youtube.com/watch?v=vaN2acVMGC8, Ark Discovery International, Inc., Sparta, Tenn., arkdiscovery.com, url: http://arkdiscovery.com/red_sea_crossing.htm. Accessed Nov. 2018. Also: "The Exodus Revealed," Questar Inc., Discovery Media Productions, https://www.youtube.com/watch?v=Lz-b4ekyX1kc&list=PLDAetAbqQFkvaL9T3wGnv4Zj-cSV2GQEz

is like Egypt, unless you are living in some other world than I am living in. It is a sinful world. Many false gods are worshipped in this world: the god of materialism, the god of selfishness, the gods of pride, of fame, and of power. Millions who have been wronged in this world cry out for justice, like the Israelites. God has promised to bring that judgment on this whole world, either while we are alive or in the next life.

All of us, like the Israelites or the Egyptians, have also sinned against God. We deserve that judgment that God is going to bring because of what we've done.

You might say, "What sin have I committed?" As we read the Scriptures, we know that we have all done things that we shouldn't have. I don't think there is a person anywhere who has never gossiped or told a "white lie" or coveted something, or lusted, or judged somebody, or tried to manipulate a situation. The Scriptures even say that everything without faith is sin.

Then, of course, there are all the things that we should have done that we didn't do. That could be a whole long list there: when somebody needed some help and we were too busy or maybe somebody was being attacked, not necessarily physically, but maybe verbally, and we thought, "That's wrong." But we were afraid to be attacked ourselves in some way.

So all of us deserve that coming judgment, but God has made a way for us to be protected from it.

In Exodus, the coming judgment was the tenth plague—the death of all first born sons in the entire the land of Egypt. Whoever lived in the land was going to lose their firstborn son. God gave the Israelites instructions on how to survive that plague, as we have noted. Every household had to take a lamb and sacrifice that lamb on the fourteenth day of the month and then put the blood of the lamb on the doorposts of the house and eat that sacrifice that night inside that house.

That night when the plague came upon all of Egypt, it would pass over that house. We can imagine that the Israelites were in their houses in great fear and awe, as they ate the sacrificed Passover lamb, and the deaths began.

God's Lamb

As each Israelite family did that Pesakh night, 1500 years later, God took a lamb for Himself and killed a Passover Lamb.

> John 1:29 *The next day, Yochanan (John) saw Yeshua coming toward him and said, "Look! God's lamb! The one who is taking away the sin of the world!*

God's Lamb was without any blemish, and God placed the Lamb's Blood on the entrance to His dwelling place—the Kingdom of God. He tells us that we can be protected from His judgment by obeying His instruction to come into that dwelling place, into the Kingdom of God. In John 5, there is this amazing verse:

> John 5:24 *Yes, indeed! I tell you that whoever hears what I am saying and trusts the One who sent me has eternal life -- that is, he will not come up for judgment but has already crossed over from death to life!*

Yeshua is that Lamb—that Passover Lamb of God. But let me ask you a question here. What is the Blood-covered entrance into God's dwelling place? It's the Cross! God placed the blood on the Cross. When we look at the Cross, that is the way into the Kingdom of God. We know that is the way in because that is where the sacrifice happened. Now here is where it all connects. What pattern did the blood make on the lintels—the doorposts—the entrance ways to the dwelling places in Egypt with it dripping down to the floor from the top? What pattern did Yeshua's Blood make on the entrance way to God's dwelling place? The same pattern. You see the parallel here?

How do we enter into that dwelling place? Through the door. In the Scriptures, Yeshua says, *"Knock and the door will be opened."* All we have to do is ask the Lord to bring us into that Kingdom and be willing to be citizens of that Kingdom, which means being willing to be obedient to the King of that Kingdom, and we will pass from judgment.

Let's go on a little bit further in that story:

> Exodus 12:29 *So it came about at midnight that ADONAI struck down all the firstborn in the land of Egypt, from the firstborn of Pharaoh sitting on his throne to the firstborn of the captive who was in the dungeon, and all the firstborn cattle.*

The plague came at midnight. The Israelites in their dwelling places who had the blood on the doors, did not go to bed. They stayed up all night. Can you imagine what it must have been like to be in one of those blood-protected households? You had seen the nine plagues before, the darkness and the blood, the frogs and the locusts—all of these things. They had seen that God was sparing Israel. I think the strongest emotion that would have been in those houses would be the incredible fear of God. Everybody would have been in the place of thinking, "Whoa! We've heard what is supposed to happen now. Oh God, may we be protected from that!" So I believe that they would have been in there praying that this plague would pass over them and their first born sons be spared. And that they would indeed, after nine tries and now a tenth try, finally be set free from the bondage of slavery.

> Exodus 12:30-31 *Then Pharaoh rose up in the night, he and all his servants and all the Egyptians, and there was loud wailing in Egypt. For there was not a house where someone was not dead. 31 So he called for Moses and Aaron at night and said, "Rise up, go out from my people, both you and Bnei-Yisrael, go, serve ADONAI as you have said.*

Pharaoh was so fearful that he didn't even wait until morning to send them out. The children of Israel left hastily.

Passover Vigil

> Exodus 12:42 (NIV) *Because the LORD kept vigil that night to bring them out of Egypt, on this night all the Israelites are to keep vigil to honor the LORD for the generations to come.*

In obedience to this command, we are to keep what is called the "Passover vigil." In Hebrew the way you say that is *la'il shimurim hu le Adonai. La'il* means *the night*. *Shimurim* is plural of *shomer* which means *watch over* like a shepherd watches over sheep or a watchmen over a city.

What is the traditional way of keeping this vigil? Stay up all night and read the Scriptures. Watch and intercede and pray for God's will to be done as they must have been doing in those households during the first Pesakh. It's very interesting because it says *"The Lord Himself kept vigil."* The Lord was watching the destroyer to make sure he didn't enter any of the houses with the blood.

Fast forward to the time of Yeshua.

I got this finally when I was watching Mel Gibson's "Passion of the Christ" movie. This was a really critical point because up to this time it says that Yeshua would not trust Himself into the hands of man because He knew man. The point we are about to come to is where He crosses over and allows Himself to be placed in the hands of man. In the movie it was so dramatic. Things were out of His control. He was trusting others who arrested Him and were going to do these things.

> Luke 22:39 *On leaving, Yeshua went as usual to the Mount of Olives; and the talmidim followed him.*

In Matthew it says He went to Gethsemane. In Hebrew, this place is *Gat shemanim*—שׁמנים גת—what it means is *the oil press*. What is that all about? It is an olive grove and is a place where olives are pressed to make olive oil.

When we were in Israel we saw a demonstration at Yod Shmoneh. They showed us that it takes a lot of pressure to extract the oil from these olives. It is very significant in the title of this place because this is a place where Yeshua was about to experience great pressure.

It is one of my favorite spots in Israel because it is just a grove of olive trees. The olive trees are so old. Olive trees don't die, they just become more and more gnarled and bigger and bigger. Some of them you can actually look through them. They are hollow inside but still alive. The understanding is that some of these trees were there at the time Yeshua was there—in this place—*Gat Shemanim*—שמנים גת—the oil press. It was not called a garden. It was called an oil or olive press. In Israel, they have now called it a garden.

> Luke 22:46b *"Pray that you won't be put to the test!"*

I struggled with the translations there but what I believe He was saying was, "Pray that you don't fall into temptation because you are going to be tempted here."

He went about a stone's throw away from them and He kneeled down and prayed. As an observant Jew, what commandment was Yeshua obeying? He was keeping the Passover vigil. On this night all the Israelites are to keep vigil to honor the Lord for generations to come. He was doing what He had probably done every year of His life after the Passover Seder: He would keep this vigil. *Gat Shemanim* שמנים גת was where He kept it.

There is an amazing thing here because the Lord, Yeshua, literally fulfilled the verse of Exodus 12:42 where we read, *The Lord kept vigil.* Isn't that amazing? *The Lord kept vigil.* Yeshua kept vigil. This is like Matthew 5:17 *"Don't think I have come to abolish the Torah and the Prophets. I've come to fulfill it."* This was a literal fulfillment of *The Lord kept vigil* that night.

> Luke 22:42 *"Father, if you are willing, take this cup away from me; still, let not my will but yours be done."*

What was this prayer all about? First of all, the "*cup*" represented the trial He was entering into: the betrayal, the arrest, the false accusations, the condemnation, the mocking, beating, whipping, the crucifixion and death. That was the cup that was being offered to Him. What He was saying to God was, "If there is another way to fulfill Your plan to bring salvation to the world, show me and we'll do that other thing because this is very difficult for me to face."

Why was He struggling? Some may think it was because of the terrible physical pain that He was about to experience—pain beyond imagination—but in the book of Hebrews, we read this.

> *Hebrews 12:2 Yeshua—who, in exchange for obtaining the joy set before him, endured execution on a stake as a criminal, scorning the shame, and has sat down at the right hand of the throne of God.*

I get the sense that the pain wasn't the issue. I believe He was struggling because He knew He was about to bear the iniquity of the whole world. When He did that, somehow He would be separated from the Father for some period of time.

We don't understand that, but in Matthew 27:46, He says *"My God, My God why have You forsaken me?"* We know that something was happening there where He wasn't connected as He had been connected. It was because He was bearing all iniquity for all time. In this place called "the oil press," He was under this intense pressure, knowing fully what He was facing.

The second half of what He prayed was still, *"Let not My will but Yours be done."* So, He was pressing in, in this place of the oil press, into the plan of God because there was no other way. This was the way, the only way that this could happen.

In the film "The Passion," if you watched the scene in Gat Shemanim, there is an amazing change in His countenance that happens as He goes from saying, *"Let this cup pass from me"* to *"not My will be done but Yours."* It is like that was the moment. That was the moment when His will became set and He said, *"I'm going to do it. It doesn't matter how much the devil tempts me. It doesn't matter how much I have fear."* In the movie He goes from struggling to—determination. It is very, very powerful.

What I began to see is that this prayer of Yeshua was actually a Passover vigil prayer. I pray you will be able to see this. What was the Father's will? It's that Yeshua give His life to pay the price for all who would turn to Him to be forgiven for their sins, and be reconciled to God, to be made citizens of the Kingdom of God—to be given the gift of Eternal Life, and be delivered from an eternity in Hell. God's will is that Israel and the whole world be set free from bondage to sin and death. When Yeshua prayed, *"Let Your will be done,"* that is what He was praying. Let there be this freedom for all.

If you think about what they would have been praying in those blood-covered houses in Egypt—what might they have been praying? *"Set us free from bondage. Free from Egyptian slavery."* In Egypt, they prayed for the protection of their families, their children, their sons especially. Yeshua was praying for His sons, His immediate disciples and all those who would follow Him over the next two thousand years..

> Luke 22:31-32 *"Shim`on [Simon], Shim`on, listen! The Adversary demanded to have you people for himself, to sift you like wheat! 32 But I prayed for you, Shim`on, that your trust might not fail. And you, once you have turned back in repentance, strengthen your brothers!"*

What was happening here was that ha-satan wanted to have those disciples. He wanted to keep them from the Kingdom of God and Eternal Life. If ha-satan had succeeded, Yeshua's work would not have endured beyond His death. There would have been nobody to carry on what He had done. He prayed and they were spared.

> Exodus 12:23 *ADONAI will pass through to strike down the Egyptians, but when He sees the blood on the crossbeam and the two doorposts, ADONAI will pass over that door, and will not allow the destroyer to come into your houses to strike you down.*

What we see there is that the destroyer actually came to each home, even those with blood over them, but the Lord was there, keeping vigil to prevent him from striking inside. In Gat Shemanim, satan came and he tempted Yeshua to deviate from God's plan. Yeshua's flesh cried out, "Let this cup depart from me." If He had departed and refused the cup, eternal death would have taken all of us, and it would have taken Him. But He said, "Not My will but Thine be done."

When He yielded to the Father's will, what we see happening there is another parallel to what happened in Egypt: the destroyer was coming and God was protecting.

> Luke 22:43 *There appeared to him an angel from heaven giving him strength, ...*

I hope you can see this that the Lord was there for Yeshua, protecting Him from ha-satan who was tempting Him at that time, and the Lord strengthened Him through this angel the same way the Lord was there in Egypt as the destroyer was coming upon the houses.

> Luke 22:44 *and in great anguish he prayed more intensely, so that his sweat became like drops of blood falling to the ground.*

I have heard people who believed that this was just descriptive. They were *like* drops of blood. But I've heard doctors talk about how this can really happen under extreme stress. When people are under such extreme stress, the capillaries that are next to the skin can expand and break and bleeding begins. This is an indication that this was happening in the oil press in the place of pressing.

Here is another parallel that I pray that you will get. Yeshua was in the oil press "*Gat Shemanim*" in that grove of olive trees, but He was also in a special dwelling place.

> John 1:14 *"The Word became flesh and dwell (or Tabernacled) among us."*

I want you to grasp that Yeshua was (is) God Himself dwelling in a human body. His dwelling place was the body He inhabited. Yeshua's blood began to come out in His sweat in the form of drops of blood all over His body. Here is another incredible parallel to Pesakh that Yeshua's Blood was placed on His dwelling place. Do you see it? It was placed on the body in which He was living. And like the blood on the doorposts of the dwelling places of the Israelites in Egypt, Yeshua's Blood protected Him from that attack of ha-satan.

This is so well done in the movie with ha-satan there telling Him, "It will never work. You're going to die." And such things. And when His sweat became as drops of blood, the angel was there to minister to Him. God was accompanying Him, preventing that destroyer from striking.

What I see here is that blood was needed in Egypt to protect the houses and the blood was needed in the oil press in "*Gat*

Shemanim" to enable Yeshua to get through this. Why the Blood? There is tremendous power in the Blood.

> *Revelation 12:11 They defeated him because of the Lamb's blood and because of the message of their witness. Even when facing death they did not cling to life.*

Protection by the Blood is part of our heritage. It is not just a "church" thing. It goes back all the way to this protection on the doorposts.

The Blood does many things. The Blood is what we are cleansed by, but what we are seeing here is that the Blood is also what we are protected by. The Blood is one of the weapons of spiritual warfare as we "apply the Blood."

What is God saying to us? All these parallels are so awesome. I hope they are awesome to you because they are testimonies that Yeshua is the Messiah because of the way in which these things line up and are fulfilled. And we just saw a new appreciation of the power of the Blood that it even protected Him. His own Blood was protecting Him.

We can see that Biblical Covenants are Blood Covenants. The Mosaic Covenant—the Sinai Covenant—is a Blood Covenant. The New Covenant—the Brit Khadashah—is a Blood Covenant. The Lord's Supper—we call the S'udat Adonai—where we partake of the memorial of the Blood—is a parallel of the blood on the doorpost and the Blood that He sweat. This blessed me so much when I first saw this. We take that Blood and we put it in our body. The blood of the Lamb is poured on the inside of us when we partake of the wine or grape juice of the S'udat Adonai (the Lord's Supper) and it is a protection.

Let's Pray

Father, I come before You right now and I thank You for all the things that we saw in this chapter. I pray that You will continue to speak to us about these parallels and their importance in proving that You are the Messiah.

Father, there may be a reader who is not sure they will be able to pass through the judgment and so I want to lift that person up to You right now. Your Word says that those who put their trust in You will not come up for judgment but have already crossed from death to life. I pray that they would see that You have made a way for them to enter into the Kingdom and to be protected from the coming judgment through that entrance way of the Blood in the same pattern as the lintel and the doorposts and the power of the Blood on the Cross where Yeshua died as the sacrificial offering.

If you have that doubt, pray in your own heart, *"Lord I receive Your sacrifice for my sin. I acknowledge that You are the Lord. I knock on that door. Please let me into Your Kingdom and Your protection."*

I pray, Father, for each of us here to have a fresh revelation of the power of Your Blood—the protecting power of Your Blood.

CHAPTER 3
MIXED MULTITUDE

Nissan, the Pesakh month, is the beginning of the year in the Biblical calendar. But if we go by the traditional Jewish calendar, which starts at Rosh Hashanah in the fall, Passover is the third of three commemorations of God's miraculous deliverance of the Jewish people. And the deliverance is in three very different ways. I had never noticed that sequence before. Maybe you have.

First it is Hanukkah in December when there was deliverance from being assimilated, from disappearing as a culture and a distinct people. That was achieved by a great and unexpected military victory by people who were not soldiers.

The second was Purim, which was a deliverance from being annihilated, and that was achieved by miraculous favor given to a young Jewish woman.

Then third we have Pesakh, which is deliverance from enslavement. It was achieved by miraculous powers given to an aged prophet. So they are very different, and yet they all end up with the same thing: God delivers His people.

---

* Photo: Yemenite Habani family celebrating the Passover Seder at their new home in Tel Aviv, 1946, Wikimedia. Public domain.

I wanted to cover something a little bit different in this chapter. There's another way in which the sacrificing of the lamb was important—another affect it had. And it's not in the Bible. So we don't know if this account is absolutely true, but the Bible certainly supports the possibility of it being true.

This is one of those Jewish roots. It's a hidden Jewish root because you have to find it in the Talmud. If you are not aware of what that is, the Talmud is a Jewish commentary on the Bible. It's something that's not to be taken as Scripture, but there is a lot we can learn from it and understand because some of the things that are written in it talk about how things were done way back in the time of Yeshua when people were much closer to the events that happened. Some of the things recorded in the Talmud are events that didn't make it into the Bible, but they certainly could be true.

So what does the Talmud say about this? It relates that something big happened in Egypt when that tenth day of Nissan came and all the heads of the households went out and got lambs for themselves. Whether they got one from their own flocks or they had to go buy one, they began rounding up the lambs. The Talmud tells us that the lamb was one of the creatures that was worshiped by the Egyptians, and so this caused a commotion.[10] Here are a couple verses in the Scripture that support this.

> Exodus 8:21 *So Pharaoh called for Moses and for Aaron and said, "Go! Sacrifice to your God— in the land.*

He didn't want to let them go out into the desert.

> Exodus 8:22 *But Moses said, "That would not be right. For the offerings we intend to sacrifice to ADONAI our God* **are an abomination to the Egyptians. If we sacrifice what is an abomination to the Egyptians, wouldn't they stone us?**

So Moses is saying here that they have to go into the wilderness to worship God by sacrificing animals. I believe it's

---

10 "War of the Egyptian Firstborn (1313 BCE)," Chabad.org, https://www.chabad.org/library/article_cdo/aid/117352/jewish/War-of-the-Egyptian-Firstborn.htm. Accessed Nov. 2018.

because of what the Talmud is saying. It's because the Egyptians worshiped these animals and to sacrifice them would've been an abomination.

So the Israelites are collecting all these lambs and the Egyptians would've said to them, "Um, what are you going to do with those lambs?"

They would've replied, "We're going to offer these to God. And it's going to happen in four days. At the stroke of midnight, God is going to pass throughout Egypt in order to execute the tenth and final plague. All the firstborn sons of Egypt will die, and the people of Israel will be free."

Try to put yourself in the place of some of the firstborn of Egypt at this point. They've gone through nine terrible plagues already. Each one happened just like Moses said it was going to happen. How would you think of this situation? You would be in great fear, right? This is not going to be just like the destruction of crops or frogs or darkness. This is the death of you! So, they would've been greatly concerned.

I began to understand a while back this whole thing about firstborns. In the ancient cultures, firstborns held very important positions in society because the inheritance always went to the firstborn. They ran the family. They led the family. After the patriarch died, the firstborn would be the one who would inherit the headship of the family.

So it was the firstborn who became the people in important positions in social structures and religious structures. They were the ones in authority. So all of those important people were going to be wiped out. This would almost be like saying something is going to happen that will wipe out all of our senators and representatives. Some of you might think that's good, but it would be like all the leaders in the government would be gone, and there wouldn't be any government anymore. So this was really very serious.

So the Talmud again relates that the firstborn of Egypt approached Pharaoh and his generals and demanded that they free the Jews! They brought forth reasons that this is in the interest of the nation.[11] Look, all of the firstborns, all of your

---

11 "War of the Egyptian Firstborn (1313 BCE)," Chabad.org, https://www.

leaders are going to die! They did this especially to protect themselves. But Pharaoh refused.

Then the Talmud also relates that the firstborn took up arms and engaged in a battle against Pharaoh and his troops, killing many of them, and Pharaoh continued to refuse to obey God.[12] So what happened next? Well, Pharaoh didn't give in. God sent the plague and all the firstborn in Egypt who didn't sacrifice a lamb and put its blood on their doorposts died. And there was great mourning. According to the Scriptures, there wasn't any house in the land of Egypt where there wasn't someone dead.

But we also read a little bit later in that same pivotal, important chapter 12 of the book of Exodus something very interesting.

> Exodus 12:38 *Also a mixed multitude went up with them along with the flocks herds and heavy livestock*

So there were people from Egypt who left Egypt with the Israelites when they went out. I believe that some of those were firstborn who had said, "I'm not going to chance this. I'm going to slaughter a lamb; and I'm going to put the blood on the doorposts of my house; and I'm going to stay in the house!" Then when everybody else was wiped out, they left with the people of Israel.

And there's another reason I would have left, if you think this through a little bit. If I as an Egyptian firstborn slaughtered a lamb and then put the blood on my doorposts, I would be in trouble with the rest of the Egyptians! They probably would be persecuting me and I would want to get out! So I would've wanted to escape with the Israelites.

Notice also that it doesn't say a few left. It says a mixed *multitude* left out of Egypt. We know there were millions of Israelites. We don't know how many a multitude is, but if you were doing like a comparative thing, you've got all these Israelites and then you've got a bunch of other people, and God says they are a multitude?! That means there's a lot of them! Otherwise compared to the Israelites, it would say there was a remnant!

---

chabad.org/library/article_cdo/aid/117352/jewish/War-of-the-Egyptian-Firstborn.htm, accessed Nov. 2018.
12 Ibid.

So a lot of people went out with the Israelites. And we don't usually think about this, but the Israelites did not reject them! They allowed them to go with them in the Exodus. And I believe they spent the next forty years in the desert with them. In fact, there's a reference to them in Numbers 11 just before Korah's rebellion. It speaks about a mixed multitude still being there.

So, like the Israelites, that generation of them also must have died before God could bring them into the Promised Land. So their children probably went into the Promised Land with the Israelites and possibly received an inheritance and assimilated and intermarried. All kinds of things could have happened with those Egyptian descendants.

It's important also to understand something else about that mixed multitude. It says "a mixed multitude." It doesn't say Egyptians. Egypt was a great empire. There may have been people from all around the world living in Egypt at this time. Many different ethnicities might have been there in this mixed multitude. Otherwise it would have just said Egyptians came out with them. So this is very interesting. And we are going to see that there's something very symbolic here, especially for those who are not Jewish, about joining with Israel at this critical time.

I actually was looking at this Biblical account a few years ago, and was interested enough to write down notes about it. Then as I was praying about it, asking God what I could say about it in my sermon, I didn't get anywhere. So I gave a totally different message for Shabbat HaGadol that year. The next year I looked at it again and saw that, oh wow, I took notes on it and didn't do anything with it. I thought, well that's kind of interesting.

So all of a sudden, after I read over it again, the Holy Spirit revealed to me that this story of the firstborns speaks prophetically of the situation that America was in at the time, and maybe still is when you are reading this. It not only gives a warning, but it also gives comfort to us. So that's where we're going to go with this now.

To set the stage, let's go back to Genesis 12 to a very familiar Scripture called the blessing of Abraham.

Genesis 12:3 *My desire is to bless those who bless you, but whoever curses you I will curse, and in you all the families of the earth will be blessed.*

I believe, like you most likely believe, that this promise of God's blessing, notice that there's a curse in there too, this blessing and curse of Abraham is to the promised child. It's through Yitz'chak (Isaac) and then through Ya'akov (Jacob) or Israel and to his descendants. I believe that our nation has experienced this blessing, especially over the past several decades, to the extent that we have blessed Israel. In a striking parallel to the firstborn in Egypt where they saw their leader, Pharaoh, oppressing the Israelites and opposing Moses, what kind of times are we in?

Several years back, we saw our government turning away from being a blessing to Israel. In the Obama administration, we even saw employees of the State Department cursing the leaders of Israel. They called Prime Minister Netanyahu derogatory names when they were talking amongst themselves. Somehow there was a hidden microphone and it got recorded. At that time, there was also outright opposition to an incredible level that we had never seen before.

Then the story came out about the meddling in the Israeli elections, of sending our tax dollars over there to support the meddling and doing everything in their power to defeat prime minister Netanyahu because he wasn't going along with our then president's program. So, many of us were fearful of the possible removal of God's blessing from our nation, and that the curse that goes with cursing Israel could come upon our nation. Many of us feared we would suffer the consequences of this militarily, politically, economically, and financially.

So can you see the parallel there? The Egyptian firstborns were crying out to Pharaoh, "Can't you see the hand of God in all those nine plagues?! Every plague that Moses said God was going to bring has come! They came because you refused to let the Israelites go. You cursed them. You kept them in slavery. All those plagues have come! We have suffered greatly! Now Moses is predicting a tenth plague worse than all the other nine combined! Yet you continue to stand against God's people. This plague is directed at us! The firstborns! If you don't let them go to worship their God the way He commanded them to worship, we're going to die!"

In the same way, we saw back then many Americans saying similar things to our leaders. When Prime Minister Netanyahu spoke before Congress in March 2015, we saw an incredible outpouring of support for him and for Israel from Congressmen.

People were saying, "Stop opposing! Stop manipulating! Stop pressuring! Stop endangering! Stop refusing to listen! Stop dishonoring! Stop audibly cursing and criticizing Israel! We believe you will be the cause of the blessing of Abraham to be removed and the curse of Abraham to come to our nation, and we will suffer the consequences!"

Who was saying that? You could see how us Jewish people would say that. But it wasn't just Jews. It was politicians. It was everyday people. It was Gentiles. It was senators and representatives. It was people all over the country saying it.

So that was how I saw this little side story from the Talmud. Again, I'm not saying it's necessarily true, but it certainly could have been true that those firstborn would've been in great fear and wondering what to do.

Question About Prayer

So in addition to that, one night that same year a question arose in our Messianic Judaism class that is opened to the public. The question was about how we are to pray and walk in the Spirit through such times. Let me give you the background to the question.

We had been studying the prophecies of Zechariah. Let's look at a couple of those prophecies. I recommend you read Zechariah chapter 12 through 14. It is an amazing passage. It reads like the current news.

> Zechariah 12:3 *Moreover, in that day I will make Jerusalem a massive stone for all the people. All who try to lift it will be cut to pieces. Nevertheless, all the nations of the earth will be gathered together against her.*

Other translations where it says "cut to pieces" say "will injure themselves." What does it mean "all who try to move or lift Jerusalem"? I think it can only mean to change who owns Jerusalem, or to move it's borders. So all who try to do that will be injured. And also it says that all the nations of the earth will be gathered together against her.

On a side note: Somebody in class asked, "Do you think it'll be the United States, too?" And someone else in the class said, "What does it say? It says 'All.'"

So we were like the firstborn of Egypt. We were seeing our nation stop being the defender of Israel and start siding with the Palestinians about lifting Jerusalem.

That's really what all the conflict is about. The Palestinians were demanding a return to the pre-1967 borders to be the starting place for negotiations. The pre-1967 borders divided Jerusalem. So they were saying the half of Jerusalem that was separate from Israel until 1967 must be ours. And we saw our State Department and our president, in all the negotiations, allowing that to go on rather than saying, "No, that's off the table. The Israeli's say that's not negotiable."

That is what Israel is saying, "We're never going to let Jerusalem become divided again." But back then our State Department was saying, "Oh no. We have to leave everything on the table."

Now understand that with this "all nations coming against Jerusalem," it's predicting a catastrophe. Zechariah is not predicting pretty things. In 14:2 he predicts the destruction of half of the city, the exile of half of the inhabitants, and rape of the women. So he's talking about there being real warfare and a terrible battle. But then in verse 3 he says this:

> Zechariah 14:3-4 *Then ADONAI will go forth and fight against those nations as He fights in a day of battle. 4 In that day His feet will stand on the Mount of Olives which lies to the east of Jerusalem, and the Mount of Olives will be split in two from east to west, forming a huge valley. Half of the mountain will move toward the north and half of it toward the south.*

You may know the rest of the verse. The Mount of Olives will split in two, and a river will flow out to the east and will turn the Dead Sea into a fresh water lake.

So this actually is the prediction of the Lord appearing in visible form. That's what this is referring to. It talks about His feet standing on the Mount of Olives, and the mountain splitting and him defeating the nations who have gathered around Jerusalem, which could include the U.S.

Then here's where it gets to be relevant to the question that was brought up in our class. In 12:10 we read this incredibly wonderful prediction:

> Zechariah 12:10 *Then I will pour out on the house of David and the inhabitants of Jerusalem a spirit of grace and supplication, when they will look toward Me whom they pierced. They will mourn for him as one mourns for an only son and grieve bitterly for him, as one grieves for a firstborn.*

Now this is in the Old Testament! This is nothing else than the prediction of the salvation of the people of Israel. How could you not recognize that this is the Messiah?! "Him whom they have pierced," "firstborn," all those things point to the Messiah. Perhaps this is what Paul was thinking of when he wrote in Romans 11:26 *all Israel will be saved.*

So here's the question that was brought up in our class. "If the Bible says that this is going to happen, including all the nations turning against Israel and this partial destruction, and then the salvation of Israel, isn't that a good thing? So shouldn't we be praying for that to happen rather than telling our Pharaoh to stop opposing Israel since it's written that he's going to do it anyway? Right?"

Do you see that it's a conundrum there? It's a paradox and a great question. I've struggled with that question. Many have struggled with this question. So I just began to pray for revelation because I really didn't have a great answer for the class. I think I said something, but it wasn't adequate.

The Mystery of Why We Pray

Here's the answer I got, and it's one of the mysteries of prayer, of why we are called to pray. Even though we know that following the battle against Jerusalem, God will save all Israel, we should not pray for the U.S. and other nations to attack Israel. Nor should we passively accept that that's what's going happen and there's nothing we can do about it.

See, here's the thing. We can't let our knowledge of the prophecies cause us to act or pray in ways that are contrary to God's heart's desire. His desire is very simply for all nations to love Israel and love the God of Israel. He doesn't want to see all these things happen. He just knows they're going to happen. Think of it this way. If we prayed that way—if we prayed, "Oh yea, let it come, Lord. Go ahead. Let's have them attack Israel, and then You will come back and we will see their salvation," we would be disobeying His command in Psalm 122:6 which you are most likely familiar with.

> Psalm 122:6 *Pray for the peace of Jerusalem*

We would be praying for the war of Jerusalem, not peace.

This would be similar to another prophesied event. We know that before the Lord returns and the great judgment happens, things are going to get worse on the earth. So you could say we should pray for it to get worse! That will hasten His return, right? No! No! That's not the way we are to pray. This is the mystery of prayer that is so hard to understand.

Here's what I saw in this: I believe that our prayers and our efforts are needed to bring about God's plan. So for the Lord to appear as predicted in Zechariah and defeat all the nations will require us praying that all Israel be saved.

That's the mystery.

Even though it seems like a terrible thing has to occur before the desired event, He wants us to be praying for His Will to be done, for Israel to be saved, for the nation to come to know Him, and then this plan will come to pass. So that's what we're to pray. We're to pray that God's faithfulness to Israel would be demonstrated in the face of all the nations turning against her at that time.

Are there any examples of that in the Bible? Well, the one I thought of was Moses. God told Moses that He was going to harden Pharaoh's heart so that He would have to bring all these plagues before they would get out, right? But Moses just continued to pray to God and plead with Pharaoh. He didn't say, "Hey, Pharaoh, it's going to happen. Too bad." No, he went and begged Pharaoh, and he prayed for God to soften his heart.

You may not be aware of this, but we get a lot of opposition in the Messianic Movement. One of the accusations from those who call themselves the "anti-missionaries" is that Messianic Jews have a hidden motive in trying to get Jewish people to believe in the Messiah. They say we do it so that the siege of Jerusalem will happen and the Messiah will return. They're saying, "You just want to see the Messiah return. That's why you're praying to have Jewish people saved. You don't care about Jewish people. You just want to see happen what you think is supposed to come to pass."

Interestingly, this is actually what the Muslims do. Have you ever read some of the stuff that Ahmadinejad was speaking when he was the president of Iran? Here's what he was saying. He believed he was called to cause chaos in the world so that the twelfth mahdi, the Muslim messiah, would show up and take over and take the world for Islam. You see, it is the same way of praying and acting. "I'll make things really bad so that God has to step in and bring judgment, and then we will have the whole world."

We are to pray for good, not evil. We're to pray for Jewish people to be saved, not attacked. The Spirit will lead us to pray according to God's heart, which is always full of mercy.

But then you might say, "Well, what about us? Are we going to die like the firstborn because the curse is going to come upon us?" Well, here's a word of encouragement about what happened there. Just as God brought the firstborn out who obeyed Him even though they were not part of Israel—that mixed multitude—God is able to bring us through these times. He's able to protect us in the midst of a nation that is turning away from Him—very clearly turning away from Him.

But He expects us to oppose that turning away, not just to go along with it. He expects us to pray that our country would turn back. We must always pray and work toward Godliness, toward God's heart and not give up because of predictions, even though the Bible says it will come about.

So what this is basically saying is that our eschatology, which is our study of predictive prophecies, should not interfere with our obedience in being led by the Spirit of God. The biggest problem I find in following eschatology is this. We don't know how those things that God says are going to happen are going to come about. Often times we think we know, but there's all these twists and turns that happen beforehand.

For instance, there are all these prophecies of Israel being reestablished and many people in the past felt that this was going to happen when the Messiah came. In fact, there was a large part of Orthodox Judaism that believed that Israel would be resettled after the Messiah returns. But what happened? Who established the State of Israel? It was secular Jewish people who didn't even believe in God! And when people saw that, they thought, "This can't be a fulfillment of prophecy!" But it was! It's so amazing. So you see what I mean? You can't know the details. You know that we are going to get to the end point, but the road may curve all around on the way there.

Actually you should be aware that this kind of eschatological thinking, making the eschatology, the future predictions, more important than the heart of God has really affected the Jewish people in a great way in terms of their salvation. Let me explain what this is. I call this the veil of dispensational theology.

Rabbi Sha'ul (Paul) said there is a veil over the hearts of Jewish people. Well, this is one of those veils. The veil of dispensational theology is this. The dispensational theologians' eschatological theories, which they believe very strongly, is that Jewish revival, actually based on Zechariah passages here, will occur after Yeshua's return and after the rapture. The people who believe this may love the Jewish people and believe that God still has a plan for Israel, but it doesn't involve Jewish people coming to the Lord until after the church is gone.

So what effect has this had? It has had an enormous affect because since a large part of the church believes that the revival of the Jewish people will happen after the rapture, they believe that the church doesn't need to work for it or apply any resources to it. It doesn't need to send any missionaries. It doesn't need to support any Jewish outreaches because it's all supposed to happen after the church is gone.

Is that correct? No! I'm a testimony that it's not correct. This Jewish person got saved before Messiah returned! The same is true for many other Jewish people!

Really, the Scripture that most supports this is Yeshua speaking to the people of Jerusalem just before He went to the Cross.

> Matthew 23:39 *For I tell you, from now on, you will not see me again until you say, "Blessed is he who comes in the name of ADONAI."*

So what is He saying here? I understand this to mean that when He comes back, He will be welcomed by the Jewish people. So that means they will already have turned to Him. They will already be seeing Him as the Messiah.

So the large number—thousands upon thousands—of Messianic Jews who are in existence today are all proof that revival is already happening. Yes, there's going to be something much bigger at the end of this battle. But that doesn't mean there isn't going to be revival leading up to this battle.

This is what my wife said to me when we were first praying about being involved in the Messianic Movement. "If you want to see Yeshua return, help reach the Jewish people with the Gospel. And if your heart aches for Jewish people who are lost, pray for them because that's the heart of God, for them and for all people."

So what could've happened if our American leadership would have gone the way it was going then, or what could happen if it would go that way again? What could happen that would actually work out for good? It is possible. Here are some things that came to my mind.

Number one, it could cause the American Jewish people to make aliya (immigrate to Israel), completing the prophecy of return from the north-south east-west. The return from the west has not happened yet.

Secondly, it could cause believers in United States to take a strong, visible stand for Israel, which would be a witness to the non-Messianic American Jews, which could bring revival in the Jewish community in the US by breaking down that opposition.

One of the major reasons why Jewish people are closed to the Gospel is their belief that Christians persecute them and hate them. So when they see a large part of the church standing up and supporting Israel, it will break that reason down. It's breaking it down in Israel.

It's wonderful that churches in many cities are holding the annual CUFI (Christians United For Israel) sponsored event called the Night to Honor Israel, because it is a way that the church visibly demonstrates that we support Israel, that we love Israel. It is a tremendous witness to the Jewish community that something has changed.

Third, I believe that a line is being drawn in the church by the Holy Spirit of deciding whether to support Israel or not, just like other lines that have been drawn over the years. Whenever those lines get drawn, there's revival in the church because the church begins to take a stand, and to say, "No, we are on this side of the line." So we hope this new line comes.

Lastly, this strong opposition that is raised to this turning away from what God has said in the Bible could cause America as a nation to turn back to God. It's not too late. This could be the issue that people take a stand about, that will cause our nation to turn back to God.

Notice that in all of these things, those walking with God are called to stand against the turning away. Even though it's predicted, we are called to work toward stopping that turning away from God. Even though we know from prophecy that it's going to happen, we still must stand and pray and work against it.

So that is my answer. On the other side of it, I think that if we get over the fear, we will see amazing works of God. For example, President Trump's decision in late 2017 to move the U.S. Embassy to Jerusalem. I think it's awesome to watch prophecy be fulfilled before our eyes. We're living in an age that nobody else ever lived in before, seeing these things happening, one after another, these prophecies coming to pass. And they're not shrouded in mystery. They're right out there.

To see "all nations turning against Israel," all you have to do is follow what the UN is doing. The General Assembly of the UN is constantly passing resolutions against Israel. The only reason they're not being put into practice is because the Security Council vetoes them.

The Security Council has veto power over what the General Assembly does. The General Assembly is 170 nations. The Security Council is about a dozen. So the Security Council, which includes the United States, vetoes those things and stops the UN from carrying out actions against Israel. But all of those other nations are already against Israel. What happens if we stop vetoing things? We don't know the details, but it would not be good.

So let's pray.

Father, we thank You as Jews, we thank You for hearing our ancestors' cries and responding to them 3500 years ago. We thank You for the great deliverance of Passover and for the Gentiles whom You have grafted in among us. We thank You that the miracles that You performed in Egypt were so great that not just a few but a multitude of Egyptians and other ethnic groups left with Israel. We also thank You that Israel welcomed that mixed multitude. They didn't chase them away, but let them leave Egypt with them.

We thank You that we are going to be remembering all this at the Passover in our homes. Father, it is so relevant today. We see our nation's leaders turning as Pharaoh did, hardening their hearts more and more almost every day. I keep thinking enough already, but new things keep coming out every day. We pray, Father, that You would help us and all who are being led by your Spirit, by Your Ruakh, to stand at this time.

Strengthen our leaders who are standing with Israel. Strengthen those senators and congressmen and those in the administration. Strengthen those in the public view who are speaking out. I pray, Father, again for Your blessing on the Night to Honor Israel. May it speak to the people in each city. May it break down that belief that I grew up with, that Christians hate us and persecuted us. Awaken a curiosity about who these people are that say that they're followers of Jesus, but they love us. And they're coming together to show their support. We pray for that to bring revival to the Jewish people around the nation. Open them up to the Good News.

I pray also for the church, Father. I know You are drawing a line in the church. You are separating those who will follow Your Spirit concerning Israel from the rest. I pray that You give strength to those who want to follow Your Spirit that this will bring revival in the church.

And I pray for those of us who are Jewish. Give us wisdom, Father, about what steps we are to take concerning Aliya (immigration to Israel). Maybe we are supposed to be actively pursuing it right now. But we understand, Lord, that right now we're not allowed to do it. The Israeli government says we cannot have citizenship. We pray that You would tear that down and give us the right of return.

Finally, we pray, Father, for the people of Israel that You would protect them as Your Word says, that You would fight against those who turn against Israel, even if it's our own nation, that You would make Yourself known as the Protector of Israel. We pray for protection specifically from Iran, the remnants of ISIS, from all the proxies of Iran, Hezbollah, Hamas, Al Qaida, all those that are active in the West Bank and Gaza and in Syria and in Africa and the Philippines and other places in the world. We pray, Father, for wisdom and for the protection of all Your people even to the point that they would see that it is You. Just as the miracle that Israel exists, that they are still there and still surviving and that it is Your miracle. We commit this to You in Yeshua's awesome Name. Amen.

CHAPTER 4
THE SERVANT AND THE SON

In this chapter, we are going look at the comparison between Moses and Yeshua and then apply what we learn to our own lives.

> Hebrews 3:5-6 *Also, Moshe was faithful in all God's house, as a servant giving witness to things God would divulge later. 6 But the Messiah, as Son, was faithful over God's house. And we are that house of his, provided we hold firmly to the courage and confidence inspired by what we hope for.*

As I was reading Hebrews a few years back, I was inspired to think about these two pillars of our faith, Moses and Yeshua. I will just briefly recount Moses' life story for you.

Moses was born in Egypt but had escaped the terrible afflictions that had befallen his people, the Israelites. The Pharaoh at the time that Moses was born had ordered the

---
* Painting: "Blood on the Doorposts," unable to find artist.

murder of all the infant sons of the Israelites. Moses escaped that because his mother hid him in a basket. He was raised by Pharaoh's daughter who had discovered the baby in the basket. But at age 40 Moses had to flee Egypt because while trying to protect an Israelite, he had killed an Egyptian slave master. After taking care of sheep in the desert for 40 years, marrying, and fathering two sons, God called him at the burning bush. In obedience, he came back to Egypt, and in the power of God, he prevailed over Pharaoh. The children of Israel were released to leave Egypt and begin to go toward the Promised Land. Pharaoh's army that chased after them was destroyed.

In reading the Exodus story again and watching the Exodus movie again that came out in 2006, I was amazed at Moses and his incredible perseverance to follow the Lord through so much tzuris—as we say in Yiddish—so many difficulties and trials, over and over again. Just think of all the things he encountered.

As I was praying about this, an outline came to me of how to learn from this. We will look at the enormous difficulties Moses faced, the fruit that he produced in overcoming those difficulties, and then we will talk about how he was able to overcome them.

Moses' Difficulties.
First let's hear from Moses himself.

Shalom, Shalom. I am Moshe *re'enu*. It is wonderful to be here to tell you some of my experiences that I went through when God called me to lead my people out of the land of Egypt. When He first called me at the burning bush, I was afraid. I was very much reluctant to go. I was afraid of the opposition that I would encounter. After all, our people were in bondage to the most powerful nation in the world—this cruel and powerful Pharaoh. He would never let them go. But God gave me things—signs—that enabled me to overcome Pharaoh.

I was also afraid that the people of Israel would not follow me because who was I? They didn't know me. I was a stranger coming back from the desert. But God gave me signs again to help persuade them.

When I came back, I first went to the people of Israel and I told them that God was going to set our people free. They asked, "How do we know?" I took the signs and I did the signs. I threw my staff to the ground and it turned into a serpent. I put my hand into my cloak and it turned white. I poured out water on the ground and it turned to blood, and they believed. They said, "We will follow you. Do what you can do."

And I said to God, "That was easy." It surprised me.

Then I went to Pharaoh and said, "Let my people go!"

Pharaoh said, "No way!" Aaron and I brought the sign that God had given me, the first plague, the plague of blood.

I said, "Let my people go!"

And Pharaoh said, "No way!"

We brought the second plague, "Let my people go!"

"Absolutely not!"

The third plague—ten terrible plagues and finally Pharaoh said, "Go! And take your people."

And I thought, "That was easy."

We went out. We crossed the Red Sea. The army of Pharaoh was destroyed by the return of the Red Sea. And I thought, "That was easy."

But then, I got out in the desert with my people. Let me tell you. That part was NOT easy!

If you have read the story, you know that I had outright rebellion. Korakh and his friends, thinking that they should be the leaders. Not just Korakh, but my own sister Miriam and my brother Aaron, thinking that they should be the leaders. Sometimes I would appoint someone to be my assistants and they would sin so terribly. Aaron with the golden calf. Aaron's sons in ways that were not approved by God. Zimri, bringing a Midianite woman in to have relations with in front of all the people! Terrible sins.

Not just my assistants. The people, so foolish and immature. Look at what they did. They complained and were ready to kill me because there was no water, not believing that God who had parted the waters of the Red

Sea could bring them water! They complained because there was no food. They complained because there was too much food. They complained about what kind of food there was. They made a golden calf, and then finally when we were about to enter in to the land that God promised, what did they do? They refused to go in.

That was not easy!

This understanding of Moses was new to me and it showed me something new about the cost of following God and leading His people. We are always in a battle. We always have opposition. My experience has been that the opposition from outside that is against us is easy to deal with. It is the struggles that come from within that are hard. I've had some outside opposition since I've been the Rabbi. I've had some non-Messianic Rabbis writing letters to the newspaper. We've had some anti-missionaries teaching against Yeshua. We've had some Christian theologians teaching Replacement Theology. But those were "easy."

The difficulty is in leading God's people. The worst difficulties are the ones that come from within.

The Fruit Moses Produced

What was the fruit of Moses' tzuris? He is revered—he was one of our greatest leaders before Yeshua. He left an incredible written legacy: the Torah! And he left a disciple named Joshua who was capable of leading the people of the Lord into the Promised Land and taking possession. Moses also had trained the people to be able to take possession of the Land, but it took forty years to train those people. Moses had amazing fruit.

How Moses was able to Overcome

How was Moses able to have this fruit in the face of such opposition from within his own community?

There are a few things I saw in here that were very interesting. First of all, Moses was called of God. Look at these verses.

> Exodus 3:4 When ADONAI saw that he turned to look, He called to him out of the midst of the bush and said, "Moses, Moses!" So he answered,

> *"Hineni." 5 Then He said, "Come no closer. Take your sandals off your feet, for the place where you are standing is holy ground." 6 Moreover He said, "I am the God of your father, the God of Abraham, Isaac and Jacob." So Moses hid his face, because he was afraid to look at God. ... 11 But Moses said to God, "Who am I, that I should go to Pharaoh, and bring Bnei-Yisrael out of Egypt?" 12 So He said, "I will surely be with you. So that will be the sign to you that it is I who have sent you. When you have brought the people out of Egypt: you will worship God on this mountain."*

Moses knew God had called him to do this thing. There was never a doubt in his mind. Secondly, Moses called on God. When the strategy—what he was supposed to do—was opposed by his people, Moses had a highly sophisticated, intellectual, elegant, dignified way of dealing with that opposition. Do you know what it was? He used it over and over again. If you read through the stories, the Scriptures tell us that he fell on his face before God. He didn't try to argue. He didn't try to bring violence. He simply fell on his face before God.

One of the things I saw as I was studying this that I hadn't seen before is conjecture, so you may disagree with me. Moses walked with God for a long time before he was called to deliver the people out of Egypt. Prior to my digging into this, I had the impression that before that experience at the burning bush, Moses was ignorant of God. If you watch the movies, that is how they portray it. He is just a shepherd, walking in the desert with his sheep and suddenly comes upon this bush, and God appears to him. In fact, in The Ten Commandments TV movie miniseries put out by Hallmark in 2006, the portrayal of how Moses was able to follow God through such adversity was a product of him hearing God audibly. They had God speaking to him at every step—a supernatural way of God imparting to him at critical moments.

To me it is hard to believe that Moses could go suddenly from a person without a relationship with God to following the Lord in the face of such tremendous opposition, displaying several of the fruits of the Spirit: patience, faithfulness, humility, and self-control. Those things don't develop quickly. I concluded that Moses had walked with God for a long time before the burning bush experience. Can I support that from the Bible? I asked the Lord, "Is this You? Is this in the Bible?" And I found some very interesting things.

I want to bring to your attention a character that is not very prominent in the story of Moses. This is the character of Moses' father-in-law Yitro (Jethro). If you want to look back at some verses in Exodus, we learn a little bit about Moses' father-in-law.

> Exodus 3:1 *Now Moses was tending the flock of his father-in-law Jethro, the priest of Midian. So he led the flock to the farthest end of the wilderness, coming to the mountain of God, Horeb.*

Jethro was a priest. In Hebrew, he was a cohane. He was the cohane of Midian where Mt. Horeb was. Horeb was a place where there was presumably a special presence of God. Was he really a priest of the true God—of the God of Israel? Was that really true? If you turn to Exodus 18, we find a very interesting verse. Just before the Israelites came to Mt. Sinai, Jethro visited Moses and brought his wife and two boys to him.

> Exodus 18:12 *Then Jethro, Moses' father-in-law, presented a burnt offering and sacrifices to God. Aaron also came along with all the elders of Israel to eat bread with Moses' father-in-law before God.*

What do you think? Was he really a priest of the one true God? I think so. This is surprising to us. How can a non-Israelite be a cohane? Well, we have Melchizedek who was not an Israelite. Balaam, also not an Israelite, was a prophet. I have concluded that we don't know what God was doing among the other peoples of the world during these times.

How does this all connect? Moses met Jethro forty years before the burning bush. He married his daughter. I have concluded that Jethro taught Moses to know the Lord forty years earlier and discipled him in walking with the Lord those forty years out there in the desert.

Why am I making a big deal about this? Why is this important to us? I believe it is very important because God wants all of us to be like Moses. Really. He wants every one of us to be like Moses. He wants every one of us to follow Him, to overcome opposition, to fall on our faces before Him when opposition comes, to persevere, to teach, to make disciples, and to leave a legacy.

The problem with the picture of Moses that we get from the movies is that Moses' ability to do those things came from some special supernatural visitation he had that maybe we've never experienced. Some of you may be hearing audible voices from God. I can say that I have never heard an audible voice. I've heard God in my inner spirit, but not in an audible voice.

The problem with seeing Moses that way is that we won't aspire to be like Moses. We will think it is too much for us. But if we see Moses as a person who walked with the Lord the way we are called to do, learning obedience by being discipled and going through trials, then we are inspired to follow the Lord through similar tzuris—through similar troubles like Moses had.

The second thing I saw about Moses is that Moses was a prince. Yes, the movie, The Prince of Egypt had it right, although not all right. (For one, I don't know where they got his brother.)

> Exodus 2:10 *After the boy grew older she brought him to Pharaoh's daughter and he became her son. So she named him Moses saying, "Because I drew him out of the water."*

Moses was raised as a son of Pharaoh's daughter. Why is it important that he was a prince? Here's the reason. The rest of the Israelites have been enslaved by the Egyptians for many, many years. What happens when people are slaves for a long time is that they develop what is called a slave mentality. They think like slaves.

The Seder foods that we eat at the Passover Seder remind us of what the people went through. At a Seder, we dip the karpas (usually parsley) in salt water, and remember the tears of slavery. Then we eat the maror (bitter herb, usually horse radish) and remember the bitterness of slavery. We eat the kharoset (a sweet apple and nut mixture) and remember the hard labor of building the buildings with mortar and brick.

As slaves for maybe 300 years (depending on how long it took the Egyptians to forget Joseph), their minds were trained to think in the ways of this world, in the ways of Egypt. Slaves generally live in fear. They live in hopelessness and have lots of hurts. Usually slaves don't have vision to do great things with their lives because they are slaves. Usually they don't have a willingness to take a risk because whenever they have done that, they have been beaten.

Usually they don't have much confidence in themselves because they have been put down. They are at the bottom of the social ladder. They don't have any expectation that they can make a difference in this world.

Usually slaves don't trust authority figures because they have been abused by authority figures. Usually slaves are not willing to sacrifice themselves for a cause because it is hard for them to believe in a cause because if they are still slaves, what good is that cause? I believe this is why Moses had so much trouble with his followers. They were coming out of hundreds of years of being slaves.

Look at Moses. What a difference it would have made because of the way he was raised, not as a slave but as a prince of Egypt. He wasn't beaten down or made to feel hopeless, fearful, rejected, abused, or despised. Moses' adoptive father was all-powerful and although he was cruel to the Israelites, I am speculating that he was good to his own family and that he loved, cared for, and cherished Moses. I speculate that Moses had everything he wanted in life because of who his father was, and that his father actually had great plans for Moses and encouraged him—opened doors for him.

Now we know Moses still had some baggage. He was raised in Egypt where they worshiped many, many gods. If you read the story, it is obvious that he had some baggage from being a prince, like when he expected people to do things when he told them to do them, which didn't always happen. That is how he got into trouble and lost his temper and ended up fleeing Egypt.

I believe it was because he was so different from the rest of the people that he was able to come in and be that spark, that one who would lead them out of Egypt. Let us compare what we have talked about here, about Moses, with someone else—Yeshua.

Our writer of Hebrews did this. We are going to go through the same outline with the same three things: the difficulties He faced, the fruit He produced, and then about how He was able to overcome.

Yeshua's Difficulties

First let us talk about Yeshua's tzuris. He had direct opposition: the Sanhedrin, the Pharisees, the Sadducees, the Scribes, and the Romans. Even some of His own people directly opposed Him. He tried to preach in His own home synagogue and they were going to throw Him off the cliff. He had direct opposition from spiritual enemies: ha-satan and demons.

How about from within? We know that one of His closest followers betrayed Him. The people whom He had spoken to and perhaps done miracles for, when asked this question, "Shall we release Yeshua or Barabbas?" What did they do? They asked for Barabbas, condemning Yeshua to death.

Then we have abandonment by His own close friends. Peter left Him when He was arrested, as did all the other disciples apparently, except John. His family, earlier in His ministry, did not want to have anything to do with Him. Many of His disciples left Him when He spoke harsh words.

Then we have the foolishness of His followers. Some of His disciples wanted to call fire down from heaven. Others argued about who was the greatest amongst them. Some of them tried to stop Him from the plan of God for His life.

Yeshua's Fruit

Yeshua persevered and became our greatest leader of all time—our Savior—and produced incredible fruit. He, also, like Moses, left a written legacy, the Brit Khadashah (New Testament) and He discipled twelve men. Those twelve men, according to the Scriptures, turned the world upside down.

How Yeshua Overcame

How was Yeshua able to follow the Lord and overcome all this opposition and bear all this fruit? Again, He was called.

> Matthew 3:17 *and a voice from heaven said, "This is my Son, whom I love; I am well pleased with him."*

He called upon God as Moses did.

> Hebrews 5:7 *During Yeshua's life on earth, he offered up prayers and petitions, crying aloud and shedding tears, to the One who had the power to deliver him from death; and he was heard because of his godliness.*

He consistently spent long hours, sometimes all night, in prayer to His Father.

Thirdly, we may not appreciate it very much, but Yeshua walked with God a long time before He began His public ministry. And He suffered many things.

> Hebrews 5:8 *Even though he was the Son, he learned obedience through his sufferings.*

I believe that as Moses who did not achieve obedience just by hearing from God the way we don't hear from God, so Yeshua was also not able to do the things He did merely because of the Divine power—special power that we don't have, even though He was the Son of God. Why do I believe that? Because in the book of Philippians, we are told that He emptied Himself of that power.

> Philippians 2:7-8 *On the contrary, he emptied himself, in that he took the form of a slave by becoming like human beings are. And when he appeared as a human being, 8 he humbled himself still more by becoming obedient even to death—death on a stake as a criminal!*

He learned obedience. He learned to overcome through the things that He struggled with, even to death.

Finally, Yeshua was raised as a Prince.

Philippians 2:6 *Though he was in the form of God, he did not regard equality with God something to be possessed by force.*

We have to understand that what the Brit Khadashah teaches us is that Yeshua existed before He came to earth as an infant. When He came to earth as an infant, He was fully a human being. He took on the form of a slave, but somehow at an early age, He came to know that His real Father was not an Israelite subject to a Roman emperor. But His real Father was the true King of the Universe—Elohenu Melekh HaOlam.

How do I know this? At age 12 or 13, His parents found Him in the Temple debating with the scholars. When his parents were rebuking Him, He said to them, "Why did you have to look for me? Did you not know that I had to be concerning myself with My Father's affairs?" So, at least from the age of 12 or 13 until He entered public ministry at 30 (18 years) He knew who He was. He knew He was the son of the King of kings. He knew He was a prince.

What does this mean? This means He was not overcome by the world's way of thinking, but He learned to think and live and act as the prince of God's Kingdom. Even though His people were subject to the Roman empire, He was a subject of a different kingdom. He was the subject of the glorious Kingdom of God. Thus, He was aware of the power of God that was available to Him. He had such trouble from His followers because they were still walking in the ways of this world. They were still walking in a slave mentality.

Let's make this a little more personal. What about you and I? The traditional Haggadah says some very wonderful things about Passover. It exhorts us that we must all make the journey out of Egypt ourselves. Spiritually, we all need to make that journey. How do we do that?

First, we need to identify with the fact that we are like slaves because of the culture that we live in—because of the way in which we think—because of the systems that we are influenced by. Each of us must be set free by King Messiah through His shed Blood, the Blood of the Lamb. We must experience His breaking the power of those enslaving forces and drowning them in the waters.

Then we must go on from that Red Sea experience and learn the Laws of this new Kingdom that we are part of and walk in those Laws. And we must trust Him, depend on Him to travel from that place to the Promised Land—from slavery in the kingdom of this world that has enslaved us—to liberty in the Kingdom of God.

Now let's use the same outline for ourselves and look at it from a personal point of view.

Our Difficulties

We all face enormous difficulties following the Lord. Do you disagree with that? I didn't think so. Every one of us faces great difficulties and great struggles. One of the real surprises of being in the ministry, one of the real struggles and one of the real delights is that you get to hear people's stories. Before I came into the ministry, I thought there were some people who just had it easy. Everything went along fine in their lives. It was just a nice walk through the garden. But you know what? I have yet to meet a person like that. I've talked and shared with many, many people that have told me their life stories. I've never met anybody who has had it easy. Everybody struggles.

Our Fruit

It is God's purpose for each one of us to overcome these difficulties. That is His purpose in our life. We are to walk through these things with His help. We are to follow Him. We are to overcome through Him. We are not to escape from the trouble; we are to overcome it. This is how we grow. This is how we bear fruit. It is God's plan that we bear fruit.

How We Overcome Difficulties

Let us take a few minutes to talk about this third aspect where the meat is of all this. How can we overcome and follow the Lord and bear fruit? Just like Moses and just like Yeshua, we all have to know that we are called. I want to tell you today that if you have given your heart to the Lord and have committed to follow and obey Him, you have been called. Don't ever doubt that you have been called. You have been called by Him for a specific role in the Kingdom of God. You have been called by Him to bear fruit.

Secondly, we all have to learn to fall on our faces when we face difficulty. That is where most of us fail because we don't have that as a natural instinct. Most of us try to do it on our own strength first. That is where Moses was such a great example to us. It wasn't that he was so strong or smart or that he was so experienced. It was that he fell on his face and depended on God.

Thirdly, we need to understand that this walk with the Lord is long term. It takes a whole life. As we walk, the trials never end. You don't just get over them and find that everything is easy from then on. It keeps coming. You have to learn to walk through those trials with Him with you and then those trials are a joy. *Count it all joy when you encounter difficulties* (See James 1:2). They are a joy. They are not easy, but they are a joy because the fruits of the Spirit begin to develop in our lives—because of the things we have to deal with—because of the struggles we go through.

Finally, we need to begin to think like princes and princesses because that is what we are. We are children of the King. Do you feel like a prince or a princess? Hopefully, by the time you finish this book, you will feel like a prince or a princess because you are. You're a child of the King of kings.

Why is that so important? We saw that many of Moses' and Yeshua's problems were caused by their followers. As we seek to follow the Lord, we often mess up because we don't think like He thinks. He calls us to step out and lead others. We encounter opposition because the people we are trying to lead don't think like He thinks. Hopefully, we are learning to line up our thoughts to think like He thinks. Listen to what God says in Isaiah 55:

> Isaiah 55:8-9 *"For My thoughts are not your thoughts, nor are your ways My ways." It is a declaration of ADONAI.* 9 *"For as the heavens are higher than earth, so are My ways higher than your ways, and My thoughts than your thoughts.*

Now here is the problem. Most of the time, we don't even know that we are missing it in this way. We are just like the Israelites. Wait, let me stop spreading it around. I am just like the Israelites. I think that the way I think is normal. It is the only way I know to think. It is the way I was raised and the way I've developed. It's how my friends around me think. But it is really of this world and not God's way of thinking.

Some of you were raised in a Godly home and you may think—we can do it. Our parents are Godly parents and they are teaching us Kingdom thoughts. That is surely a tremendous advantage, but the world is still constantly bombarding us with its way of thinking. As you go out into the world, even the young person being raised in a Godly home or even going to a Godly school, thinking Godly thoughts, you are going to encounter over and over again this pressure from the world to think the way the world thinks, like a slave. Why do I call it a slave mentality? That is a hard word, but it is true.

> John 8:34 *Yeshua answered them, "Yes, indeed! I tell you that everyone who practices sin is a slave of sin."*

That sin can be "B-Y" sin—Before Yeshua. In other words, the things that you got into before you turned to the Lord are still affecting your life. There may still be some chains that are binding you. Or you could have fallen, as many of us do, into "A-Y"—After Yeshua. Things that happened after you come to Yeshua can bring bondage to your life also.

I would like to expand on what Yeshua said there to something a little bigger because the things that enslave us are not necessarily the result of our own sin. Sometimes they are a result of other people's sin. Maybe our parent, or sibling, or someone else or even a government abused us or hurt us or something happened that traumatized us. All those things that are a result of sin that affect us have the potential of putting us into bondage.

This has been very clear to me because over the last two decades, we have been working with people who have come out of a communist culture. One thing that communism strongly teaches is atheism. But it teaches more than that. It instills fear and is very controlling. All kinds of negative things were going on in that culture. The government kept the people in poverty while the communist party officials lived well. Some people had to steal just to survive the system.

One day we were talking with Russian-speaking people about sin. We asked, "What are some of the things that are sins?" Stealing came up.

One woman said, "I don't think stealing is always a sin."

"Oh? Why not?"

"Well, when you steal from someone who has more than you do, it is not a sin."

"What? What about when someone who has less than you, steals from you?"

"Oh, then it is a sin."

That was the culture they were brought up in. We need to be asking God to show us in what ways our thinking does not line up with His thinking. In what ways are we still thinking in the ways of this world? How are we displaying a slave mentality rather than the Kingdom mentality—the mentality of a Prince?

Take the time to make a list—be open and honest with yourself.

On the following page, there is a list in which worldly thinking is contrasted with Biblical, Kingdom thinking.

WORLDLY THINKING	KINGDOM THINKING
No absolute truth	I am the Truth
Everyone should look out for #1	Give and it shall be given unto you.
There is never enough. (slave mentality of want)	There is plenty. (Prince mentality)
I do not have resources	I have all the riches of my Father.

[God wants us to understand that there is no lack with Him. If we are doing His will, He will provide abundantly. We have such a struggle to do this.]

WORLDLY THINKING	KINGDOM THINKING
No one can get away with doing that to me. I'll make them pay.	Beloved do not give way to vengeance. "Vengeance is mine, says the Lord."
How can that person do such a terrible thing?	"Judge not that you be not judged."
Eat, drink and be merry because that is the only reason we are here.	"If anyone wants to come after Me, let him say "no" to himself, take up his execution stake (cross) and follow Me.
My worth is dependent on what I own, control, know, do, who likes me, what I have accomplished	"What will it benefit a person if he gains the whole world an loses his soul"
Do unto others before they can do it unto you.	"Do unto others as you would have them do unto you.
I am not accepted, by God, by people	"He made us accepted in the beloved."

[Many people suffer or struggle with rejection. "People reject me. People don't love me." But God says, "You are my child. I love you and I accept you."]

WORLDLY THINKING	KINGDOM THINKING
I'm too stupid, ugly, weak, sinful, ignorant, old, young to be used by God.	"You did not choose Me but I chose you. I have commissioned you to go and bear fruit that will last."
I have no purpose in life. Life is meaningless	"I know the thoughts that I think toward, you, thoughts of peace and not of evil, a future and a hope." God has a plan for each of our lives.
If I submit to Godly authority I'll be controlled, I'll be abused. I'm going to be independent. I'm going to do my own think.	"It must not be like that among you. Whoever wants to be your leader must become your servant."
No one truly loves me.	"You have loved them just as much as You have loved Me." (said to His Father)

[The love by which God loves His Son is the same love by which He loves you.]

WORLDLY THINKING	KINGDOM THINKING
No one will stand by me. They will all desert me.	"I will never leave you nor forsake you."
I don't want to be disciplined.	"For the Lord disciplines those He loves."
I can't ask big things of God. I don't deserve them.	"Have no fear little flock for your father has resolved to give you the Kingdom."

Yeshua wants to deal with our worldly mindsets and our worldly mentality.

> Romans 12:1-2 *I exhort you, therefore, brothers, in view of God's mercies, to offer yourselves as a sacrifice, living and set apart for God. This will please him; it is the logical "Temple worship" for you. 2 In other words, do not let yourselves be conformed to the standards of the 'olam hazeh. Instead, keep letting yourselves be transformed by the renewing of your minds; so that you will know what God wants and will agree that what he wants is good, satisfying and able to succeed.*

How do we get our minds renewed? First of all we offer ourselves as a living sacrifice. We offer to serve Him. Then we let Him transform our minds. How does He do that? He uses a very specific process. It is His Word that transforms our minds.

> Ephesians 5:26 (KJV): *That he might sanctify and cleanse it with the washing of water by the word,* CJB: *making it clean through immersion in the mikveh, so to speak,*

> Isaiah 55:11 *so My word will be that goes out from My mouth. It will not return to Me in vain, but will accomplish what I intend, and will succeed in what I sent it for.*

Let us pray

Father, we thank You for this season in the year and for the awesome things You did at this time. We thank You for what Moses did and for what Yeshua did. We believe that You have called us to do "exploits." Help us to be like Moses. We know we're not going to do exactly what Moses did, but You have something for each of us to do.

Father, I pray that Your Spirit would confirm Your call on every person who reads this book. That You would be speaking to hearts and that every person would know that if they have turned their hearts to You, if they have committed to following

You, You have a call on their lives. You have a plan for them. You have something for them to do that will bear fruit.

Father, I pray that we would have patience to let Your fruit grow as we walk with You through every trial. Lord, I pray for a supernatural revelation of how our thinking is not in line with Your way of thinking and how we have adopted the ways of the world and how those ways have seeped into us.

Lord, we pray that You would renew our minds that we might begin to think as princes and princesses, sons and daughters of the King. We pray that You would wash us with the water of Your Word. Wash out those worldly ways of thinking and enable us to bear much fruit.

I pray especially for those who have heard the call to leadership. I pray they will be able to persevere because of the example of Moses and the example of Yeshua—to persevere through those difficulties of leading, to understand that nothing comes easy, but that everything is possible to those who believe. We thank You in the mighty Name of Yeshua. Amein.

CHAPTER 5
Removing Khametz

I was going to call this chapter, "Matzah Balls." But I decided to be more serious and include a Hebrew word you are going to learn, the word khametz (also spelled hametz). [The kh is a guttural sound in the back of your throat.]

Passover is part of *Khag HaMatzah* (Feast of Unleavened Bread), in which we eat no leaven for seven days, sometimes referred to as the Passover Week. We are going to learn a little bit about it. Every year when we come around to these holidays I think, "Is there anything new, Lord?" I've been talking about them for so many years, but every year there is something new! One year I realized I had never studied Khag HaMatzah. I had studied Passover and Resurrection Day but never this. I was excited.

> Exodus 12:19 *For seven days no hametz (khametz) is to be found in your houses, for whoever eats hametz, that soul will be cut off from the congregation of Israel, whether he is an outsider or one who is born in the land. 20 You*

---
* Illustration: "The Searching for Leaven" by French Engraver, Bernard Picart, circa 1733–1739. Public domain.

73

are to eat no hametz; in all your houses you are to eat matzot.

Khametz (also spelled hametz) is anything that will make bread or food rise. Sourdough, yeast, baking soda or anything else that makes things rise is forbidden.

You can see that this commandment is quite severe. It is commanded for us as Jews to keep this. It is optional, as we know from Acts 15, for those who are not Jewish, but it is a very strong commandment. We will be cut off from Israel if we don't keep it.

The most significant and hardest part of these seven days for us is being forbidden to eat any leaven. After our Passover Seder one year, on a Tuesday night, I slept in a bit that Wednesday, and when I woke, I came downstairs. Wednesday is usually my fast day when I only drink fruit juice, but my normal routine on a non-fasting day is that I get an orange first thing. I came downstairs, went to the refrigerator, grabbed an orange, and sat down and started eating it. About half way through, I thought, "Oh my! Today is Wednesday, my fast day. Why am I eating this orange?"

The Lord spoke to me and said, "It's a Feast, Jim. You're not supposed to be fasting on a Feast day."

I said, "But Lord, it's not really a feast because we're eating unleavened bread which is not something we want to eat! We are fasting leaven."

Then He said, "Look it up."

So, I looked it up and sure enough the word is khag which means festival or feast. This is interesting because, if you think about it, it is a feast but in terms of a denial. What I understand, in studying the history, is the Egyptians were expert bakers.[15] One of the things the Israelites enjoyed very much was all the pastries and breads. Now when they came out, God was saying, "None of that."

So, it's a feast but we are being denied, it seems like. But we are going to see why it is not being denied on the spiritual level.

---

15 April Sanders, "What Are Some of Ancient Egypt's Dessert Dishes," TheClassroom.com, https://classroom.synonym.com/ancient-egypts-dessert-dishes-15909.html. Accessed Nov. 2018.

What is the Scriptural reason that we eat matzah?

> Exodus 12:39 *They had baked matzot cakes from the dough that they brought out of Egypt. It had no hametz, because they were thrust out of Egypt and could not delay, so they had not made provisions for themselves.*

They left hastily. The Egyptians said, "Get out of here!" They were fearful of any more plagues. What I get out of this is that they had the dough mixed. If you've ever made bread, you know that you let it sit in a warm place undisturbed and it rises. They would've probably made bread from sourdough which takes several days to rise rather than just hours.

What happened was that because it was already mixed they just grabbed it and left. The Bible talks about it being in their kneading troughs and so they just wrapped it up and took it, but because it was taken out of that warm place and shaken up, it did not rise. When they had their first stop and tried to bake it—instead of it rising, it just sat there and this was the flat bread that is called Matzah.

The spiritual meaning in Judaism, as you can read in any Haggadah, is that it is because our forefathers were to leave behind the sins of Egypt. The Khametz or leaven represented sin. You hear people say that leaven represents sin, but many times they don't understand where that came from. It came from Khag HaMatzah because when we went out, we were leaving behind all the sins of Egypt.

Khametz was chosen by God as a symbol of sin. Without khametz, their bread was flat. They were supposed to see it as the symbolism that they left behind the sins of Egypt.

As I mentioned before, if you read in any Haggadah, there is this wonderful phrase, "All of us have to come out of Egypt." What does that mean? It means all of us have to come out of the ways of the world and leave those things behind which are represented by the khametz.

Some of the traditions around Khag HaMatzah actually begin before Passover because it is not only a question of not eating leaven, there is a cleansing of the houses that is supposed to go on ahead of time. An interesting tradition has developed because of it, which is based on this verse:

> Exodus 12:18-19 *During the first month in the evening of the fourteenth day of the month, you are to eat matzot, until the evening of the twenty-first day of the month. For seven days no hametz is to be found in your houses, for whoever eats hametz, that soul will be cut off from the congregation of Israel, whether he is an outsider or one who is born in the land.*

This has led to this being a time of spring cleaning in the Jewish culture, making sure your houses are all clean and all the leaven is removed. I think Judaism can actually take credit for the whole idea of spring cleaning. Every year before Passover, observant Jewish mothers are exhausted from cleaning their houses because it is the tradition to clean the whole house top to bottom in preparation for Passover in obedience to that Scripture. Then there is a cute tradition involving the father and his children, which we will get into later.

It's not a trivial thing to get rid of your khametz because you've got to get it off your property.

> Deuteronomy 16:4 *No hametz should be seen with you in all your territory for seven days....*

So that means that even if you decide to throw khametz away, if your trash bin is still there on your property, it's still there! I jokingly tell my congregants, "Don't bring it here to the synagogue and put it in our trash bin either." ☺

The Matzah rules and traditions are interesting. If you go to the store, like in November, you can buy Matzah there, but the package won't say, "kosher for Passover." It is important to understand what "kosher for Passover" means. Special Matzahs are made for Passover.

The Rabbis have built what is called *"a fence around the law."* That is, there are rules around rules in Judaism that keep us from breaking the Law of God. (More on that in a later chapter.)

Matzah that is "kosher for Passover" is made in a very special way. The flour and water are mixed and baked in less than 18 minutes from when they are mixed. The reason for this is that the rabbis actually researched this and found that if you take flour and water and put them together and you wait 18 minutes, they begin to ferment. That fermentation is what we call "sourdough." The souring is the fermenting process and it begins in 18 minutes. Regular matzah can be over 18 minutes, but Passover Matzah must be baked in less than 18 minutes.

You are also not supposed to keep a box of Matzah from one year to the next even if it is kosher for Passover because the researchers have found that if you leave the matzah for a certain length of time, the microbes will get on it and it will start to ferment. They're saying that there could be some microscopic fermentation activity that goes on if the matzahs are out too long, even though they're sealed in a bag. So last year's matzah is not kosher for this year's Passover. Now, I have my doubts about that because I've left Matzah around for a year and it doesn't look any different to me, but that is the conclusion from the scientific studies they've done.

Another interesting thing in Ashkenazi tradition is that not only do we not eat leavened bread, but we don't use flour at all. This is pretty far out, but instead of using flour, they take matzahs that are already baked and can't ferment any more and grind them up into Matzah meal. We use that to make things like breading for a chicken, for example. You can't bread it with flour, you bread it with ground up Matzah meal. A further Ashkenazi tradition is that there are no grains or legumes used at all for this whole week because we can't eat anything that expands when it is cooked. So this rules out corn, rice, beans, lentils, pasta, none of which have leaven in them. But traditionally you can't eat any of those things because that's the tradition.

So we make delicious food with the Matzah meal. We make matzah balls for matzah ball soup and all kinds of different things to make it a feast (such as those listed in chapter one). It takes a special effort and creativity to think of festive dishes that are kosher for Passover according to all the rules.

It is always interesting to me how they have taken the basic Laws of God and over the years the rabbis and traditions have made them stricter and stricter.

Whenever I study the Moadim—the Appointed Times—I always ask myself three questions about them. The first question is, "How does this Appointed Time point to Yeshua being the Messiah?" The second question is, "How did Yeshua celebrate this? How did He use the ordinances for that Appointed Time and the traditions that developed around it to enrich or enhance His teachings?" The third question is, "How did Yeshua fulfill it? How did He take what was portrayed there as a physical thing and through what He did, spiritually fulfill it?"

Often times you hear people say, "Yeshua fulfilled this." They are thinking of Matthew 5:17. But many times they forget the other two aspects, that they point to Him, and that He observed them and used them.

Now, let's look at Khag HaMatzah and answer those three questions.

How Does the Appointed Time of Passover Point to Yeshua Being the Messiah?

If you've gone to a Passover Seder, you remember the Afikomen ceremony. To me that is the most incredibly detailed, spectacular picture in this Moad that points to Yeshua being the Messiah. If you remember, we take the middle Matzah, the center one of three, and we break it in two. We take one half and wrap it in a white linen napkin. It is called the Afikomen, a Greek word that means *He comes*. Later during the Seder the leader hides the Afikomen. Then when the children have finished their food and the adults are still talking, the children are told to search for the Afikomen. The child who finds it returns it to the Seder leader and receives a gift.

When you lay this out, you see that this is the story of Yeshua and what He suffered. The matzah is pierced in a pattern of stripes and is browned in its cooking so it looks like it has been bruised. So, the Afikomen ceremony is the story of the crucifixion, the resurrection, and the gift of Eternal Life that the finders of Him get. It is powerful in the way it points to Yeshua being the Messiah.

The most amazing thing about it is that in every Jewish household around the world—Jewish people who don't believe

He is the Messiah or that actively reject that He is the Messiah—do this ceremony at their Passover Seders. The picture is painted before them over and over again every year. My childhood growing up included our yearly Orthodox Passover Seders. When I read the Gospel story, I was astounded at the similarities to the Afikomen. When you hear more details about that ceremony, it will astound you, too. Read on.

How did Yeshua Use the Traditions Around This Moad in His Teachings?

Tzfoon Ceremony

We are going to look at two ways in which Yeshua used the ordinances and the traditions that developed around this Moad to enrich or enhance His teachings. The first way is that He built on what is called the Tzfoon ceremony in the Seder, which is the last part of the Afikomen ceremony.

I want to explain something to you. I hope you grasp this because this is really amazing when you understand what was going on here. After the Afikomen is found by the child, he is given a gift. It is redeemed, bought back with a gift, and the leader of the Seder now has the Afikomen.

The leader unwraps it and breaks it up and distributes it to all the people. It is considered the dessert. It is the last thing we eat after any other dessert. What happened then is that Yeshua took that Afikomen and made it the Matzah of the *S'udat Adonai* the *Lord's Supper*. We know this because in the Scriptures it says it was *after the supper*. So that would have been the Afikomen after the supper because that is the only time Matzah is eaten after the supper.

He took that and said, *"This is My body which is broken for you."* Here is what is strange about that. Lamb was still being eaten during Passover Seders when Yeshua walked this earth. It specifically commanded that they eat lamb at their Seders. We understand from the Talmud about Jewish tradition, that lamb was to be the last thing that was eaten. You were supposed to leave the Seder with the taste of lamb in your mouth because the lamb was what was sacrificed.[16] The lamb was the most important food of the whole ceremony. The Matzah is important and the bitter herbs are important, but the lamb was the most important thing.

From the time of Moses until the year 70 AD, Jewish people ate lamb at their Passover Seders. It was a roasted lamb. They followed all of God's commandments about it. They didn't break its bones and ate it all before morning—all those commanded things they observed for the food of the Covenant. In the year 70 AD, the Temple was destroyed by the Romans. A couple of years after that, the rabbis concluded that we could no longer eat lamb at Passover because without a Temple, we couldn't sacrifice them anymore.

So today, Jewish people purposely choose meat for the Seder meal that could not be sacrificed. So, for example in our family we didn't use beef because cattle could be sacrificed. We would have chicken because chicken was never taken to the Temple to be sacrificed. Chicken could be the food.

What happened then was that the Afikomen, the Matzah after the meal, became the memorial of the lamb.[17] We eat the Afikomen after the meal to remember the lamb, which we now cannot eat. The last thing we taste before we leave the Seder is the Afikomen, just like it was the lamb.

Here is the thing. Yeshua is the Lamb of God. He went to the Cross in the year 33 AD, 37 years before the destruction of the Temple. Lamb was being eaten at that time. Wouldn't it make sense that when He decided to give us something to remember Him by, He would have said, "Take and eat this lamb…? Do this in remembrance of Me."? Wouldn't that make sense? And yet He chose the Matzah. There is something a little bit strange about this.

Here is my conclusion as to why He did that. God, of course, knew the destruction of the Temple was coming and He knew that

---

16 Executive Committee of the Editorial Board, Jacob Zallel Lauterbach, "PASSOVER SACRIFICE (Hebrew, "zebah Pesah"; lit. "sacrifice of exemption")," JewishEncyclopedia.com, http://www.jewishencyclopedia.com/articles/11934-passover-sacrifice. Accessed Nov. 2018.
17 "The Origin of The Afikomen," ChosenPeopleMinistries.com, https://www.chosenpeople.com/site/the-origin-of-the-afikomen/. Accessed Nov. 2018.

following the year 70 AD, for thousands of years, Jewish people wouldn't eat lamb, but they would eat the Afikomen Matzah. Isn't that amazing? He took the Matzah instead of the lamb, and in the process was predicting that the lamb would no longer be eaten.

[Some scholars believe because the Afikomen so much tells the story of Yeshua, that before the time of Yeshua it was part of an established Messianic ritual observed during the Passover and that Yeshua built on the significance of this ritual, and then it was adopted by all the Jews after the year 70 AD because they couldn't eat lamb anymore.[18]]

Get Rid of Khametz

We see a second way in which Yeshua used tradition to teach us and His disciples something. Remember what I said that the spiritual meaning of Khag HaMatzah is that when our forefathers left Egypt, they were to leave the sins of Egypt behind. Why does khametz represent sin?

One reason is it puffs up. Think about this. Look at a piece of leavened bread. Do you know what it is mostly made up of? Air. The puffing up is the little pockets of air—the little circular things you see when you cut through it. The fermentation process puts those little bubbles of air in there. What a pertinent picture of the worst thing we struggle with. Pride. It graphically demonstrates the sin of pride. Being puffed up. Being full of hot air.

The other reason is that a tiny little bit of leaven leavens the whole lump. If you've ever baked bread, you know that you take a tiny quarter teaspoon of yeast and you put it in a big batch of dough, and that little yeast leavens the whole lump of dough.

What is that all about? Well, a little bit of sin—just giving in a little bit—goes a long way. We have all experienced that at some point in our lives. You do one little wrong thing and it snowballs. I think the classic example is the little tiny lie that you tell to get out of something. Then you need another lie to cover up the tiny lie, and then you have to lie some more to cover up the bigger lie. Soon you're into big trouble.

---

18 Paul Sumner, "HE WHO IS COMING: The Hidden Afikoman," Hebrew-Streams.org, http://www.hebrew-streams.org/works/judaism/afikoman.html. Accessed Nov. 2018.

Look at what Yeshua said in Matthew 16 and also in Luke 8:15 and Luke 12:1 where He speaks of khametz

> Matthew 16:6 ..."Watch out! Guard yourselves against the hametz of the P'rushim and Tz'dukim,"

Yeshua kept Khag HaMatzah all his life, certainly for the seven days. Even in that last year He kept it for one day because He died after the first Seder and before that second Seder. So when Yeshua said this, He knew very well what khametz was and He had taken care to avoid it every year for the Feast of Unleavened Bread.

However, He isn't telling us here to guard against leaven in what we eat in our food, He is warning us to guard ourselves against sin. He used this particular symbol of khametz as sin repeatedly. He was teaching His disciples and us that spiritually we are to live as if it is always the Feast of Unleavened Bread, avoiding spiritual khametz. He has specific teachings about what the spiritual khametz is. It is the khametz of the Pharisees and of the Sadducees and the khametz of Herod. These were all leaders. And He was very specific about what the sin of these leaders were.

Let's take a look.

> Matthew 16:12 Then they understood—they were to guard themselves not from yeast for bread but from the teaching of the P'rushim (Pharisees) and Tz'dukim (Sadducees).

> Matthew 23:2-3 "The Torah-teachers and the P'rushim," he said, "sit in the seat of Moshe. 3 So whatever they tell you, take care to do it. But don't do what they do, because they talk but don't act!"

This is important to understand. It wasn't actually the verbal teaching of the Pharisees that Yeshua was telling His disciples to avoid because they were teaching from the Scriptures, but their teaching by example was what we were to avoid. That was the khametz. What they did, not what they said, was the khametz. Let's look at their teaching.

As we go into this, I just want to take a moment and suggest to you that what I did in this study is something I recommend people do when studying the Bible, and that is to look for the context.

So Yeshua said this in Matthew 16:6. What I did is I looked before and I looked after. Then I looked before and after in Luke where Yeshua said this. I asked myself, "What was He talking about?" By looking at that, I began to see that He was telling us what the khametz of the Pharisees is just before and just after and all around when he actually said this.

So I found ten different types of khametz of the Pharisees that He warned about. This makes sense because when we bake, there are different kinds of khametz that we use. There's yeast, right? But there's also baking soda and baking powder, and there's sourdough yeast. So there's more than one type of khametz, and I found ten kinds that He warned about.

1. Unbelief: Expecting a sign from the Sky to prove He is the Messiah
2. Hypocrisy: Washing Only the Outside Of The Cup
3. Personal Legalism: Obeying tiny things, while ignoring big things
4. Self Exaltation: Seeking To Be Seen By Others As Righteous and Important
5. Institutional Legalism: Burdening people with rules
6. Intellectualism: Taking away the key of knowledge and preventing others from entering the Kingdom of God
7. Deception: Their false teachings
8. Do What I Say, Not What I Do
9. Fear Of Man Rather Than Fear Of God
10. Covetousness, laying up treasure on earth

1. Khametz of Asking for a Sign

The first is they were expecting a sign from the sky to prove He was the Messiah. We're going to start with where He said it in Matthew 16, but to understand this you have to backup into Matthew 15. Don't be distracted by the chapter headings because they weren't there in the original text.

> Matthew 15:30-31 *and large crowds came to him, bringing with them the lame, the blind, the*

> crippled, the mute and many others. They laid them at his feet, and he healed them. 31 The people were amazed as they saw mute people speaking, crippled people cured, lame people walking and blind people seeing; and they said a b'rakhah [blessing] to the God of Isra'el.

So Yeshua was doing amazing, amazing miracles in healing and delivering people. And then Yeshua realized that the crowd become hungry and had nothing to eat.

> Matthew 15:35-38 After telling the crowd to sit down on the ground, 36 he took the seven loaves and the fish, made a b'rakhah, broke the loaves and gave them to the talmidim, who gave them to the people. 37 Every one ate his fill, and they took seven large baskets full of the leftover pieces. 38 Those eating numbered four thousand men, plus women and children.

So He healed, delivered, and He provided here.

> Matthew 16:1 Then some P'rushim and Tz'dukim came to trap Yeshua by asking him to show them a miraculous sign from Heaven.

Let's just grasp that. After what He had just been doing, they say, "Show us a sign." Now obviously they knew about His teachings. They knew about His miracles and His deliverances and provision. By asking for a sign, what they're saying is, "We don't consider those miracles a miraculous sign. We want a sign from Heaven. We want something to appear in the sky before we'll believe that You are the Messiah and put our trust in You." Yeshua did not react pleasantly.

> Mark 8:11-12 With a sigh that came straight from his heart, he said, "Why does this generation want a sign? Yes! I tell you, no sign will be given to this generation!"

When you see that phrase, *with a sigh that came from His heart,* what do you see? I see Him looking very disappointed and sad. It was really troubling to Him, that they were asking for this sign.

> Mark 8:13-15 *With that, he left them, got into the boat again and went off to the other side of the lake. 14 Now the talmidim had forgotten to bring bread and had with them in the boat only one loaf. ... 15 ... Yeshua said to them, "Watch out! Guard yourselves from the hametz of the P'rushim and the hametz of Herod,"*

What is the khametz that He is telling them to guard themselves against? Unbelief! Asking for a sign. It brought forth from Yeshua a very strong rebuke.

> Matthew 16:4 *A wicked and adulterous generation is asking for a sign? It will certainly not be given a sign -- except the sign of Yonah!" With that he left them and went off.*

He walked away from them. (Of course the sign of Jonah is referring to His being three days and three nights in the belly of the earth before He resurrected.) Why did the Lord consider this so wicked? It doesn't seem so wicked, asking for a sign.

Let's look at the last verse in the Gospels:

> John 21:25 *But there are also many other things Yeshua did; and if they were all to be recorded, I don't think the whole world could contain the books that would have to be written!*

What is He saying there? There had been a multitude of signs, healings, and deliverances, fulfillment of the prophesies of Scriptures, and yet these guys were asking for a sign. So what do you think? Do people fall into this error today? Yes, this great wickedness is something we do ourselves. Don't point your finger at the Pharisees. The wickedness here is the demanding from God the sign that *we* want to see and not accepting the signs that He has already given.

I've been frustrated sometimes when I've been working with unbelievers. You may have experienced this too. After praying for them in Yeshua's Name, there might be something so miraculous, a healing or something and then you ask, "Does that convince you?" And they say, "Oh no, I still have my doubts. I've got to think about it." They're still not sure. They need a bigger sign. It can be very discouraging to see them react like that.

It is putting God in a box of our preconceived ideas of how He will do things, expecting Him to do things in the way we have imagined or we've been taught or we figured out and not recognizing His hand when He actually does miracles. We don't even realize that it is a miracle or a sign. We say, "We want to see this and we want to see that. Why don't we ever see these things?" We need to be careful of that.

Now, I have to admit that I've seen this in my own life. Here's the way it happens. God does something wonderful, rescues me from some trial, provides miraculously, and then another trial comes up and what happens? I get all anxious about this other trial and I'm not trusting God, even though He just did this amazing, miraculous thing for me. Have you ever done that?

When my wife and I bought our first house, God provided amazingly for us to make the down payment and then start making all the payments and all of the costs of it. That was in the fall. So we got through the winter. We were able to pay the heating bills and all that. Spring came and we didn't have a lawn mower. I was worried, "Where am I going to get a lawn mower?" God had just provided like thousands of dollars, but now I was anxious about getting a lawnmower.

So we're prone to that, and Yeshua said we're to guard against this khametz. So how are we to do that? Well, in this next passage, it says something else about the khametz that's interesting.

> Exodus 12:15 *For seven days you are to eat matzot, but on the first day you must remove hametz from your houses, for whoever eats hametz from the first day until the seventh day, that soul will be cut off from Israel.*

So as we pointed out before, God's instructions about khametz during Passover is more than don't eat it. Remember?

He says, "Remove it from your house!" Having it around even defiles you, even if you are not going to eat it. So guarding against the khametz of the Pharisees is more than just avoiding it. You need to remove it from your house, from your property, from your spirit, from your heart, from your life. If you've been caught up in it, repent of it, renounce it, take authority over it, and resist it coming back. Get rid of it.

2. Khametz of Hypocrisy

Let's move on now from Matthew to Luke. Luke gives the same warning in 12:1. But again let's go back and look at the context in chapter 11.

> Luke 11:37-38 *As Yeshua spoke, a Parush asked him to eat dinner with him; so he went in and took his place at the table; 38 and the Parush was surprised that he didn't begin by doing n'tilat yadayim before the meal.*

That's the ritual handwashing tradition that Jewish people do before a meal.

> Luke 11:39 *However, the Lord said to him, "Now then, you P'rushim, you clean the outside of the cup and plate; but inside, you are full of robbery and wickedness.*

I wonder if He finished the meal?

What this is describing is a cup that may look clean from the outside but inside it is all cruddy and moldy and yucky. Inside of you, *you are full of robbery and wickedness.* What is this that He is talking about? This is what I think it is. People who appear to be righteous on the outside—good and kind—but inside are scheming for ways to obtain riches or power in ways that are within the law. It is not even visible to others because it is inside the cup.

What would this be? This would be like a banker who professes to be a Godly man who upholds the law, but is within his rights to foreclose on that poor widow and take her house away. That is the inside being wicked. The outside is clean and the inside is lawful, but it is not good. Is this something people do today? Sure. This is hypocrisy.

It is doing outwardly righteous things but neglecting inward righteousness. Doing visibly good things like giving to charity, going to services while harboring bitterness, greed, anger, unforgiveness, pride, fear, resentment, lust, envy, and jealousy—harboring those things in your heart but doing outwardly good things.

> Luke 11:40-41 *Fools! Didn't the One who made the outside make the inside too? 41 Rather, give as alms what is inside, and then everything will be clean for you!*

He is using strong language here. Deut. 16:20 says, *Justice, justice you must pursue, so that you may live and possess the land that ADONAI your God is giving you.*

In other words what I see here is, "Don't try to get ahead by taking advantage of others, even if it is by lawful means." There are many people who try to do this. But we are to pursue justice. Pursue fairness for others less skilled or those with less resources or who are not connected—show that kind of kindness. What He says here is, then everything will be clean. If you are pursuing that kind of *doing unto others as you would have them do unto you* on the inside, you'll be pure in God's eyes.

3. Khametz of Personal Legalism

> Luke 11:42 *But woe to you P'rushim! You pay your tithes of mint and rue and every garden herb, but you ignore justice and the love of God. You have an obligation to do these things—but without disregarding the others!*

Mint and rue are just tiny crops. A farmer may have a whole field of corn, but just a little patch of mint. They were tithing on that. They would give a tenth of that to the Lord. Why? To be able to say, "I am righteous!" But what were they ignoring? Justice and the love of God.

What is this khametz? This is legalism. Doing all the right things and keeping all the rules, even tiny ones, but ignoring the big things like love. The word *love* here could be interpreted two ways. It says the love of God. In other words, your relationship with God, or the love of God that you are supposed to show to others. It could be either one.

He's not saying that you don't need to tithe. He is saying you should do that but don't disregard love and justice. He is saying, stand up for justice. Champion the oppressed. Expose corruption, and share the love of God

4. Khametz of Self Exaltation

> Luke 11:43 *"Woe to you P'rushim, because you love the best seat in the synagogues and being greeted deferentially in the marketplaces!*

Do you recognize this type of khametz? Pride and self exaltation. Seeking to be seen by others as righteous, as important, seeking to be well-liked or popular, seeking the praises of man basically, wanting privileges and recognition and being honored rather than what? Whose approval should we be seeking after? God's approval.

> Luke 11:44 *"Woe to you, because you are like unmarked graves, which people walk over without knowing it."*

In Jewish tradition, back in the days of the Temple, if a person walked over a grave, it would ceremonially defile them. Unmarked graves were a great danger because you might accidentally walk on them. They were a greater danger than marked graves.

Here we have a very significant picture. These people, the Pharisees, are very religious people. They might not be believers in Yeshua but they are very religious. They are dangerous like unmarked graves because they appear to be good but they are not. They are full of wickedness: Pride, legalism, hypocrisy, etc. You look at them and say, "I want to be just like them. They look so nice." That is the danger because they could draw people in—to defilement. That is what an unmarked grave does. It defiles somebody by surprise. They don't even know they're being defiled. This is also the khametz of hypocrisy.

5. Khametz of Institutional Legalism

At this point, Yeshua includes a khametz of the scribes. Before He was talking about the Pharisees and the Sadducees, but now He mentions the Torah teachers.

> Luke 11:46 *Woe to you Torah experts too! You load people down with burdens they can hardly bear, and you won't lift a finger to help them!*

So this is what I saw as the sixth type of khametz: burdening people with rules, especially ones that require more of people than God's Word says He requires, making the keeping of God's law more difficult when most of God's Laws are very simple.

What is this khametz? This is a religious spirit. This is what Judaism and Catholicism have done with all their rules.

The rules of Judaism are overwhelming if you try to be Orthodox. You can become loaded down with those rules. Khag HaMatzah is a vivid example. The Bible says don't eat khametz for seven days and have no leaven on your property. The Ashkenazi tradition for Passover is not just no khametz but no flour or anything that swells when wet. Do you think God meant that?

Now, there are two valid reasons to keep Ashkenazi traditions. So for those who are Ashkenazi, I want to encourage you.

Number one: If you have an Ashkenazi Jewish friend and you want to show them that you are indeed keeping Passover according to their Jewish traditions, you have to keep it the way they keep it. And if you want to have them come over during Passover, you need to be keeping it their way.

Number two: If you were raised with Ashkenazi traditions and that's what you love, and you want to honor them, that's fine if you want to do that. The point is to realize that it's a tradition. It's not what the Bible says. The Bible just says to get the khametz out your house, and don't eat it. Again these things and many other areas of Judaism become a burden, and that's what Yeshua is saying.

In fact, I was thinking about this. Three times a year God commands us to do things that require self-denial. Right? On Passover: eat no leaven. On Yom Kippur: don't eat at all. Fast. And on Sukkot: set up a sukkah where you don't have substantial shelter. Those are three times in the year when God says you must deny yourself in these ways.

But if you look at them, they're not that difficult to do. Even the thing about the sukkah, when you read the Scripture about it, it says only native born Israelites need to live in the sukkah for seven days. God understood that in cold climates it would be really hard, and He said you don't have to do it.

But traditional Judaism again has made two of them harder. Passover with this expanded tradition about leaven until it's difficult to obey. And on Yom Kippur the Jewish tradition is not just fasting food, but also fasting water, which makes it much harder. But that wasn't God's intention. It's amazing to me how easy God made it. For self-denial, He gave straightforward instructions that are pretty easy.

What about all the rules of Catholicism? It is legalism, but it is institutionalized legalism. One kind of legalism is being legalistic about our own lives. But this legalism is that they are the Torah teachers and they are putting this burden on others. This doesn't just happen in Judaism. It is in other religions, too. It is khametz, and it is a dangerous one.

6. Khametz of Intellectualism

> Luke 11:52 *Woe to you Torah experts! For you have taken away the key of knowledge! Not only did you yourselves not go in, you also have stopped those who were trying to enter!*

This is another specific form of khametz. What is this form? It's the pride of being an expert. It's religious intellectualism. We are surrounded by this. This is the intellectuals who think only they can interpret the Scriptures. They rationalize it and make it into something that is unbelief. The "God is dead" philosophers and those who say Yeshua never really lived, which is even in some forms of Christianity.

It is big in Rabbinical Judaism. You need to be familiar with the Jewish way of doing this. They say "You can't understand the Scriptures until you know what all the rabbis and sages have to say about them." "You can't understand a passage of Scripture unless you know what the Talmud has said about it." Each Bible verse has reams of stuff attached to it. You have to study the Talmud for years and years to find out what all the ancient sages said. They see you as just an ignorant person if you are trying to understand the Bible by yourself. This is a big thing. Judaism has suffered from this for hundreds of years.

And the church—think about what the Catholic Church did. Who could interpret the Scriptures for the millennium that the Catholic Church ruled the world? Only the priests. They taught that the common people could not understand the Scriptures. They didn't allow it to be translated into the common language.

In fact, Catholic authorities executed the first people who translated the Scriptures. They burned them at the stake because they didn't want people to be able to read the Scriptures for themselves. So do you see how that fulfills that? They were taking the key of knowledge and keeping it for themselves, not letting the people have it.

In traditional Judaism, we do our whole Synagogue service in America in Hebrew. Do the people understand Hebrew? No, but we do them in Hebrew anyway. Are they learning anything? No, but they shouldn't. Only the rabbis can teach them. This is the khametz. It is big. It has had a powerful effect on this world.

7. Khametz of False Teachings

The disciples understood this khametz because Yeshua actually tells them what it is in the next passage and it's a big type. He tells them this after He's told them to guard themselves.

> Matthew 16:12 *Then they understood—they were to guard themselves not from yeast for bread but from the teaching of the P'rushim and Tz'dukim.*

So this seventh type of khametz is their teaching or their doctrine as some translations put it. So what were they teaching?

One thing we learned already is they were teaching that there would be a sign in the sky from the Messiah. Yeshua is saying that teaching is wrong. God will choose what signs you will get.

I would guess that if I were to talk with you, I would find out that you experienced signs that turned your heart to the Lord, and it is probably different from what other people experienced. It might have been a revelation, it might have been a healing, it might have been a provision, but everybody gets different signs. That's the amazing thing about God.

My sign, if you remember my story, was that I did not have a reaction to a bee sting for the first time in many, many years and then I was stung by a bee again the next day.[19] That was my sign. See it is very different from being healed and other things like that.

Now today, non-Messianic Jewish leaders teach a doctrine similar to the Pharisees about signs. We learn about this in the *Messianic Judaism Class* books.[20] The main one about signs that is taught by the non-Messianic rabbis is that when the Messiah comes, He will bring peace. They get that based on Isaiah 11 where it says that the lion will lie down with the lamb and in Micah and Joel where it talks about beating the swords into pruning hooks. So they say Yeshua can't be the Messiah because obviously since He has come, the world has not had peace. That's their teaching.

Here's how I respond. You can plagiarize me all you want. I respond by saying Yeshua has brought peace to this world. He brings peace with God in the heart of every person who receives Him as Lord and receives His atoning sacrifice. That's the peace He brought me, and that's the peace He gives to everyone who gives their heart to Him.

What other khametz or wrong teachings of the Pharisees, or shall we say religious leaders, is with us today? Now understand that rabbinic, or traditional or what we call non-Messianic

---

19 "Meet Rabbi Jim," About the Rabbi, Congregation Shema Yisrael, http://www.shemayisrael.org/about-the-rabbi. Accessed Nov. 2018.
20 Rabbi James Appel, Rabbi Jonathan Bernis, and Rabbi David Levine, *Messianic Judaism Class Teacher Book*, Olive Press Messianic and Christian Publisher, http://olivepresspublisher.com/messianic-judaism-class-teacher-book.html . Accessed Nov. 2018.

Judaism, actually originated with the Pharisees. So the non-Messianic rabbis of today are the descendants of the Pharisees, and they have many teachings that have a lot of pharisaic khametz in them. That was one.

Another one that I think is the most destructive khametz teaching is that you can't be Jewish and believe in Jesus. If you believe in Jesus, you're not a Jew anymore. Have you heard that teaching? Well, that's khametz. This type of khametz is still being taught very strongly by traditional rabbis all around the world.

But the other thing is that this was also taught by the church for about seventeen centuries. It's only been the last couple decades that they stopped teaching it. The reason is because the Messianic Movement has developed and pastors are seeing that there are Jews who believe in Yeshua and they're still living as Jews.

What is the effect of this khametz? Well, it should be obvious. It makes Jewish people closed to the Gospel.

There's another equally destructive khametz. It says that Messianic Jews are Christian missionaries in disguise attempting not only to make Jewish people believe in Jesus but to convert them to Christianity so that they will assimilate and not be Jewish anymore, to steal them away from their own heritage.

Another of the khametz teachings is "Jesus was a great prophet and teacher, but He wasn't the Messiah." They say that often. But this is incredibly contradictory. How can you consider Him a great teacher when He Himself claimed to be the Messiah and you deny that? You must believe either that He was lying or He was delusional. You can't say He was a great teacher and then say the main thing that He taught is false. How could He be a great teacher if you believe that? It is sort of George Orwellian doublespeak there.

Another khametz teaching is that Yeshua cannot be divine because that violates Judaism's foundational revelation that there is one God and God cannot take on physical form and come as a man. This sounds pretty convincing. After all, we recite the Shema that says, *"God is One."* So if Yeshua is divine and there is also the Father that means there are two gods. And, of course, there's the Holy Spirit, too, so that would be three gods.

However, there's a big contradiction in that teaching. The contradiction is that the Tanakh (Old Testament) records at least five times when God took on the form of a man and appeared.

He appeared to Abraham as a man. He appeared to Jacob and wrestled with him. He appeared to Moses when he was in the cleft of the rock. God talked to him face-to-face. He appeared to Joshua as the captain of the Lord of Hosts. He appeared as the fourth figure in the fire when the three men were thrown into the furnace. So God *can* come as a man. I believe that's who Yeshua is, God come as a man.

There are many other doctrines today that are being taught by "Pharisees and Sadducees." Who are they? They're the religious leaders, both in Judaism and in the church. There are many khametz doctrines being taught by them. I'll just list a few of them in the world today:

1. Yeshua is not divine.   (We talked about that one.)
2. God's Word is not inspired. It's just a bunch of myths.
3. There are many ways to God.
4. Jews have their own covenant with God. They don't need Yeshua as the Messiah.
5. Marriage can be between two people of the same gender.
6. Prayer cannot be allowed in government functions.
7. There are no negative consequences to breaking God's law. Just repent and ask Jesus to forgive you.
8. Israel has no right to the Land. The Palestinians were there first.

Have you heard any of those false teachings? The danger is that as they're frequently repeated, many receive them and begin to believe that they're the truth, but they're not. They're false. So those are some of the khametz teachings. There are more. I'm sure if we thought about it, we could probably come up with 50 or 60 more.

8. Do What I Say, Not What I Do
Luke records another warning about khametz.

> Luke 12:1 *Meanwhile, as a crowd in the tens of thousands gathered so closely as to trample each other down, Yeshua began to say to his talmidim first, "Guard yourselves from the hametz of the P'rushim, by which I mean their hypocrisy.*

This is another form of hypocrisy. Do what I say and not what I do. We have seen a lot of that just in the last couple of decades in the church unfortunately. We've seen prominent ministers who preach against sin, falling into gross sin. It's usually over power, sex, or money, and it is an abomination. But there is also a great danger for all of us in this, especially those of us who are raising children. When telling them to obey, share, not complain, stop whining, clean up after yourself, be respectful, listen carefully, we have to guard ourselves that we don't do those things ourselves, because that would be hypocrisy.

9. Fear of Man Rather Than Fear of God

> Luke 12:4-5 *"My friends, I tell you: don't fear those who kill the body but then have nothing more they can do. 5 I will show you whom to fear: fear him who after killing you has authority to throw you into Gei-Hinnom! [Hell!] Yes, I tell you, this is the one to fear!*

10. Covetousness: Laying up Treasure on Earth
And finally the tenth type of khametz.

> Luke 12:15 *Then to the people he said, "Be careful to guard against all forms of greed, because even if someone is rich, his life does not consist in what he owns."*

So the tenth type of khametz is covetousness, laying up treasure on earth. And that's something that we all have to guard against.

Here's a list of the ten khametz again.
- Unbelief
- Hypocrisy
- Personal Legalism
- Self-exaltation
- Religious legalism
- Religious Intellectualism
- Deception
- Inconsistency
- Fear of Man
- Covetousness

1. Unbelief: Expecting a sign from the sky to prove He is the Messiah
2. Hypocrisy: Washing only the outside of the cup
3. Personal Legalism: Obeying tiny things, while ignoring big things
4. Self Exaltation: Seeking to be seen by others as righteous and important
5. Religious Legalism: Burdening people with rules
6. Religious Intellectualism: Taking away the key of knowledge and preventing others from entering the Kingdom of God
7. Deception: Their false teachings
8. Inconsistency: Do what I say, not what I do
9. Fear of Man rather than fear of God
10. Covetousness: Laying up treasure on earth

This is pretty heavy stuff. Yeshua used the Feast of Unleavened Bread to teach us to search for the khametz and get it out! That is what He was telling His disciples. Get the khametz out of your life! They had lived all their lives under the teaching of these folks, the Pharisees and Scribes and Sadducees.

Spiritual Bread - The Word

Look at how beautiful this analogy is:

> Deuteronomy 8:3 *He afflicted you and let you hunger, then He fed you manna—which neither*

you nor your fathers had known—in order to make you understand that man does not live by bread alone but by every word that comes from the mouth of Adonai.

What is bread a symbol for? The Word, the teaching. The word *Torah* doesn't just mean the writing, it means the teaching or instruction of God. During Khag HaMatzah we still eat bread, but it is without khametz. What is the application? We need to receive the teaching of God, the Word of God but with no khametz mixed in it.

How Did Yeshua fulfill this Moad?

That leads us to how Yeshua fulfilled this Moad and we will see the answer to this problem of how we get the teaching without the khametz.

> I Corinthians 5:7 *Get rid of the old hametz, so that you can be a new batch of dough, because in reality you are unleavened. For our Pesach lamb, the Messiah, has been sacrificed.*

What is Rabbi Sha'ul (Paul) telling us here? Get rid of the old khametz which we now understand are teachings, false doctrines, bad doctrines and behaviors. It is beautiful the way he says this, because you **are**—not because you "will be"—because you **are** unleavened. In other words, the Spirit of God, when you receive Yeshua and His sacrifice, has come into you and has removed the khametz. He has taken out the khametz just like the night before Passover when we are searching for the khametz. Let me describe that because it is a beautiful picture.

The father takes a candle and a feather and a little dustpan. The wife has cleaned the house already but he goes around and inspects and sees if he can find any khametz. The feather is like a little brush and the candle is so he can look in the dark places. There is a beautiful picture there. The Holy Spirit is the candle illuminating those dark places.

> I Corinthians 5:8 *So let us celebrate the Seder not with leftover hametz, the hametz of*

wickedness and evil, but with the matzah of purity and truth.

What is the *leftover khametz?* It is the sins of this world that we are called out of. It is the teachings of this world that might still be clinging to us—the list we just went over. Even if we are religious and went to synagogue or church all our lives, we've got all of that stuff—the legalism, the intellectualism, the hypocrisy. That is what the *leftover khametz* is. That is where it comes from.

I need to stop and define legalism here. It doesn't mean obeying the commandments or the Torah. Rabbi Sha'ul (Paul) really didn't have a word to use like *legalism* in Greek. Legalism is when you believe that you are made *righteous* by the keeping of the Law or Torah. The Law/Torah of God is good. But when you begin to see that the keeping of that Law is what makes you righteous, that is legalism. It is keeping the letter of the Torah without the spirit of the Torah, without the mercy and grace of the Torah.

What has happened in Judaism is there are rules and rules, and rules on top of rules. It is a burden. It is a heavy burden to carry to be right with God the legalistic way. The Torah of God gives a simple command, "Don't eat khametz." Judaism has made a big thing out of it. It has to be baked before 18 minutes, and you can't keep it until next year, etc. It even gets bigger with other sets of rules around that, requiring a whole separate set of dishes for Passover to avoid any trace of khametz left on them, etc. All of that can take the focus off of the intent of the commandment.

Matzah of Life

Rabbi Sha'ul says the intent is not to just get rid of the khametz amongst us but to keep the feast with purity and truth. What is the Matzah of purity and truth?

Yeshua said:

> John 6:35 *I am the bread which is life! Whoever comes to me will never go hungry, and whoever trusts in me will never be thirsty.*

When we partake of Him, we are partaking of the pure Matzah—the teaching of God. When we receive His sacrifice, when we receive His teaching, when we have a relationship with Him, when we are connected to the vine, when we see Him and obey Him as Lord, we are eating the spiritual Bread of Life, which is without khametz. He is our *unleavened bread.* That is how He fulfilled the Feast. He is our Bread, free of khametz.

Remember what He said about the Pharisees. It wasn't just what they taught. It was their actions. How do we know that He is the Bread without khametz? It is by the test which He gave us in Matthew 7.

> **Matthew 7:15-18** *Beware of the false prophets! They come to you wearing sheep's clothing, but underneath they are hungry wolves! 16 You will recognize them by their fruit. Can people pick grapes from thorn bushes, or figs from thistles? 17 Likewise, every healthy tree produces good fruit, but a poor tree produces bad fruit. 18 A healthy tree cannot bear bad fruit, or a poor tree good fruit.*

What is Yeshua's fruit to prove that He is our Matzah of Life? It is clear. He laid down His life as the sacrificed Lamb. He became like the Afikomen. He was pierced, bruised, and broken for us. We, and millions of people, are His fruit. Therefore we know that He is the true Matzah.

It is good to clean house and keep Khag HaMatzah. But it is also good to remind ourselves yearly that we need to clean house not only physically but spiritually. We need to clean our spiritual house every day.

There's one more thing I learned during this study. The word *Matzah* comes from the Hebrew word for sweet, *matzatz*. Sourdough was the way they caused bread to rise—it was sour. Matzah, because it does not sour, tastes sweet. People full of khametz are often sour people. When we get rid of khametz and allow Messiah to make us more like Him, we start to become sweet like He is, true, Living Matzah.

I saw something else really interesting, too. Think about the difference between a wheat tortilla and a Matzah. A flour tortilla is soft and a Matzah is hard. A flour tortilla can be torn. You can't say "I broke a tortilla" because it is soft, not hard. If you cooked a flour tortilla until it was hard, it would most likely burn up.

Why is a Matzah able to be cooked until it is hard? The piercing! It is the piercing that allows the Matzah to get hard. The bruising shows that it gets a little bit burned. But if it was flat like a flour tortilla it would be all burned. The piercing creates that striped look. Matzahs can be broken.

What I saw there was the Lord could not have given us His body as a tortilla or a pita. There is a big difference between what we take sometimes as bread for the Lord's Supper and tear it off and say it is broken, but really only with a Matzah can you see true brokenness. And you can see the piercings and the bruising. Because He submitted to those things, His body (His skin, not His bones) indeed was broken.

Let's Pray

We thank You, Yeshua, for fulfilling Khag HaMatzah. We thank You, Lord, that You showed us that we need to get rid of the leaven, the khametz. We ask Your Holy Spirit to search us right now, like that little candle searching for the khametz. We ask that if there are any of these things in us, that You would convict us and bring us to a place of repentance.

We ask that You show us if there is any unbelief, any asking for a sign that we want to see when You are doing signs all around us.

Father, we ask that You reveal if there is any personal legalism in us. Considering ourselves righteous because we do this or that or keep this law or that law.

Lord, we ask You to put Your Light on us and show us if there is any hypocrisy in us. Trying to appear pious and righteous and harboring something inside, whether it is unforgiveness or envy or lust or desire for power or self exaltation or any of these things inside of us that we cover over.

Show us, Lord, if we are like that cup that is clean on the outside but dirty on the inside. We want to be rid of it, O God.

Show us, O Lord, if there is any intellectualism in us where we think that we are better because we know more. And Lord, deliver us from anything that might have been on us from the past, from being part of organizations that promoted that. Deliver us from that, Lord, from legalism.

Keep us from pride. That is the big one that the khametz represents. Show us ways in which we think that we are better than others. Just deflate us, Lord. Let Your spirit be like a sharp instrument to deflate us. And if there are ways in which we try to exalt ourselves and suppress others and have that need to be recognized, Lord, reveal that to us and we repent of that.

Anything that You have revealed, we repent of that and ask for forgiveness. We see You as the search light but in that tradition we wield the feather, so help us to do our part, O Lord, in ridding ourselves of these things, standing against habits that we might have. Help us to be honest with ourselves and with You.

We also pray, Father, for the Jewish community, that You would open peoples eyes to the truth that the legalistic burdens they've been carrying, laid on them by men, are not from You. They are the legalistic teachings of men. And we pray that You break the deception of those false teachings. Break that teaching that has deceived people about the Messiah, that He's supposed to have brought world peace, that God cannot come as a man, that Yeshua was a great prophet even though He said He was the Messiah, that believing in Yeshua means you're not Jewish anymore and that Messianic Jews are driving people away from being Jewish when we're doing just the opposite.

So we thank You, Lord. And I pray, Father, that as Your Holy Spirit works in our lives, that You would show us if there's a pharisaical attitude that we've fallen into, any false teaching, any khametz in our lives. Help us to get that khametz out of our spiritual houses, out of our hearts.

Finally, Father, we recognize that You are the Bread of Life, that You are the Matzah that is unleavened—pure—without any leaven. And we thank You that not only was Your life lived without any leaven—any sin—but Your doctrine and Your teachings are pure and there is no leaven in it. Your fruit and Your actions testify to Your pureness. We pray, "Give us this Bread of life."

Lord, this is a feast even though sometimes we see it as a time of deprivation—and yet, Lord, we need to come to the place as seeing this as the better bread —the pure bread—You are the pure Bread of Life. Thank You for being the Bread of Life for us.

We just thank You that You've laid this all out for us, Father. Thank You for the Feast of Unleavened Bread. May it strengthen our resolve as we commit to removing all khametz through Your overcoming power. In Yeshua's awesome, awesome Name. Amein.

Chapter 6
Two Seders

Let's open this chapter with prayer.

Heavenly Father, You gave us Torah—instruction, and we thank You that the New Covenant became instruction for us also, and that we can look into Your Word, both the Tanakh and the New Covenant, and it is instruction. So we just commit ourselves to receiving Your instructions today, to opening up our ears in our minds and hearts, not only to receive it, but to be doers of Your Word. In Yeshua's Name. Amen.

Once more, here are the instructions for Khag HaMatzah:

> Lev. 23:6 *On the fifteenth day of the same month is the Feast of Matzot to ADONAI. For seven days you are to eat matzah* [unleavened bread].

So from the day of Passover you count seven days that you have to eat Matzah. That's how it is according to the Bible, and interestingly also according to reform Judaism in America, and for the people in Israel. It also includes me because I decided to follow the Biblical instruction, instead of tradition.

---

* Illustration: "The Passover of the Portuguese Jews" by French Engraver, Bernard Picart, 1723. Public domain.

Two Passover Days Tradition

But for some people it is eight days. That's another Jewish tradition. It is the tradition of Orthodox and Conservative Judaism outside of Israel. The reason is that in the Diaspora [the Jewish people living outside Israel] a second day is added to Passover. So they celebrate Passover for two days. Then they count seven days starting on the second Passover.

The reason for the two days is very interesting and has some amazing spiritual significance. Each month of the Jewish calendar starts with the sighting of the first sliver of the moon. It's a lunar calendar. In Yeshua's time, astronomy had not yet developed the ability to predict the dates of the new moon. What the Jewish people did back then is we sent two men to the top of a mountain in Israel to watch for the first sliver of the moon to appear to determine when the month began and especially this month because Passover had to be celebrated on the 14th day.

When they saw the sliver of the moon, they did something right out of "The Lord of the Rings." They lit a bonfire on top of the mountain. Some people were assigned to be on top of hills all through the nation. When the first bonfire was lit, the others lit bonfires one after another all over the nation to let everybody know that this was the beginning of the month. Then they would know when any Moadim in that month were to be observed. Remember that incident in "The Lord of the Rings" where they communicate by the bonfires? Well, they got it from this Jewish practice.

So in the month of Nissan, everyone would count 14 days and would know when to keep Passover. However, with typical zeal to obey God's laws, the rabbis worried about something. They asked questions like, "What if it's cloudy and they miss the first appearance of that sliver? Or what if they fall asleep on the mountain and miss it? Then we would be at least a day late in celebrating Passover.

Their solution was that, when the first sliver of the moon would be sighted, they would count instead of fourteen days, thirteen days, and they would have Passover twice, on the thirteenth day and on the fourteenth day. That way they could be sure they always made it on the actual fourteenth day. And so they would have two Seders.[22]

Also the other issue with this without modern communications was, "What about the people that live far away, especially those who lived outside of Israel in the Diaspora?" Well, on the night when the moon was first sighted, messages were sent to Jewish communities in the other parts of the world and it took time to get there to tell these people. Some places were more than 14 days away, but the places that they could reach within 14 days were notified that this is the day you're supposed to keep Passover. So there was this uncertainty of communicating when to keep Passover to the Diaspora also. So in the Diaspora, they adopted the custom of the two Seders, as well, just to be sure.

When astronomical calculations developed, they switched to one Seder, one day for Passover in Israel. However the custom was kept in the Diaspora, but because we now knew which day is Passover, the custom was shifted to the 14th and 15th days instead of the 13th and 14th days because we're absolutely sure as to when it is. So some people count the seven days of unleavened bread from the second day of Passover.

Now I said that there is some amazing spiritual significance to this. So what is that?

> Luke 22:15   [Yeshua] *said to them, "I have really wanted so much to celebrate this Seder with you before I die!*

Yeshua said this at the Last Supper. Again, this and many other things tell us that the Last Supper was a Passover Seder. Right? Now, if you've seen that, you might wonder the same thing that hit me as a question a long time ago.

After they had the Last Supper, which is recorded in detail in John chapters 13-17, they went to the Garden of Gethsemane, right? Then He was arrested and was tried by the religious leaders, and then He was brought to the Roman governor. Then in John 18:20, we have this verse which makes absolutely no sense unless you understand the traditions of Judaism. Remember, Yeshua and His disciples had just celebrated Passover.

---

22 Mishna: Tractate Rosh Hashanah: chapters 1 and 2.

> John 18:28a *They led Yeshua from Kayafa to the governor's headquarters. By now it was early morning.*

This was the morning after the Last Supper.

> John 18:28b *They did not enter the headquarters building because they didn't want to become ritually defiled and thus unable to eat the Pesach meal.*

Do you see what that is saying? There was going to be another Passover that night. And if you didn't understand these customs, you would say, "What's going on? How could they have just had Passover and Passover is still coming?

Why would they worry about being ritually defiled? It was because they had to remain ritually clean because they were going to keep Passover again that evening. This was because it was in the time before modern astronomy when they were following the tradition of the two Seders. The second Seder was on the correct evening and the first was the night before because astronomy had not developed yet to be able to accurately predict the time of the new moon.

The Significance of Two Seders

So what's the amazing significance of this? Well, I think it's just mind-boggling. The tradition of having two Seders enabled Yeshua to have a Seder with his disciples at which He gave us the New Covenant, basically, building it on the Seder, which was the ceremonial renewal meal of the Mosaic Covenant thereby showing the connectedness between the two Covenants. And then to actually die on the Cross the next day at the Biblically correct time for the lambs to be slaughtered for the second Seder which was the correct Seder, thus fulfilling his role as the Lamb of God, dying at the time the lambs were being slaughtered.

Do you get it? Isn't that amazing? If there wasn't this tradition of the two Seders, He couldn't have done that. He couldn't have had a Seder with His disciples and died at same time that the lambs were being slaughtered. So I marvel at that because it's one thing when Yeshua fulfills the laws of Moses. It is another thing when He fulfills the traditions that developed around the laws, or He uses them to enable Him to do what He needs to do. I'm glad you know this now. It is amazing.

In the last chapter, we learned five things about the Pesakh matzah.

1. We eat it to remember that our ancestors had to leave Egypt in haste and their dough didn't rise.
2. Eating bread without khametz represented leaving the sins of Egypt and the sinful, polytheistic culture of Egypt behind.
3. We learned that when the Temple was destroyed in the year 70 AD, the matzah became a memorial for the meat of the Passover lamb. Up to that time lamb was eaten at the Passover Seder, but after the year 70 AD, because you could no longer sacrifice animals, matzah became the memorial for the meat of the Passover lamb at the Seder.
4. We learned that the traditional way the matzah is made and used during the Seder in the Afikomen ceremony actually tells the story of Yeshua's last hours and His purpose, which is another amazing fulfillment of tradition.
5. We know that Yeshua took matzah without khametz and made it the covenant renewal food of the New Covenant, and said it was a memorial of His body broken for us.

We learned all of that plus a lot about khametz. It's a lot to digest, no pun intended. But it is all so marvelous.

Let's Pray

Heavenly Father, we thank You for the amazing coincidence of the two Passover Seder's, the amazing way in which You orchestrated that, so that You could be further confirmed as being the Messiah. May it strengthen our faith, and we just commit our whole Passover season to You. In Yeshua's awesome, awesome Name. Amein.

CHAPTER 7
MUST BE RITUALLY PURE

So as we have learned, preparation for Pesakh involves a time of spring cleansing. In this chapter we will look at another type of cleansing that is required in addition to removing khametz.

Some of the material that I want to share now is from a very special book that I was given one year: *Carta's Encyclopedia of the Holy Temple in Jerusalem*.[24] The thing that stood out to me as I studied the Passover in this book is that in Yeshua's time, there was a much greater emphasis on the need for cleansing of the people in order to participate in Pesakh. That seems to have been lost today. It was more than just that you had to get the leaven out of the home, there were other cleansings that needed to be done by the people.

Why the need for cleansing? In Deuteronomy, the Scriptures speak of three "pilgrimage feasts."

> Deuteronomy 16:16 *Three times a year all your males are to appear before Adonai your God in*

---

* Photo: Haggadah from Trieste, Italy, 1864, edited by Abraham Hai Morqugo, printed by Jonah, Cohen, Library of Congress, public domain.
24 Ariel, Israel, and Richman, Chaim, Carta's Illustrated Encyclopedia of the Holy Temple in Jerusalem, co-published by The Temple Institute and Carta, Jerusalem, Israel, 2005.

> the place He chooses—at the Feast of Matzot,
> the Feast of Shavuot, and the Feast of Sukkot. No
> one should appear before Adonai empty-handed—

All the men of Israel had to go to Jerusalem three times a year to keep those three feasts. Many of the men would bring their families. Remember, when Yeshua was twelve years old His family came with His father for Passover. So this was a tremendous time of gathering as throngs of people came up to those feasts. It is called "coming up to Jerusalem" because the Temple is on a mountain, so no matter which direction you are coming from, you are going up.

So, all the men would come up for Passover and go into the Temple courts with their Passover lambs.

> Deuteronomy 16:5-6 *You may not sacrifice the Passover offering within any of your gates that Adonai your God is giving you. 6 Rather, at the place Adonai your God chooses to make His Name dwell, there you will sacrifice the Passover offering in the evening at sunset—the time of your coming out from Egypt.*

Everybody had to sacrifice a Passover lamb. Try to grasp the magnitude of this. There were probably more than a million lambs to be sacrificed. They all had to be done between noon and sundown on the day of Passover.

There would've been lines and lines of the people coming in to make their sacrifices, while the Levites played instruments, welcoming them. The book shows a picture of the line of the cohanim (priests) sacrificing the lambs.[25] The blood of each lamb had to be splashed on the altar, so they have vessels in their hands which are being passed down the line, and it is then splashed on the altar.

> Numbers 19:13 *But the person who is clean and not away on a journey, yet neglects to celebrate Passover, that soul shall be cut off from his people because that person did not present ADONAI's offering at the appointed time. That man will bear his sin.*

---
25 Carta's p. 228.

As you can see here in the commandments, which were followed closely in Yeshua's time, there was a severe penalty of the threat of being cut off from Israel if you did not participate in this. So there was no question that everyone was going to participate in Passover. It was not optional. If you were part of the nation, you had to participate.

However, as you begin to study this, you discover that there were some pretty interesting conditions as to who could participate.

> Numbers 19:13 *But the person who is clean and ... yet neglects to celebrate Passover, that soul shall be cut off from his people....*

> Numbers 19:10-11 *If any man, whether you or your descendants, becomes unclean because of a dead body, or is away on a long journey, he may yet observe Adonai's Passover. 11 They are to celebrate it at twilight on the fourteenth day of the second month.*

This meant that a person had to fulfill this thing of being purified in order to celebrate the Passover because he had to go into the Temple to keep the Passover (Deuteronomy 16:5-6 above). An unclean person could not enter into the Temple grounds, yet everybody was commanded to come and be on the Temple grounds.

> Leviticus 22:3 *Tell them, if anyone of all your offspring throughout your generations approaches the holy things, which Bnei-Yisrael consecrate to ADONAI, while in a state of uncleanness, that soul will be cut off from before Me. I am ADONAI.*

> Numbers 19:20 *...that man who is unclean but does not purify himself will be cut off from the community. He has defiled the Sanctuary of ADONAI, since the cleansing water was not sprinkled on him.*

This passage is referring to those in the priestly family, but in the exile to Babylon when the Israelites were without a Temple, it was decided that this applies to all people. So in Yeshua's time, everyone was subject to this ruling.

Why was it so important to eat the Passover? Because it was the Covenant meal that needed to be renewed. It was very important to keep it, but you had to be clean and purified to do so.

What does this mean to be clean—to be purified? Well, the ways in which a person becomes unclean are listed right after the verse above in Leviticus 22 and also in Leviticus 11:

> WAYS YOU BECOME UNCLEAN
> - If you touch an unclean animal (any animal that is not kosher, like a pig or a lobster or insect or rodent or reptile – alive or dead) this makes you unclean and unqualified to go into the Temple.
> - A woman is unclean for seven days after the birth of a son and fourteen days after the birth of a daughter.
> - If you have a skin infection or mold on your clothing, you would be considered unclean.
> - If you have a discharge or running sore.
> - A menstrual discharge or a man's nocturnal emission made you unclean.
> - Eating the kill of a predator. In other words if you found an animal killed in the field and you took it home and ate it, that would make you unclean.
> - Eating an animal that died naturally would make you unclean.
> - If you have leprosy (or a skin disease).
> - Touching a corpse or grave would make you unclean. [Anyone out in the open field who touches a dead body, whether killed by a sword or was killed by a natural cause, or touches a human bone or a grave, shall be unclean seven days (Numbers 19:16).]

That last item has got to be a big problem because what if someone you knew died and you had to help bury them? And who would know if you had accidentally walked over an unmarked grave? Apparently, this was a problem because Yeshua mentions it.

> Luke 11:44 *"Woe to you, because you are like unmarked graves, which people walk over without knowing it."*

There is also the part of the commandment that says even if you were touched by someone who was unclean or you touched something they touched, that made you unclean.

> Leviticus 15:5-7, 10-11 *Whoever touches his bed is to wash his clothes and bathe himself in water, and be unclean until the evening. 6 Whoever sits on anything on which the man who has the discharge sat is to wash his clothes and bathe himself in water, and be unclean until the evening. 7 Whoever touches the body of the one who has the discharge is to wash his clothes and bathe himself in water, and be unclean until the evening. ... 9 "Any saddle the one who has the discharge rides on will be unclean. 10 Whoever touches anything that was under him will be unclean until the evening. Whoever carries them is to wash his clothes and bathe himself in water, and be unclean until the evening.*

> Numbers 19:22 *Anything touched by an unclean person becomes unclean, and anyone touching it will be unclean until evening."*

It became as we say in Yiddish "a gonsa magila" which means "a big production" to try to be clean. The penalty for violating these rules was very severe.

Running Water - Mikveh

Notice that for the defilements mentioned in Leviticus 15 above, the cleansing process required only bathing or immersing in water. One passage says it has to be running water.

> Leviticus 15:13 *When the one who has a fluid discharge is cleansed of his issue, then he is to count for himself seven days for his purification and wash his clothes. Then he is to bathe his body in running water, and he will be clean.*

By Yeshua's day, running water was required for all such defilements. (Excluding touching a dead body or bone or grave which required much more extensive cleansing. More on that later.) A special bath, called a mikveh, had been designed which had to be connected to a stream somehow so that a trickle of water was always running into it to provide clean, running water. Most wealthy people had these outside their homes, and there were many public ones. The Pool of Siloam at the bottom of the hill below the Temple was actually a huge mikveh. This immersion cleansing was its main purpose.

Because of these cleansing commandments, everyone had to be cleansed in a mikveh before they could enter the Temple. Today, in Orthodox communities, it is required to enter a synagogue.

Cut Off From the People

Here again, we see how serious cleansing is.

> Leviticus 7:20 *The soul who eats of the meat of the sacrifice of fellowship offerings belonging to ADONAI, having his uncleanness on him, that soul is to be cut off from his people.*

It doesn't designate who was going to cut them off. You would think that perhaps the judges had to decide that this person is exiled, but no, it has been interpreted as meaning the Lord will cut you off! So, people would do everything they could do to obey this because God could cut you off.

How does this relate to Passover? If you were unclean, you couldn't enter the Temple. It was as simple as that. You had to remain clean. However, Passover was so important that God, in His grace, made a provision for those who did not manage to get cleansed or purified by the time Passover came around.

Passover Grace

> Numbers 9:10-11 *If any man, whether you or your descendants, becomes unclean because of a dead body, or is away on a long journey, he may yet observe Adonai's Passover. 11 They are to celebrate*

> it at twilight on the fourteenth day of the second month. With matzot and bitter herbs they are to eat it.

This shows the amazingness of God's grace but also the importance of Passover. In other words, if you can't keep it in the first month because you were not cleansed, well, get yourself cleansed, wait until the second month, and you can keep it then. But how did a person get purified from touching a dead body or bone or grave, etc? This is a very interesting subject in the Tanakh.

The Red Heifer

> Numbers 19:1-3 *ADONAI spoke to Moses and Aaron saying, 2 "This is the statute of the Torah which ADONAI commanded saying: Speak to Bnei-Yisrael that they bring to you a flawless red heifer on which there is no blemish and on which has never been a yoke. 3 Give her to Eleazar the kohen. He will take her outside the camp and slaughter her in his presence.*

Notice that this Red Heifer, which is a young cow who hasn't been impregnated yet, must be a special red heifer without any blemish. This means it can have no non-red hairs. This is the famous red heifer that so many were talking about a few years back. There are currently, in Israel, many active attempts to breed a red heifer without a blemish. They have been trying for decades to do this, but, as of this writing, though they've been close a couple times (thinking they had one until they found a white hair), they have not come up with a pure red heifer yet.

Notice also that this Red Heifer is to be slaughtered outside the camp. (So this could be done before the Third Temple is built.) The location where they burnt the Red Heifer in the past was on the Mount of Olives. There was a bridge going from there to the Temple Mount.[26] (Jewish authorities believe that this bridge will be built again in the future.) There would have always been a crowd watching.[27]

The High Priest was commanded to put cedar wood, hyssop, and scarlet wool on the fire with the heifer.

---
26 Carta's pp. 211, 212.
27 Ibid.pp. 210-214

> Numbers 19:5-6 *While watching, he is to burn the heifer, her hide, flesh, blood and refuse. 6 The kohen is to take some cedar wood, hyssop and scarlet wool, and cast them into the midst of the burning heifer.*

After the Red Heifer was consumed and it had all become a pile of ashes, we read what is to be done next:

> Numbers 19:9 *A clean man is to gather up the ashes of the heifer and put them in a clean place outside the camp. They are to be for the community of Bnei-Yisrael to use as water of purification from sin.*

This water was the prescribed way for how a person who had touched a dead body or bone or a grave, etc., could become clean and purified, so he could be able to enter into the Temple and keep the Passover. The water used to mix with the ashes of the Red Heifer actually came from the Pool of Siloam in Jerusalem,[28] which you have probably read about in the Gospels.

The reason they are trying to breed a Red Heifer now is because there is a whole group of people, Orthodox Jews, in Israel that are working on rebuilding the Temple, the Third Temple. They are preparing all the materials that are needed for the rebuilding of it. They have already made the clothing for the priest, all the utensils, etc.

Every year they even bring a cornerstone for the Temple to the Temple Mount during the Feast of Tabernacles. Of course, they are stopped by the Israeli police because, if you know anything about the politics of what is going on over there, the Temple Mount now belongs to the Muslims. They have a mosque on that Mount, so if the Jewish people announce that they are going to build the Temple, we would have WWIII immediately.

The police try to stop them from bringing up this cornerstone, but I believe, the Bible predicts that someday this will happen. If you don't believe it, read through the book of Daniel where the anti-Christ will perform a sacrifice in the Temple, the abomination

---

28 Carta's p.212.

of desolation (Daniel 9:27; 11:31; 12:11). There has to be a Temple for that to happen.

The ashes of this heifer will be mixed with the water from the Pool of Siloam to make the water of purification, and it will be used to cleanse the utensils for the Third Temple and everything else that will be used in the Temple. Everything! The clothing, everything will be cleansed by that purification water.

Seven Days of Cleansing

To get back to the Passover and the cleansing, when a person was defiled by touching a dead body or a grave or whatever it was, here is what they had to do:

> Numbers 19:11-12 *Whoever touches any dead body will be unclean for seven days. 12 He is to purify himself on the third day and on the seventh day. Then he will be clean. But if he does not purify himself on the third and seventh days, he will not be clean.*

What this is saying is that after a person realized that they had been defiled by doing one of these things, they had to go and be purified with this water on the third day and on the seventh day.

So, when this happened, you had to go to Jerusalem and then you had to stay in Jerusalem at least four days because you had to have the water put on you on the third day and on the seventh day. Bear with me and think about this for a minute. What about a person who became unclean in Haifa or Be'er-Sheva? Do you know how far away they are from Jerusalem? Back then it was like a three days' journey. Can you see what a production this was to get yourself cleansed?

So, let's say you had this happen and you got cleansed and then you went home for a while and you were very careful not to get defiled again, but now you had to take a journey back again to Jerusalem for the Passover. Who knows what you were going to encounter on that journey. I am getting a new mental picture about how difficult it was and the lengths people had to go through to be able to keep this commandment. Are you?

Staying Cleansed

In the book I mentioned in the beginning of this chapter, *Carta's Encyclopedia of the Holy Temple in Jerusalem*, it talks about how at this time of year the streets were cleaned to make sure there wasn't anything that could defile anyone while they were walking on the street.[29] They had an actual rule that those who were cleansed walked down the middle of the street and people who knew they were unclean would walk on the sides so that they wouldn't touch each other because that would defile them.[30]

Do you remember that phrase that Yeshua used in the Gospels, *whitewashed tombs*? We don't whitewash our tombs, but they did. Every year they went out and whitewashed the tombs in order to prevent anyone from stepping on something that was unclean[31] Even if they just stepped on a human bone fragment, that also would make them unclean. If these things happened to them and they entered the Temple, they could be cut off by God. Not because someone saw it, but because God would know.

Here's an interesting side note. Have you ever noticed in the news whenever there's a terrible suicide bombing or shooting or killing in Israel that after they take care of the injured people, this squad of Orthodox men comes in and cleans everything up? They are cleaning up body fragments. This commandment is why. They clean up every little piece of skin or bone. It comes out of this same understanding about touching a human bone fragment.

Let's apply this to what we read in the Gospels. There are some very interesting things that you begin to see. For example, take the story of the Good Samaritan. Why did the Cohane and the Levite pass by the injured man? Because he might have been dead and they were on their way to Jerusalem. If they touched a dead body, they would be defiled. It wasn't that they were mean or heartless. They knew what a tremendous production it was to become clean again.

How about the Pharisee that was outraged because Yeshua allowed a prostitute to touch Him? She was unclean. Prostitutes were unclean according to their rules. Touching them made a

---
29 Carta's p. 206
30 Ibid. pp. 213-215
31 Ibid. p. 206

person unclean. This is why the man said, "If He knew who was touching Him, He would not let her."(See Luke 7:39.)

How about the leper? (See Matthew 8:1-4; Mark 1:40-45; and Luke 5:12-16.) The leper must have been amazed when Yeshua touched him. That was against the rules. Yeshua actually violated these rules other times, too: when He touched the dead girl and resurrected her (Matthew 9:23-25; Mark 5:22-24,38-42; and Luke 8:41-42,49-56) and when He touched the widow's son who was being carried away to a funeral (Luke 7:11-15).

This is also the reason why the Centurion, when he asked Yeshua to heal his servant said, "Don't come in my house." (See Matthew 8:5-13; and Luke 7:1-10.) Jews would not go to the house of a Gentile because you never knew what you would touch in that house. If the Gentiles were eating pork or shellfish or something—it wasn't just a question of eating it—it was if you touched it. This would defile you and you would have to go through this whole rigamarole to get cleansed.

In the story toward the end of Yeshua's life, after He's been put on the Cross, we read that the Sanhedrin officers went to Pilate requesting to take the body down, but they wouldn't go in to Pilate's courtyard because it says that they had to eat the Passover. That would have defiled them to go into the courtyard of a Gentile. It's the same reason that in Acts 10 Peter had to get a vision from heaven to persuade him to go into the house of Cornelius, a Gentile. All this was because of these rules.

Finally this also helps us understand something more about foot washing. This was a new revelation for me as to why there is a foot washing in the Seder. It was during a Passover Seder. The reason for it was, "Well, we're still not sure if we are really cleansed...so before we eat the Passover, we are going to cleanse ourselves one more time." Yeshua said that even if your body is cleansed your feet are still dirty. The foot washing was another outgrowth of these rules.

Why did God command all these rules of cleanliness? Well, a lot of them can be seen as health reasons. You never know if someone has a contagious disease. If somebody touches something they touched, that disease can be transmitted.

Millions of Jewish people lived in Europe in the Middle Ages during the times of the terrible world epidemic of the Bubonic plague, also called the Black Death. This plague did not harm the Jewish communities as much as others because Jewish people practiced these laws of staying away from unclean things.

Spiritual Cleansing

There is a spiritual reason for all of this, too. It wasn't just for physical cleansing. It is to teach us how to come into His presence. What do we need to be cleansed of spiritually? Sin.

These were pictures of the tremendous need for cleansing. We all need cleansing, and God has provided a way for that cleansing. In the Tanakh the way was the water of purification and the mikveh. How can people be cleansed today so we can eat the Passover? So that we can come into God's presence? Well, even though there is no Temple today and there is no heifer, listen to what the author of Hebrews tells us:

> Hebrews 4:16 *Therefore, let us confidently approach the throne from which God gives grace, so that we may receive mercy and find grace in our time of need.*

So we are told, "Come into the presence of God." But how can we come? Again God made a way. He made a way by sending His Son, Yeshua. What is new to me, and I hope it is new to you, is this whole cleansing side of His atonement. We've talked about the cleansing of sin, but this is a picture from the Tanakh of this being a huge ordeal. Let's read a little bit more from the book of Hebrews. We will see the way in which he connects it with the Red Heifer.

> Hebrews 13:12 *So too Yeshua suffered death outside the gate, in order to make the people holy through his own blood.*

Where was the Red Heifer? Outside the gate. This is a reference by the author of Hebrews to Yeshua fulfilling the unblemished Red Heifer, which I haven't heard people talking about much. Of course, He was the fulfillment of other sacrifices:

the Passover lamb, the Yom Kippur goats, etc., but we can see here that He was also a fulfillment of the Red Heifer.

Since the Temple's destruction—since the year 70 A.D.—nobody could be cleansed the way we talked about here because there was no Temple and no Red Heifer. Nobody could come into God's presence. The only way anybody can now come is by receiving the cleansing Yeshua made for us.

I am hoping that understanding these laws of purity will give us a new appreciation of the awesome thing that God has done—the awesome cleansing power of Yeshua's atonement. We talk about His sacrifice for sin, iniquities, and transgressions, but I believe He also made a cleansing for all these things we don't even think about. We are certainly subject to these defilements, which Scripture says disqualifies us from eating the Passover and from coming into the presence of God. How can a person be made clean? Yeshua made the way.

Three Spiritual Cleansing Agents

There are three detergents in the Kingdom of God—three cleansing agents that God has provided for us. The first one is the Blood of Yeshua.

> Hebrews 9:13-14 *For if sprinkling ceremonially unclean persons with the blood of goats and bulls and the ashes of a heifer restores their outward purity; 14 then how much more the blood of the Messiah, who, through the eternal Spirit, offered himself to God as a sacrifice without blemish, will purify our conscience from works that lead to death, so that we can serve the living God!*

How much more powerful is Yeshua's cleansing Blood? It cleanses people inside where the ashes and the water can't reach. It cleanses us of our sin, our iniquity, and our transgressions. As the blood of the sacrifice is sprinkled on the altar, so the Blood of Yeshua is the first thing that cleanses, but the Scripture also says:

> Ephesians 5:26 (KJV) *That he might sanctify and cleanse it with the washing of water by the*

word.... [CJB: *in order to set it apart for God, making it clean through immersion in the mikveh, so to speak.*

So the second detergent in the Kingdom of God is the Word. It is the Word that keeps us clean, because if we are not regularly in the Word, we don't stay clean. But by staying in the Word, by continuing to have God's Word flowing through our minds and hearts, we can stay clean. It is an ongoing cleanser.

Finally, there is another cleansing agent.

Matthew 3:11b-12 *It's true that I am immersing you in water so that you might turn from sin to God; but the one coming after me is more powerful than I—I'm not worthy even to carry his sandals—and he will immerse you in the Ruach HaKodesh and in fire.*

The third cleansing agent we have available to us is the Holy Spirit, the Ruakh HaKodesh. How does the Ruakh HaKodesh cleanse us? There are certain gifts that we are given through the Holy Spirit: the discerning of spirits, prophecy, and words of knowledge and wisdom. A part of the reason for those gifts is so that we can discern unclean spirits. The fire of the Ruakh HaKodesh deals with those unclean spirits.

Understand that in the New Covenant, there are many mentions of the word "unclean." Do you know what it refers to every time? Spirits. It all has to do with unclean spirits. The Holy Spirit needs to open our eyes to be able to see how we have become defiled through these harassing spirits—these unclean spirits that get into our lives and defile us and keep us from all that God has for us.

Let's ask the Lord to purify us in preparation for the Passover. Some people do some fasting for this time of cleansing. It is all about coming into the Lord's presence. It is not just about getting the khametz out of our houses, but about cleansing our hearts.

What do we need to be cleansed of? From touching a dead body or an unclean animal—the things in the Torah—yes, but also from our sin, and our iniquity, known and unknown, and from these unclean spirits that get into our lives. We don't even know they are there because ha-satan's main way of dealing with us is through deception. He assigns things to us without our knowledge, if we aren't alert to it. All of a sudden something seems difficult or we just keep falling into a sin.

I was watching a documentary about underwater creatures. It showed whales having tons of barnacles stuck to them. They seemed to not even be aware that these parasites were on them. That is how these unclean spirits are. They sneak in and they get ahold of us. They harass and deceive us and manipulate us and we don't even know they are there. The Holy Spirit can reveal them to us. Now is the season for cleansing.

Let's pray

Heavenly Father, we pray that we would have a new appreciation of what it takes for You to cleanse us, so we can come into Your presence. Give us a new revelation to see how Holy You are and how we are so unworthy of coming into Your presence without that cleansing that only You can provide. I thank You for Your atoning sacrifice today, Lord. I thank You for Your Blood. I pray that we would receive the Blood upon us to cleanse us, O God, in preparation for Passover. We pray that in preparation for the remembrance of Your death and Resurrection, that You would pour Your Blood upon us today and cleanse us. That You would continue to cleanse us by Your Word. That Your Word would stay in us and keep us clean.

Lord, we ask for the cleansing of Your fire—Your Ruakh HaKodesh—Your Holy Spirit fire. I particularly ask that You would open the eyes of our hearts and give us discerning of spirits, O God, that we might see the devices of our enemy that are against us. Open the eyes of our hearts, O God, to burn up that which is not of You. May we eat the Pesakh, the Passover this year with a new appreciation of what You have done to enable us to eat it. In Yeshua's name, AMEN.

*Artwork: Seder Table, 1867 Haggadah, printed in Livorno, Italy, public domain.

CHAPTER 8

YESHUA'S PURITY PARADIGM SHIFT

So, now we have seen that the Torah required people to be clean to partake of Pesakh. Yeshua entered into Jerusalem on the day the lambs were chosen. Of course He had to be ritually clean also when He entered Jerusalem for two reasons. One was because He had to be ritually pure to celebrate Passover and the other was because He was going to be the Passover Lamb! He had to be pure and unblemished for that. So, he had to be doubly clean.

During the next four days you find that the religious leaders in Jerusalem tried to show that he was unclean. They tried to trip him up and show that he was a false teacher. They questioned him about paying taxes, about whose wife a four-time widow will be in the resurrection, about the greatest commandment, etc. All these questions came in order to trap Him in His Words. We will read them later and will see how incredibly He answered them; how He confounded every one of His questioners.

> Matthew 22:46 *No one could think of anything to say in reply; and from that day on, no one dared put to him another sh'eilah* (the Hebrew word for question).

They were unable to prove any unrighteousness in Him. So we know that Yeshua obeyed the purity laws or else they would've been able to find fault with Him. But they couldn't, which meant that He was pure and clean and holy and therefore qualified not only to eat the Passover, but to be the unblemished Passover Lamb.

Fence Around the Law

Let's turn now and look at how, by Yeshua's day, the laws for cleanliness had grown and become quite extensive from what the Torah says.

If you are familiar with Orthodox Judaism and the Talmud (or remember from the Khametz chapter), you know that the main idea of it is to build a "*fence around the law.*" The purpose for the "fence" is to make completely sure that we don't break the commandments. So we put an extra set of rules around them so that there is not even a possibility that we will break them. The thinking is that if we get too close to the edge of the law, we might break it. The analogy is of a cliff. Breaking the law is like stepping off a cliff. So if we are going to build a fence so that you don't step off the cliff, we will build it quite a ways from the edge of the cliff, rather than right on the edge where there would still be danger of falling.

Interpretation Is Needed

The thing we have to understand is that God's Torah/Law does require interpretation and application. How did God plan that this would be done? This was one of the roles of the cohanim (priests). They are commanded to do this.

> Leviticus 10:8,10 *ADONAI spoke to Aaron saying: 9 "Do not drink wine or fermented drink, neither you nor your sons with you, when you go into the Tent of Meeting, so that you do not die.*

> This is to be a statute forever throughout your generations. 10 You are to make a distinction between the holy and the common and between the unclean and the clean.
>
> Deuteronomy 17:8-11 "Suppose a matter arises that is too hard for you to judge—over bloodshed, legal claims or assault—matters of controversy within your gates. Then you should go up to the place ADONAI your God chooses, 9 and come to the Levitical kohanim [priests] and the judge in charge at that time. And you will inquire, and they will tell you the sentence of judgment. 10 You are to act according to the sentence they tell you from that place Adonai chooses, and take care to do all that they instruct you. 11 You are to act according to the instruction they teach you and the judgment they tell you—you must not turn aside from the sentence they tell you, to the right or to the left.

This was the priestly role to discern between the clean and the unclean and to interpret the Torah. They were supposed to do this. That was part of their job. The question however was: How were they to do this interpreting?

Go to God to Get the Interpretation

In the book of Numbers and in many other places in the Torah, we see the pattern of how they are to make these interpretations. In Numbers 27 there was the case of women's inheritance rights.

> Numbers 27:1-11 The daughters of Zelophehad ... of the families of Manasseh son of Joseph ... 2 stood before Moses, Eleazar the kohen and the princes of the entire assembly at the entrance to the Tent of Meeting and said, 3 "Our father died in the wilderness. ... Yet he had no sons. 4 Why should our father's name diminish from his family just because he had no son? Give to us property among our father's brothers."

> 5 So Moses brought their issue before ADONAI, 6 and ADONAI spoke to Moses saying, 7 "The daughters of Zelophehad are right in saying you should give them property by inheritance among their father's relatives. You are to turn over the inheritance of their father to them."
>
> 8 "Furthermore, you are to speak to Bnei-Yisrael saying: If a man dies without a son, you are to transfer his inheritance to his daughter. ... 10 ... This is to be a legal statute for Bnei-Yisrael, just as ADONAI commanded to Moses."

What is this saying? This is saying to interpret the Laws of God, go to God and get revelation from the Spirit of God. Don't just try to interpret the Laws by your own wisdom or thinking. Man tries to interpret the Laws of God without revelation, which leads to legalism, hypocrisy, and bondage. This has been a pattern throughout history.

This is not just a pattern among Jewish people. The Church has done the same thing. It is taking the Laws of God and adding to them and interpreting them in ways that are not the "Spirit of the law." When a judge or jury is trying to decide a case, they try to find this out. They ask themselves, "Did they violate the spirit of the law?"

Contradict Scripture

Sometimes the manmade laws actually contradict Scripture. We can see this in this next passage. Haggai lived during the time of the Babylonian exile after the first Temple had been destroyed by King Nebuchadnezzar and the Israelites had to figure out how to continue to follow Torah—God's Laws—without a Temple. This is the era when the "fence building" around the laws began in earnest.

> Haggai 2:12-13 "If a person carries consecrated meat in the corner of his garment, and with his corner he touches bread, stew, wine, oil or any food, will it become holy too?" Then the kohanim answered and said, "No."

> 13 So Haggai said, "If one who is unclean by contact with a corpse touches any of these, does it become unclean?"
> The kohanim answered and said, "It does become unclean."

Look at the actual laws about sacrificial meat in the Torah.

> Leviticus 6:10-11, 18-19 (English Bibles: 6:17-18, 27) ... *It is most holy, like the sin offering and like the trespass offering. 11 Every male among the children of Aaron may eat it, as their portion forever throughout your generations from the offerings of ADONAI made by fire.* **Whoever touches them will become holy.** *... 18 ...This is the Torah of the sin offering. In the place where the burnt offering is slaughtered, the sin offering is to be slaughtered before ADONAI. It is most holy. 19 The kohen who offers it for sin should eat it. .... 20* **Whatever touches its flesh will be holy.**

Do you see that? The Torah says that people or things that touch the sacrificial meat become holy, not the other way around as the cohanim in Haggai are saying. [It is only the peace offering that cannot be touched by anything unclean, most likely because it is eaten by the person sacrificing it rather than by the cohanim in a sanctified place (Lev.7:18-19).]

This Haggai Scripture shows the beginning of these extra rules of impurity. Understand that the word that is used is the word we often sing—*Kadosh*—*holy*. So it doesn't mean clean as in no dirt on it. It means *holy*. It means *set apart to God*. Really, I think the thing we ought to grasp about this is that it means *able to come into God's presence*. So when they are talking about this meat offering, they are asking, could it have been offered to God? Was it fitting to be offered to God or not because it had touched other food or had been contaminated by an unclean person?

I encourage you to go back and read through the Gospels to see that the daily society at that time had been dominated by the wisdom of man in many things, including their interpretation of God's Laws of ritual purity.

It is not difficult to see examples of this today if you go and learn about the Orthodox Jewish communities. It is very similar. They have what is called the "Oral Law." It was oral for a long time and then it was written down in what we call the Talmud. There are many rules from the Talmud that you have to keep about Shabbat and about foods, etc. They are manmade rules. They are not in the Bible. They are the interpretations of men that have been added to God's rules, and sometimes they actually go against His original rules.

Manmade Laws Cause Barriers

Some of these rules, especially the ritual cleansing ones, created barriers within the community in the nation of Israel concerning who is in and who is out. Inside the boundaries were what you called the "elite" people—the cohanim, the Sadducees, the Pharisees, the scribes, the educated, those in the royal Davidic line or of the tribe of Judah, etc., and pretty much the wealthy people because they could afford to have their own mikveh, etc. On the outside were the uneducated, the sick, the blemished, the lepers, the beggars, the impure, the women, the Gentiles, the prostitutes, and slaves—all these were outside the elite—the insiders club. (In Orthodox communities still today, for example, a man cannot shake hands with a woman because what if she is having menstrual flow and is therefore unclean?) The way to become an insider was through knowing all the Torah laws and the "Oral Laws" from the Talmud and keeping them.

These extra laws of purity that developed during the time prior to Yeshua had a great effect on that society. As we saw in the last chapter, according to the Torah purity laws, they had to avoid things, like stepping on graves, touching someone who was sick or had any kind of a running sore or discharge.

But their extra *fence around the laws* went farther. The extra fence required they separate themselves and not touch someone who was injured because they might die and then they would be in the presence of a dead person. It also required they separate themselves from sinners, for instance a prostitute or a drunkard or a thief. These people were declared unclean, and their uncleanness could also be communicated through touch.

The other group they had to separate themselves from were non-Jews because you never knew if a Gentile was clean. They are perpetually unclean because they never go through the ritual cleansing. So if you touched them, you were unclean, and now you would have to go all the way to Jerusalem, spend three days there and get cleansed. This was a big thing and it dramatically affected the society. We saw in the last chapter that this was why it took a vision for Peter to be convinced that God wanted him to go to Gentile Cornelius's house.

Yeshua's Halachic Judgment

Let's look at how Yeshua dealt with this question of purity, which is really a question of holiness and of who is part of the Kingdom. Yeshua did not agree with the teachings of the religious leaders of the day. He was strongly in disagreement on many of their rulings. Where does He get His authority to disagree with them? Well, being God Himself come in the flesh, He knew how these Laws were to be handled.

He is our Great High Priest. This was a priestly role as we noted—interpreting the Torah and discerning between the clean and the unclean. He is also the Word of God that was *in the beginning with God*, and the Word of the Torah that God spoke to Moses. He knows the Spirit of the Law (Torah) because He IS the Torah! So here is how the Torah Himself saw things.

He saw people's physical and spiritual health as more important than the Torah Laws of purity. It has a higher priority. He was making what we call a "halachic judgment." He was saying, "This law takes priority over that law." It was very simple. Healing those that are sick and diseased takes priority over worrying about becoming defiled yourself. When He began to do this, He caused a tremendous paradigm shift in that culture.

Paradigm Shifts

Here is the definition of a paradigm shift. It is a significant change from one fundamental view to another that allows the creation of a new condition previously thought impossible or unacceptable. The shift can be in one individual or in a whole society.

Let me give you a few examples. We are actually seeing a few paradigm shifts in the Body of Messiah. The churches being supportive of Israel is a huge paradigm shift. And if it works like we hope, there will be another enormous shift: Jewish people will begin to see Christians as their friends instead of their enemies.

There have been more that you might not be aware of. One is that a few decades back, it was thought that Believers should not be involved in politics. That was considered dirty stuff. We've gone through a paradigm shift. Now the Body is very strongly involved in politics.

Another is that humanitarian aid used to be called a "Social gospel." Churches used to reach out and help the poor, but they would never really share the Gospel with them. Now many congregations are moving in the direction of sharing the Gospel while they help the needy. It is important to see this in light of Passover because in the traditional Haggadah it says, "Let all who are hungry, come." So, there is traditionally always the thing of wanting to help the needy.

Yeshua's Major Paradigm Shift

Yeshua showed people that inner purity and holiness is more important than outward cleanliness. Let me give you an example of this new paradigm.

> Luke 5:12 *Once, when Yeshua was in one of the towns, there came a man completely covered with tzara`at* [skin disease]. *On seeing Yeshua, he fell on his face and begged him, "Sir, if you are willing, you can make me clean."*

According to the Torah laws, this man cannot come into the Temple, into the presence of God! So, he might be afraid that even when he dies he cannot go to be with God. The issue was bigger than physical healing. It was also spiritual. This is not just Talmudic. As we have pointed out, the Scriptures say that someone who has a running sore or leprosy is unclean.

And apparently being healed and cleansed from leprosy was a very rare thing. It did occur as we see with Simon the leper in Matthew 26:6. (We know this Simon was healed because people could come into his house. If he had still been a leper, he would have had to "dwell outside the camp" away from people per the Torah Law. See Numbers 5:2.)

> Luke 5:13 *Yeshua reached out his hand and touched him, saying, "I am willing! Be cleansed!" Immediately the tzara`at [skin disease] left him.*

This was a major miracle. It wasn't like the man went home and over a few days was healed. Visibly the sores instantaneously healed up.

> Luke 5:14 *Then Yeshua warned him not to tell anyone. "Instead, as a testimony to the people, go straight to the cohen (priest) and make an offering for your cleansing, as Moshe commanded."*

In other words Yeshua was telling him to go be assessed by the Cohen and make the required offerings and go through the whole eight-day ceremonial cleansing, which included being cleansed with the special holy water that is to be made specifically for him for cleansing from leprosy. It also included shaving all bodily hair twice on different days and bathing and washing his clothes and finally, a special ritual sacrifice and anointing ceremony. (See Leviticus 14:1-20.)

Yeshua Touched the Defiled

Today we know there are good health reasons for not touching certain sick people because many diseases are contagious. We know when somebody is hacking and coughing, we don't want to breathe that air, etc.

Yeshua had done something radically different. He touched a leper! It was a real paradigm shift. It might not seem that radical to us today, but to them it was earth-shaking. People in that culture did not touch a leper because once you did, you became unclean and had to go through this cleansing.

But when Yeshua touched the leper, look what happened. Rather than Yeshua becoming defiled, what happened? The leper was the opposite of defiled—un-defiled—he was cleansed. He was no longer impure. The skin disease actually left.

The physical healing was actually proof that rather than Yeshua becoming defiled, the leper was cleansed. It was proof that Yeshua's power to purify was greater than the power of this disease that made this person unclean. Notice also that the last thing Yeshua says to him is, "Go and make the offering." Because He wanted to make sure this was done according to the Scriptural commands.

This is the same dynamic that was operating around the Sabbath. Yeshua kept the Scriptural Laws about Sabbath perfectly. He would heal people on the Sabbath without breaking God's Law. But the legalistic leaders got upset with Him because He was violating *their* rules of the Sabbath.

This was just one of the several paradigm shifting things Yeshua did concerning the ritual purity laws. Another one was the way He treated the centurion who had a servant who was sick. Yeshua said, "I'll go to your house." He ended up not needing to go there because of the centurion's faith. (See Matthew 8:5-13; and Luke 7:1-10.) But the fact that Yeshua was willing to go to his house was totally against the rabbinical rules.

Let's just review some of the things we mentioned in the last chapter. In Luke 7:38, Yeshua allowed a prostitute to touch Him. In Luke 8:41-42,49-56, the leader of a synagogue's daughter is dying. He calls Yeshua to come and lay hands on her. She dies in the meantime. He goes anyway. What does He do? He took her by the hand. He touched her, unconcerned that He would become ritually impure. She came back to life as a testimony.

What is happening here? He is reversing the Torah cleansing laws. When He touched someone unclean, He was not defiled. Instead, that person became clean. He conveyed purity to the impure. What was unclean He made clean. What was sinful He made holy. What was unfit to come into God's presence, He made fit to enter.

Insiders With Yeshua

What about the idea I mentioned earlier about who is in and who is out? Yeshua had some profound things to say about that, too. He really turned it upside down. Before it depended on ritual purity, on birth status, or on wealth and ancestry. But look at this Scripture:

> Mark 3:31-35 *Then his mother and brothers arrived. Standing outside, they sent a message asking for him.* ***32*** *A crowd was sitting around him; and they said to him, "Your mother and your brothers are outside, asking for you."* ***33*** *He replied, "Who are my mother and my brothers?"* ***34*** *Looking at those seated in a circle around him, he said, "See! Here are my mother and my brothers!* ***35*** *Whoever does what God wants is my brother, sister and mother!"*

"My mother and my brothers" are who? Those who hear God's message and act on it. Inclusion into the Kingdom of God, Yeshua's Kingdom—the way of access—is dependent on these three things: hearing His Word, obeying it and acting on it.

The way of access into the presence of God is no longer through ritual purity, but through a relationship—through hearing Him and obeying Him—through having a relationship with Mashiakh—Messiah. We must understand that that relationship is the only way to really come into God's presence.

Here are a couple of passages where He speaks about how to keep in God's presence. *"If you love me, keep my commandments"* (John 14:15). Paul says *"All who are led by God's Spirit are part of the family – Sons and daughters* (Romans 8:14). This is how we come into the Kingdom and how we stay in the Kingdom—through this relationship.

Yeshua Was Not Defiled by Touching the Unclean

The question is: How could Yeshua do this? Why was He not defiled when He touched unclean people? The Scriptures said that they were unclean. I believe it's because the Holy Spirit's power was so great in Him. The Spirit was like this protective shield around Him. If you can envision this, the Spirit that came out of Him was like a protective shield and a mighty cleansing power so that as He touched someone He didn't "catch" what they had. Instead, they "caught" what He had! They caught the Spirit of God and overcame by His power.

Why did He have such power? Because He was God himself come as a man. Also, because He walked in the power of the Spirit every day. He was anointed by the oil of the Holy Spirit. That was His lifestyle. He was walking in the power of the Spirit.

Let me show you something really amazing about this. Yeshua said:

> Matthew 12:6 *But I say to you that something greater than the temple is here.*

Look at this law from the Torah about the Temple. This is from God's instructions for making the special oil for anointing the cohanim and all the things in the Temple to cleanse them.

> Exodus 30:25-28 *You are to make holy anointing oil from it, a fragrant mixture, blended as the work of a perfumer. It will be holy anointing oil. 26 You are to anoint the Tent of Meeting with it, the Ark of the Testimony, 27 as well as the table and all its articles, the menorah and its articles, the altar of incense, 28 the altar of burnt offering with all its utensils, and the basin along with its stand.*

So anointing these things with this oil made these things clean and holy. Now listen to what God says happens if something unclean touches them.

> Exodus 30:29 *You are to consecrate them so that they will be most holy.* **Whatever touches them will become holy.**

So you see, Yeshua is greater than the Temple. He has the powerful anointing oil of the Ruakh HaKodesh on Him. When He touched unclean people, they become clean.

Even touching sinful people didn't make Yeshua impure. The woman who was the prostitute confirmed that this was really what was happening because she repented. He said, *"Your sins are forgiven"* (Luke 7:48). She went off and changed her life.

So we see that He had authority over sin—the authority to take what was sinful and impure and turn it into what was pure and holy. Touching the demon-possessed did not separate Yeshua from God. That was confirmed by their deliverance when He spoke. That demonstrated His authority over ha-satan and all of his forces. Touching the dead did not separate Yeshua from God. How was that confirmed? When He touched them, they rose from the dead.

To tie this to Passover, His own death as the Passover Lamb did separate Him from God, but only for a moment. When He was hanging on the Cross, He said, *"My God, My God, why have you forsaken me."* People thought now God has left Him because He went too far. He really wasn't who He said He was. But He rose from the dead! This confirmed that He really did have authority over death and hell. We can see that Yeshua was moving in a different paradigm. It was so radically different from what was happening around Him.

Is This For Us Today?

The question I want us to end up with is, "How do we function in that paradigm?" That paradigm is for His followers, too. So, get ready. This is important. The last instruction Yeshua gave to His followers, which you are probably very familiar with but never saw them from this light, is called "The Great Commission."

> Matthew 28:18-20 *Yeshua came and talked with them. He said, "All authority in heaven and on earth has been given to me. 19 Therefore, go and make people from all nations into talmidim (disciples), immersing them into the reality of the Father, the Son and the Ruach HaKodesh, 20 and teaching them to obey everything that I have commanded you. And remember! I will be with you always, yes, even until the end of the age."*

Why is the "therefore" there? Because I have all authority, you go with My authority. Where do you go? To all the nations. To the Gentiles. But they are unclean! They are heathens! Idolaters! They are even cannibals! You go to all of them—places where God is not honored—where people are defiled—and make them into disciples.

I had never seen this before, but look at the first thing they have to do when they become disciples. *"Immersing them into the reality of the Father, the Son, and the Ruach HaKodesh."* What is this "immersing" about? It is about cleansing. It is symbolic of the cleansing that happens when a person is immersed in water.

He continues, *"and teaching them to obey everything that I have commanded you. And remember! I will be with you always, yes, even until the end of the age."* Why immerse them? To cleanse them from the uncleanness they have been walking in. Why teach them? So that they can stay clean. Otherwise they will go right back into the mire. I like Mark's version of this because it says something interesting too.

> Mark 16:15-16 *Then he said to them, "As you go throughout the world, proclaim the Good News to all creation. 16 Whoever trusts and is immersed will be saved; whoever does not trust will be condemned.*

What I like about this passage is the inclusiveness. "Whoever." "Everyone who trusts—everyone who believes."

> Mark 16:17 *And these signs will accompany those who do trust: in my name they will drive out demons, speak with new tongues,*

He is giving His authority to His followers to make even demon-possessed people clean.

> Mark 16:18 *not be injured if they handle snakes or drink poison, and heal the sick by laying hands on them."*

Heal the sick. How? By laying hands on them, by touching them! In our culture, maybe we take this for granted because we see people praying for the sick all the time. Please understand that in that culture, this was forbidden and unheard of! If you touched a sick person, you became unclean.

Authority Over Four Things

So, why can we do this? Because He gives us His authority over four things here: sin, sickness, demons, and death. Those are the four things He gives us authority over. He tells us, "Don't just sit there with it. Go and use it!" Not on the healthy and righteous. They don't need it. Use it on the sinful. The sick. The harassed. The dying. Those are the ones we are to go to.

If you can grasp how radical this was for the first disciples when they obeyed His command because they were going against everything they had learned all through their upbringing. They were going against their community. They were going to lay hands on the sick. They were moving into that new paradigm, dealing with these laws of purity.

How does this apply to our lives? To you and me? We need to see ourselves walking in this power. Do you hear that? You and me, we are the light of what? The world! So what happens when we go into a place of darkness? It lights up. Darkness does not overcome the light. Light always overcomes the darkness.

I hear you saying, "Amen." But do you really believe this? We are to go into the dark places?

Power With the Authority

Here is another way of looking at it. We use this analogy around Passover of the little bit of leaven leavening the dough. Yeshua uses it in a positive sense too. He says that we—those in the Kingdom of God—are like leaven. When just a little bit—a little pinch—is mixed into the huge lump of dough, the whole dough rises.

> Matthew 13:33 *And he told them yet another parable. "The Kingdom of Heaven is like yeast that a woman took and mixed with a bushel of flour, then waited until the whole batch of dough rose."*

What is He saying? All it takes is a little bit of the people of God filled with this power, and it will affect the world around them. Here is another analogy. When you are put into a barrel of bad apples, apples get good. It isn't "One apple spoils the barrel," that is true in the natural, but in the spiritual, "One good apple makes the whole barrel good" supernaturally in the Kingdom of God.

This is why when Yeshua speaks about drinking from Him in John 7:38, He doesn't say, "A little trickle of Living Water will come out of you." He says, "Rivers of Living Water will come out of you and change the landscape around you." This happens only when we have that boldness to identify who we are when we go to the dark places of the world where there are lots of defiled people.

In Acts, Yeshua points out that there is power that comes with this authority that we get through the outpouring of the Ruakh HaKodesh. He does not give us the authority without the power to carry it out.

> Acts 1:8 *But you will receive power when the Ruach HaKodesh comes upon you; you will be my witnesses both in Yerushalayim and in all Y'hudah and Shomron, indeed to the ends of the earth!"*

My Personal Testimony

I want to share a story about my own life. I used to work at Xerox and over the years I had opportunities to share with many of the people there. However, there were a few that I hadn't. I still remember the day when one of the people I had shared with, Ken, was in his office talking with a man named Frank whom I had not talked with. I just happened to walk in the door at that moment. Frank was telling a dirty joke. He is continuing on with this dirty joke and I see the look on Ken's face because I am in the room. He can't believe I am in the room and Frank is still telling this dirty joke. It was terrible. That was the effect of my having witnessed to Ken. Ken was not a believer at the time. But it was like the light had been there and he knew that this was not cool.

On the other side of that, we need to be led by the Spirit. If you are a recovering alcoholic, the day after you become saved is not the time to be going back to the bars to be telling everyone about Yeshua. You might get drawn back in. I know this from experience.

I was quite involved with the whole drug scene before I came to the Lord. Soon after I had come to salvation, I had all these friends who were still doing drugs. I wanted to share about the

Lord with them. But I didn't want to come in there and act like I was holy now, so I said, "I'll go back in there and smoke the stuff with them, and then I'll tell them about Yeshua." And I did! But it didn't work. I immediately saw that it started to affect me. I was getting defiled by it.

It took a couple of years before I was able to go back to some of those people to share with them and be strong enough to say, "I'm not going to take any of that, but I want to tell you about the Lord." You have to have that wisdom to know when you are strong enough to do that.

Our Feet Get Contaminated

So when we work with non-believers or new believers, there can be many ungodly attitudes in people. We have to be able to deal with that. People don't turn into showing forth all the fruits of the Spirit in one night. It takes a long time. At Yeshua's Last Seder, He dealt with this in one of the elements of the Passover Seder—when He washed their feet. (See John 13:3-15.)

We will go into much more detail on this in a later chapter, but listen to this because it is totally applicable to how we walk in this world. In those days people's feet got dirty all the time because they walked on dirt roads and they wore sandals. I believe back then the Passover tradition was to wash feet rather than hands as we do today.

This is what happened. Yeshua offered to wash His disciple's feet. Shimon Kefa (Peter), after first refusing, said, "not only my feet, but my hands and my head too." Yeshua said, "A man who has had a bath does not need to wash except his feet. His body is already clean." What is He saying? "Peter, you are already clean. You have been obeying My Word, which cleanses you. You have been acting on My Word."

I believe this is a daily thing. When we encounter the world we may feel defiled by it. So, daily we need to come before the Lord and ask Him if there is any sin in us and repent of that, believing that the Lord forgives us. But we also need to ask Him to cleanse us if there is anything that we have "picked up." What I mean by that is, for instance, if you hear somebody saying something that isn't quite "kosher" or believing something that isn't quite Scripture, and you find you are saying it or thinking it or believing it later. We can pick up sinful things almost without realizing it. Sometimes we are subconsciously thinking that if it is okay for them to do this, it is okay for me too.

Prayer

I pray for everyone reading this book to grasp the magnitude of this paradigm shift that You put into place. Help us understand how big it is and how important it is that people be cleansed enough to come before You. I pray that we would grasp the authority You have given us for this cleansing process. That we have really been given authority over sin, over sickness, over demons, and over death!

If you need a boost in this area, just pray "Lord, increase my sense of authority over those things."

Father, we need to know that You have given us authority over these things. That all other powers have to bow their knee to the mighty Name of Yeshua. We want to see more healings because we believe there is authority over those things. We want to see deliverances. We want to see people repenting of their sins. So, we pray for that authority, O God. Build it up in us.

We also understand that that authority is there when we walk in obedience to You, when we stay cleansed by being immersed in Your Word. So, bring to mind anything that we have picked up, any "junk," and come and wash our feet and cleanse us of this. Also when you spoke in the book of Acts, You said that with that authority comes power, so I pray for power to overcome all these forces of darkness in the lives of the people that we encounter in the Name of Yeshua. Amen."

CHAPTER 9
SHABBAT HaGADOL

In this chapter we are going to talk about the Shabbat before Pesakh called Shabbat HaGadol, the Great Shabbat ("gadol" means "great"). Passover activities actually last nearly a whole month. The first day of the month, Rosh Chodesh (new moon), is actually the Biblical New Year. Then it is spring cleaning and preparation time. Pesakh comes on the eve of the 14th and then Unleavened bread lasts for seven days after that.

The Name of the Month

The month has two names. One is Nissan, which comes from the root of "bud" and "miracles." Spring is here and everything is budding, and also there was a great miracle that happened at this time. The other name that you hear is Aviv. "Aviv" also means "spring." It actually describes the little ears, the "protrusions" as they call them, on the barley crop, which tells the barley growers when it's going to be ripe, which says when the firstfruits will come. So that's the two names of the month and Passover, of course, is the main event of the month.

* Photo: Arnold Eagle, photographer, from his Sabbath Study Series, 1937, The Jewish Museum, public domain.

Foreigners/Gerim Can Keep Pesakh

Who can keep the Passover? In Scripture, as we have learned, it says that all Israel had to keep it. But also, if you're not Jewish, all the non Jewish people who were living amongst Israel, called the Ger or Gerim for plural, were also invited to keep Passover.

However, they had to be circumcised. They had to be clean. They couldn't be defiled from touching anything unclean. If they did touch anything, especially if it was a dead body, they had to go through the week-long cleansing process just like the Israelites did. But notice something in this Scripture:

> Exodus 12:19 *For seven days no hametz is to be found in your houses, for whoever eats hametz, that soul will be cut off from the congregation of Israel, whether he is an outsider or one who is born in the land.*

Notice that it doesn't matter whether he is a native or a foreigner. Did you see that? This cleansing of khametz also had to be done by the Gerim. Their homes had to be prepared, too, which as we've said, today means changing all the dishes over to the pots and pans and a set of dishes designated as Passover pans and dishes. This had to all be done by the day before Passover.

Passover Parasha

The Parasha reading for the week before Passover one year was the one called Acharai Mot, "After the death." It is Leviticus 16-18. It is referring to the death of Aaron's sons. (Parasha passages are named from the first couple of Hebrew words of the passage.) This is a really powerful Parasha. It has the explanation of what's to happen on Yom Kippur. Then the next chapter is about the importance of the blood for atonement— just very powerful stuff.

It's really not about Passover at all. It seems a little bit disconnected. So when I finished reading it that year, I thought, "Well, I'll take a look at the haftarah and see what's about for this week. (The word *haftarah* means *parting* or *taking leave*.) Maybe there will be something there that is relevant for

Passover." So I went online to look at the Jewish calendar to see what the haftarah was for that week. (This was when I first began using the Parasha readings for my sermons.)

Let me give you a little explanation of what a Parasha reading is. Thousands of years ago, the Jewish leaders divided the Torah, the five books of Moses, into weekly reading portions. Each Parasha, each portion, has a specific haftarah reading with it, usually from one of the prophetic books, that has some relevance to it. That's how the reading schedule was developed.

Usually the haftarah that's associated with this Parasha, Acharai Mot, is either from Ezekiel 22 or Amos 9. It can be either one of those. But when I looked on the calendar because Shabbat that week was Shabbat HaGadol, I saw that there's a special haftarah that's always read on this Shabbat, independent of what the Parasha is. (Because of the way the lunar calendar is set up, you can have different Parashas for that week, but no matter what the Parasha is, you always also read this special haftarah portion.) It is Malachi chapters 3-4 (4-6 in English Bibles), starting at verse 4 of chapter 3.

By the way, Malachi is an interesting name. A lot of people think it's an Italian prophet, but actually it is Hebrew for *messenger*. It's the same word as *angel*. People aren't sure whether it's his name or his title.

So I read this haftarah, expecting it to have great meaning for Passover since it was especially chosen for the Shabbat before it. Well, it is very interesting. In Malachi 3:5-15, the prophet threatens judgment on Israel for all kinds of sinfulness. It actually includes the verses about tithing, about bringing the full tithe in to the storehouses, and of course, the rebuke to Israel for not having done that. Then it talks about the people who wanted to follow the Lord. The Lord actually wrote their names all down, and He says that He will especially bless them because they are committed to being followers after Him.

Then it has a promise of judgment on the wicked. And it says that those who are covenanted with God will be spared. It ends with a promise of sending Eliyahu (Elijah) to turn the hearts of the fathers to the sons before the great day of the Lord, which is a very familiar passage.

So I finished reading it and I thought, "This is good stuff but what's it got to do with Passover? Absolutely nothing!" I don't know if you can see anything there. The only thing I could see was the warning about sin. You could say it is about cleansing, but really it isn't very much. So I was kind of amazed that the special haftarah for the Shabbat before Passover doesn't relate to Passover at all. ......Unless.......you're a Messianic Jew.

Yeshua Fulfilled the Haftarah Reading

If you look in the New Covenant to see what Yeshua was doing on that weekend before Passover, all of a sudden you see that there are many things that are spoken of in this haftarah portion that He actually fulfilled. What I began to see was that He didn't just fulfill Passover day, He fulfilled the whole season starting with the Shabbat before Passover.

> Exodus 12:3 *Tell all the congregation of Israel that on the tenth day of this month, each man is to take a lamb for his family one lamb for the household.*

It's very easy to know what Yeshua was doing that week before Pesakh because in John 12 it actually tells us.

> John 12:1 *Six days before Pesakh, he rode into Jerusalem*

So Yeshua came to Elezar's (Lazarus's) house. Verses 2-11 describe what happened on that day, which is all really amazing. That was six days before Passover.

> John 12:12 **The next day** *the large crowd that had come for the festival heard that Yeshua was on his way into Yerushalayim. 13 They took palm branches and went out to meet him, shouting, "Deliver us!" "Blessed is he who comes in the name of ADONAI (the Lord), the King of Isra'el!"*

So on the next day, we would be in the fifth day before Pesakh, which starts on the 14th day at sundown. But the actual day of Pesakh is the 15th day of the month. So five days before Pesakh would've been what? The tenth day! He would've entered Jerusalem on the tenth day.

So Yeshua who is known as the Lamb of God entered Jerusalem on the day of the selection of the lambs, the 10th day, probably on a Sunday because He would not have traveled on Shabbat. He went from Bet'Aniah (Bethany) into Jerusalem. This day is known as the day of His triumphal entry, also called Palm Sunday by the church because, as we just read, the people brought palm branches.

So, if the tenth day of Nissan was on a Sunday, then the day Yeshua died wasn't on a Friday, it was on a Thursday. Thursday was the 14th. Thursday was the Passover eve or Preparation Day, the day the lambs were being slaughtered. So He would've died at the same time they were being slaughtered.

So if we back up four days from Thursday, we get to Palm Sunday, the day when He entered into Jerusalem, riding on the colt, and the people were waving the palm branches at Him. It's amazing that God gave us this calendar that we can commemorate things in the Old Covenant and things in the New Covenant on the same day.

So I went back to the Malachi haftarah to see if He fulfilled any of the things predicted there. Interestingly, there are actually three things that He fulfilled on the day that He came into Jerusalem. That's why I said that if you are a Messianic Jew, this does connect with Passover. So let's take a look at them.

> Mal'akhi 3:19 (Jewish Bibles) (4:1 in English Bibles) *For the day is coming, burning like a furnace, when all the proud and evildoers will be stubble; the day that is coming will set them ablaze," says ADONAI-Tzva'ot (the Lord of Hosts), "and leave them neither root nor branch.*

So we look through the Gospels and we find something in Luke. Listen to what Yeshua prophesied:

> Luke 19:43-44 *For the days are coming upon you when your enemies will set up a barricade around you, encircle you, hem you in on every side, 44 and dash you to the ground, you and your children within your walls, leaving not one stone*

> standing on another—and all because you did not
> recognize your opportunity when God offered it!"

So I could see that He is kind of just repeating this prophesy that Malachi had said for this day.

> Mal'akhi 3:20 (4:2) *But to you who fear my name, the sun of righteousness will rise with healing in its wings; and you will break out leaping, like calves released from the stall.*

That's probably a very familiar verse to you. But there's two very interesting things about it. The first is that in the Hebrew, the word there is "shemesh" translated as "sun." And it's not "son." It's "sun." They are very different words in Hebrew although they sound identical in English. Many English speakers think this is a title of the Messiah, the "son of righteousness," but it's not.

The other word that is interesting in there is "healing in its wings." "Wings" is the Hebrew word "k'nahfeyha" or "corners," like the corners of the Tallit (prayer shawl). The imagery here is righteousness rising like the sun with rays ("k'nahfeyha") of healing.

We know about the woman who had an issue of blood who came to Yeshua for healing, and she touched His k'nahfeyha, the hem or corners of His Tallit because she knew this prophecy—healing in the wings, the corners, the k'nahfeyha of the Tallit.

So what happened on that day when Yeshua entered Jerusalem?

> Matthew 21:14 *Blind and lame people came up to him in the Temple, and he healed them.*

So we see a second fulfillment of the haftarah's prediction. Finally, at the end of that haftarah portion, we read this:

> Mal'akhi 3:23 *Look, I will send to you Eliyahu the prophet before the coming of the great and terrible Day of ADONAI.*

The coming of that great day is always associated with the Second Coming of the Messiah, as King Messiah, as Messiah Ben David, instead of coming as the suffering servant. Of course we know that Yeshua said that Eliyahu has already come. It was Yochanan the Immerser (John the Baptist) who came and prepared the way for Yeshua.

How did Yeshua enter the city on this day?

> John 12:14 *After finding a donkey colt, Yeshua mounted it...*

I'm sure you've seen pictures of Yeshua riding into the city on a colt of a donkey. Well, this was a fulfillment of a prophesy in the book of Zechariah.

> Zechariah 9:9 *Rejoice with all your heart, daughter of Tziyon! Shout out loud, daughter of Yerushalayim! Look! Your king is coming to you. He is righteous, and he is victorious. Yet he is humble—he's riding on a donkey, yes, on a lowly donkey's colt.*

So when He entered Jerusalem that day, He came not as the suffering servant but as the King Messiah. And that's very rare. In the whole time that we read about Yeshua in the Gospels, He doesn't take on His Kingly role. He hides it because this was His time to come as a suffering servant, but that day He rode into Jerusalem as the great King.

So I began to see that to a Messianic Jew, this haftarah portion, read on Shabbat HaGadol, really does speak about Passover. But then something else came to my mind. Maybe it did to you, too. The haftarah portion started in the middle of a chapter in verse 4, and I remembered that somewhere in chapter 3 there were some other very powerful Messianic prophecies. I decided to go back and take a look at that. And here's what I saw. Look at how Messianic this is.

> Mal'akhi 3:1 *"Look! I am sending my messenger to clear the way before me; and the Lord, whom you seek, will suddenly come to his temple. Yes, the messenger of the covenant, in whom you take such delight—look! Here he comes," says ADONAI-Tzva'ot*

So understand that Malachi was written during the time of Ezra and Nehemiah. It was after the rebuilding of the second

Temple. But the glory of God had not come to that Temple. It had filled Solomon's Temple, but not the rebuilt one. So there was no visible presence of God in that Temple like there was 500 years before in Solomon's Temple.

At the time of Yeshua, this second Temple had stood several hundred years. It had been refurbished by King Herod and was a marvelous structure. But the one thing that made the Temple the Temple was not there—the glory of God.

Malachi, who was prophesying during the time when the Temple had just been rebuilt and had no glory, was saying the Lord Himself is going to come to this Temple. In fact, he says, *"The Lord whom you seek."* How can you understand this other than, it will be a person. It won't be just a spirit. What will it be? It will be the Lord Himself coming.

So this is about as Messianic and amazing as you can imagine. And, of course, in three out of the four Gospels, it is recorded that Yeshua entered the Temple grounds.

> Matthew 21:12 *Yeshua entered the Temple grounds...*

So He went directly to the Temple. So this was a powerful prophetic fulfillment. Then there's another one. Look at the next two verses still before the haftarah portion:

> Mal'akhi 3:2-3 *But who can endure the day when he comes? Who can stand when he appears? For he will be like a refiner's fire, like the soapmaker's lye. 3 He will sit, testing and purifying the silver; he will purify the sons of Levi, refining them like gold and silver, so that they can bring offerings to ADONAI uprightly.*

What's Malachi predicting here? That when the Lord comes to His Temple, it's not going to be just to stand there and be worshipped. What's going to happen? He's going to refine the people. He's going to speak words of division. So let's see what happened on that day in the Temple. Did He come there to worship? Do you remember?

Matthew 21:12-13 ... and drove out those who were doing business there, both the merchants and their customers. He upset the desks of the money changers and knocked over the benches of those who were selling pigeons. 13 He said to them, "It has been written, `My house will be called a house of prayer.' But you are making it into a den of robbers!"

How much of a fulfillment of Malachi's prophecy was that? Dividing, refining, and bringing to conviction. In fact, stopping the worship that was going on. So it's incredible to see those three verses just before the haftarah actually predict most of what took place on that week before Passover.

Were Verses Removed from the Haftarah?

Then I began to wonder why they started the haftarah portion in the middle of the chapter. After all, the chapter divisions in the Tanakh were made by the Jewish people. They weren't made by Christians, they were made by Jewish leaders, yet they decided to start this haftarah portion in verse 4! Can you see the clue here? I believe verses 1-3 were removed from this haftarah portion by the Jewish religious leaders after Yeshua's time on earth to avoid the amazing, obvious connections to Yeshua. They didn't want us to read in the haftarah about the Lord coming to His Temple on the actual day that He came to His Temple in the form of the Messiah!

Removing verses from haftarah readings sounds very familiar. You might know about another removal. If you look through the reading portions of Isaiah, they go from chapter 49 to 50, 51, 52, 54, 55, 56, etc. What do they skip? Isaiah 53! Why? Obviously, it is because that chapter is so clearly talking about Yeshua being the Messiah.

So I was so amazed. This haftarah portion was chosen for Messianic Jews! Nobody really knows how those reading schedules got selected. I was even thinking maybe it was a believer in Yeshua that chose this haftarah portion and stuck it in there and then later the rabbis took out the really good part and left the rest because they didn't want to make it too obvious that they had done this? Anyway, it was amazing to see that on the same week that this haftarah portion is read about Him coming to the Temple, He came to the Temple and did what it says.

Yeshua Fulfilled Shabbat HaGadol

I had another flash of revelation about the calendar the Lord gave us in Leviticus 23, that the days that God appointed for special things were days that Yeshua did special things. If we keep God's Biblical calendar, we end up worshiping and commemorating things that God said to commemorate on actual days that Yeshua did amazing things.

Then I realized that Shabbat HaGadol is one of those days. It was appointed that this be the Shabbat before the Passover, so it's a special day, and Yeshua did something special when He entered Jerusalem.

Now, you might be thinking that Shabbat HaGadol sounds like a traditional thing rather than a time appointed by God. Is there anything Scriptural to support that this is really an Appointed Time of God? Let me tell you what I learned as I dug into this. God actually did appoint something very significant to happen on this day, just four days before Passover. Here's the verse again:

> Exodus 12:3 Tell all the congregation of Israel that on the tenth day of this month, each man is to take a lamb for his family one lamb for the household.

On the Chabad website, we find an interesting Jewish tradition about this. They say that the Jewish Rabbis and Sages have taught for a long time that the tenth day of this month in the year of the Exodus was on a Shabbat, and that's why it is Shabbat HaGadol, and the commemoration or remembering of the 10th of Nissan has been transferred to Shabbat HaGadol.[34]

So there are two reasons why Shabbat HaGadol is so special. It's the Shabbat before Pesakh plus it's the commemoration of the 10th of Nissan, the day the lambs were selected.

---

34 Eliyahu Kitov, "Shabbat HaGadol," Chabad.org, https://www.chabad.org/holidays/passover/pesach_cdo/aid/1692/jewish/Shabbat-Hagadol.htm. Accessed Nov. 2018.

But Shabbat HaGadol is even more interesting than that. The reason that it was selected as a Biblical special day, as a miraculous day was because as we touched on in chapter 3, it turns out that one of the gods of Egypt was called *amun*, the ram god, a sheep god. So, again, imagine the people of Israel are getting this instruction that they're supposed to take a sheep, a lamb, a god of Egypt, and sacrifice it to the One True God. What would the Egyptians have thought of that?

According to the Talmud, the Egyptians were very divided over this. Some of them after going through nine plagues said, "Let them do it! In fact, we'll do it, too, to survive!" But others said, "No, we can't let them sacrifice sheep because that's one of our gods!" The miracle that happened here was that the Egyptians allowed Israel to sacrifice the lambs on that day.[35]

So here we see this evidence that the Messiah was not just in the Passover day itself. (Jews for Jesus made the term very popular: Christ in the Passover. I usually say "Messiah in the Passover.") But we see here that Messiah was in more than the Passover. He was in the week preceding the Passover.

So let's take a look at what happened during those four days because this goes on with the fulfillments.

> Exodus 12:5-6 *Your lamb is to be without blemish* [תמים *tami'im*], *a year old male. You may take it from the sheep or from the goats. 6 You must watch over* [משמרת *mishmerit*] *it until the fourteenth day of the same month.*

The lamb had to be תמים *tami'im*. *Tami'im* is the Hebrew word for *unblemished*. No defect. No injury. No disease in this animal. Think back over the Book of Genesis. Abel, Abraham, Noah. They all offered animals, but this is the first time that God commanded that the animal be unblemished. Also notice the word משמרת *mishmerit*. It means *observe*. So for four days, they were to observe the lamb for defects.

In the text, if you caught it, the lamb went from being "a lamb" to being "your lamb" in those four days. Again, lambs are very loveable creatures. It would've become a pet to them.

---

35 Midrash Tehilim 136:6 and Ancient Tanchuma Bo 18, according to Rabbi Ari Kahn, "Shabbat HaGadol," Eish.com, http://www.aish.com/tp/i/moha/48942426.html#5. (See footnote 5.) Accessed Nov. 2018.

Yeshua entered Jerusalem on the day that the lambs were selected.

> John 12:13 (TLV) So they took palm branches and went out to meet Him, shouting, "'Hoshiana! Baruch ha-ba b'shem Adonai! Blessed is He who comes in the name of the Lord!' The King of Israel!"

Hoshiana means *"Save us."* His followers and the people of Jerusalem were acknowledging His Messiahship at this time and it happened on that 10th day of the month. And as we noted earlier, it happens to have been, in that year, on a Sunday called "Palm Sunday," but waving Palm branches wasn't a Pesakh custom or tradition. Palm trees are one of the four species in the commandments for Sukkot. Shouting "Hoshiana" was a Sukkot tradition, and kings were customarily inaugurated on Sukkot. The people were saying, "Well, this isn't Sukkot, but we want Him as our King Messiah, so let's quick get palm branches."

[As a side note, this account of the waving of palm branches and shouting "Hoshiana" on Pesakh is what makes some Jewish authorities mock Christianity. They say the New Testament can't be true because it doesn't even get the Moadim correct. But they don't understand what the people were conveying here.]

Cross Examined

Then what happened to Him during the next four days? He was *mishmerit*. He was watched by the religious authorities, by the scribes, the Torah teachers, the Pharisees, and the lawyers who were not happy about the people wanting Him to be their Messiah. They were trying to trip Him up in His Words to trap Him to prove that He was not *tami'im*, and so prove that He could not be the Messiah.

> Matthew 21:23 *He went into the Temple area; and as he was teaching, the head cohanim and the elders of the people approached him and demanded, "What s'mikhah* [authority] *do you have that authorizes you to do these things? And who gave you this s'mikhah* [authority]*?"*

They were challenging Him because He had actually stopped certain activities in the Temple as you see in this passage.

> Mark 11:15-16 *On reaching Yerushalayim [Jerusalem], he entered the Temple courts and began driving out those who were carrying on business there, both the merchants and their customers. He also knocked over the desks of the money-changers, upset the benches of the pigeon-dealers, 16 and refused to let anyone carry merchandise through the Temple courts.*

He was not allowing the purchasing of animals and birds for sacrifice to go on anymore in the Temple courts. So they were asking Him, "How do You have the authority to do these things?" And how did Yeshua deal with these accusations? Well, He dealt with it in a very Jewish way. He was asked a question, so He asked them a question.

He asked them where Yochanan's (John's) authority had come from. This confounded them because they had already recognized Yochanan as a true prophet, and he predicted that Yeshua would come as the Messiah. So they were unable to convict Him of sin in this. They were unable to find a blemish in Him. What would have been the sin? It would've been coming against the recognized authority of the Sanhedrin. According to their laws, only the Sanhedrin could decide when and how worship activities go on in the Temple.

So that was their first attempt to find a blemish on Him. It's interesting, first it was about the Sanhedrin. Next they laid a trap to accuse Him before the Roman authorities. There were actually four of these traps—these searches for a blemish—possibly one each day.

> Matthew 22:17-22 (CJB) *So tell us your opinion: does Torah permit paying taxes to the Roman Emperor or not?" 18 Yeshua, however, knowing their malicious intent, said, "You hypocrites! Why are you trying to trap me? 19 Show me the coin used to pay the tax!" They brought him a denarius; 20 and he asked them, "Whose name*

> and picture are these?" 21 "The Emperor's," they replied. Yeshua said to them, "Nu, give the Emperor what belongs to the Emperor. And give to God what belongs to God!" 22 On hearing this, they were amazed; and they left him and went away.

He confounded them again because you see the trap here was that if He had said, "Don't pay taxes to the emperor," they would've reported Him to the Roman authorities and He would've been in big trouble with them. If He had said to pay taxes to the emperor, they would've accused Him of being complicit with Rome and He would've been in big trouble with all the patriots who were trying to drive Rome out. But they were unable to find a blemish in Him either way.

So we've got the authority of the Sanhedrin and the authority of Rome. Next it was the Sadducees.

Now we need to understand the societal structure at the time. The Pharisees were one sect, kind of like one of our political parties. The Sadducees were the other political party. They each had power in the Sanhedrin. The Sadducees' thing was that they didn't believe in the resurrection of the dead. So they laid a trap for Him concerning a woman who had been married multiple times and her husbands had died. They asked, "Who would she be married to in heaven?" Here is Yeshua's reply:

> Matthew 22:30-32 (CJB) *"For in the Resurrection, neither men nor women will marry; rather, they will be like angels in heaven. 31 And as for whether the dead are resurrected,* [Notice He addresses their issue directly.] *haven't you read what God said to you, 32 `I am the God of Avraham, the God of Yitz'chak and the God of Ya`akov'? He is God not of the dead but of the living!"*

I remember when I first read this it was so powerful! What is He saying? He's saying it in the present tense, "I **AM** the God of Abraham." So Abraham is still alive! So the Sadducees were unable to find sin in Him against their belief.

Finally, they tested Him against the Torah. Remember all of these tests were during those four days when the lambs were being examined. They asked Him, "Which of the mitzvot (commandments) in the Torah is most important?"

> Matthew 22:35-40 (CJB) *... and one of them who was a Torah expert asked a sh'eilah (difficult question) to trap him: 36 "Rabbi, which of the mitzvot (commandment) in the Torah is the most important?" 37 He told him, "`You are to love ADONAI your God with all your heart and with all your soul and with all your strength.' 38 This is the greatest and most important mitzvah. 39 And a second is similar to it, `You are to love your neighbor as yourself.' 40 All of the Torah and the Prophets are dependent on these two mitzvot (commandments)."*

So in this fourth area that they tested Him, they were unable to find any sin in Him, even against the Word, the Torah. Then Yeshua turned the tables on them. He began to put to them a testing question. It was, "If Messiah is to be David's son, why would he call Him, my Lord in Psalm 2?" And, of course, they couldn't answer that question. It says that after that they just left Him alone.

> Matthew 22:41-46 *Then, turning to the assembled P'rushim, Yeshua put a sh'eilah (question) to them: 42 "Tell me your view concerning the Messiah: whose son is he?" They said to him, "David's." 43 "Then how is it," he asked them, "that David, inspired by the Spirit, calls him `Lord,' when he says, 44 `ADONAI said to my Lord, "Sit here at my right hand until I put your enemies under your feet"'? 45 If David thus calls him `Lord,' how is he his son?" 46 No one could think of anything to say in reply; and from that day on, no one dared put to him another sh'eilah (question).*

So what happened? They failed to find a blemish in Yeshua. They failed in every attempt to confound Him in His Words. All of this was a prophetic fulfillment of the command that the Passover Lamb must be *tami'im*, be unblemished.

Then in the next chapter, in Matthew 23, He turned the tables on them even more and began to speak against all of His accusers. That's that great passage where He speaks against the hypocrites and the Pharisees and pronounces a very powerful judgment upon them.

My point in telling you all of this is to show you that He didn't just fulfill Passover, He fulfilled the tenth day of Nissan when the lambs were selected. And He fulfilled the eleventh, twelfth, thirteenth, and fourteenth days when the lambs were being carefully examined. All the things He did, the healings, His teachings, His actions in the Temple, Him being tested, all of them were ways in which He fulfilled not just the day, but the whole season.

Two Words For Freedom

As I came to this conclusion, I realized that I had read something about this. It came back to me that in our tradition, there is a term for this season of the year. It is *z'man kheyrutenu,* זְמַן חֵירוּתֵנוּ *the season of our liberation* or *the season of our freedom*. Of course, this is referring to our people being liberated from slavery in Egypt, which is the heart of Passover. But there was another thing that this brought forth that is really very relevant to us today. If you look at this word, *z'man kheyrutenu,* it's from the Hebrew root word *kheyrut* חֵרוּת. In Hebrew there are two ideas of freedom expressed in two separate Hebrew words. In English we have only one word: freedom.

Here are the two words. The first Hebrew word for freedom is *khofesh* חוֹפֶשׁ. This means freedom from external constraints; the freedom, in a sense, to do whatever you want to do; the freedom to do your own thing. So *khofesh* is how our culture that we live in today defines freedom. No constraints by any moral or spiritual authority, that's our culture. You can do whatever feels good as long as it doesn't hurt anyone else. Have you ever heard that before? That's the tone of our culture. That's where it has been taking us.

This is most frequently expressed as the freedom to behave sexually without any Biblical constraints. I believe that the key event in the bringing forth of this cultural archetype, you could call it, which means the way the whole culture thinks, was the invention of the birth control pill. I was a teen when they were invented. All of a sudden it was like, "Oh we don't have to worry about getting pregnant anymore, so why keep all these taboos about fornication? They're not needed anymore."

That's how liberation from spiritual restraints started. That's how people talked about it. It started with fornication, but it went on to pornography and even incest and then homosexuality, which has led to very significant negative changes in our society, and, of course, abortion is a product of this lack of restraint.

The other side of this, the other *khofesh* freedom, which is still happening in some places, and people are still lobbying for it in other places, is the freedom to partake in intoxicating substances legally. We have had a whole movement to legalize marijuana. And now we have several states where it is legal.

And then there's the freedom to explore the occult. And the freedom to use foul language, not only when nobody is listening, but on television and in movies all the time.

And then there's the freedom to lie when convenient, which is what we often find happening with people who are in important positions. How often do they fall out of those positions because of what? Because someone catches them in a lie. Or the other one, which is to just steal a little bit out of the treasury when nobody is watching. This is also another reason for their downfall. In fact, this is the reason for some of the downfalls within the Body in recent years.

So this *khofesh* freedom is really the freedom to indulge in anything we want without any fear of God's judgment. But it's not true freedom.

> John 8:34 *Yeshua answered them, "Yes, indeed! I tell you that everyone who practices sin is a slave of sin.*

So *khofesh*—being able to practice all of these things without worrying about judgment—is not true freedom. What is true freedom? Well, in Hebrew, as I said, there's another word for freedom. This really shows a lack in the English language that we only have one word for freedom. I think it really confuses us. *Kheyrut* is the other Hebrew word. It means the freedom to do what you *should* do; freedom to act responsibly; freedom to choose according to the light and moral truth available to you. Is that different from *khofesh*? It is really different. Read the definition again to let it sink in.

So Passover is the season called *z'man kheyrutenu*, the season of that kind of freedom; the season of liberation to true freedom. Two verses later, Yeshua says this:

> John 8:36 (NIV) *So if the Son frees you, you will be free indeed* [really free]!

We need to understand that this is the kind of freedom that Yeshua brings to us. He doesn't bring us *khofesh,* He brings us *kheyrut.* Many people misinterpret this. It was interesting to me when I went back and looked at something in the Scriptures. Around the time of the original Passover in Egypt, I could see the desire for this kind of freedom in a very unlikely place, amongst a group of people that you really don't think are important concerning Passover.

This is part of the reason why this Shabbat is called great, as I explained. It's the day the Egyptians allowed the Israelites to take the lambs. Remember I said there was great controversy among the Egyptians. What that means is that there were some who were in agreement with letting the Israelites sacrifice the lambs, but others couldn't stand to see the humiliation of their gods. In the Talmud, it says this day is great because God miraculously allowed them to sacrifice the lambs.[36]

Then remember the *mixed multitude.*

> Exodus 12:38   *Also a mixed multitude went up with them, along with the flocks, herds and heavy livestock.*

So who were the people in the *mixed multitude*? They weren't Israelites. These were people who most likely when the Israelites put the blood on their doorposts, they did it too, and then they left with Israel. (See chapter 3.)

---

[36] Midrash Tehilim 136:6 and Ancient Tanchuma Bo 18, according to Rabbi Ari Kahn, "Shabbat HaGadol," Eish.com, http://www.aish.com/tp/i/moha/48942426.html#5. (See footnote 5.) Accessed Nov. 2018.

But wait a minute. They weren't slaves. They were free people. So why did they go? Well, they were living in the Egyptian culture where they were not *kheyrut*. They had *khofesh*, but they did not have *kheyrut*. They did not have the freedom in that culture to live their life according to how they had gotten spiritual instruction from Moses. In other words, they were not free to worship the One True God whom they now recognized as the God of Israel. So they decided that rather than stay here and have all the comforts and *khofesh*—the ability to do whatever we want—in Egypt, we're going to leave with the Israelites. And they became the mixed multitude.

They saw what the One True God was doing with Israel, and they left with them. Rather than stick with the *khofesh* they had in Egypt, they chose to leave. They gave up everything to have the freedom to follow God.

How Does This Apply to Us?

So what's the application of this to our lives today? Well, most likely you are already free from slavery to sin and ha-satan because you gave your life to Yeshua and received Yeshua's atoning sacrifice. Maybe you did this recently or maybe a long time ago.

So I think the tendency is to kind of look at Passover and say, "Oh this is such a wonderful thing to see this freedom. I'm so glad I came out of bondage to sin! I got out of Egypt 5 years ago; 10 years ago; last year, and now I can look back at that and rejoice." And that's great. Yes, you can do that.

But what I saw in this whole *Khofesh* and *kheyrut* thing is that the enemy has ways to keep us from full *kheyrut*—the freedom to do whatever the Lord has told us to do through the Light of His revelation. I find that ha-satan is working constantly to keep me and to keep you from that true freedom.

Let me give you some examples. First of all, fear can keep us from obeying God. Do you agree? How? Well, Yeshua says this:

> Mark 16:15 ... *"As you go throughout the world, proclaim the Good News to all creation."*

So why don't we? We are held back by fear of man, fear of rejection, fear of putting a stumbling block before a person. So what does that mean? What kind of condition are we in if we are being held back by fear from sharing the Good News? We're not free. We're not in *kheyrut* because we're not able to do what we really know is the right thing to do. The Light of moral and spiritual truth has said to go and tell all creation, but we hold back.

What does this do to us? We don't fulfill God's full calling on our lives. We each have our own Promised Land, and that's doing everything God wants us to accomplish in this life, and becoming everything God wants us to become. So, if we are being held back by fear, we are in bondage. It's still not freedom. If we had the full freedom, we would proclaim the Gospel.

What other ways is the enemy keeping us from true freedom? It's another fear. It is fear of lack of provision. God says, "Go there." We say, "Well, it's going to take some airfare. It's going to take time to go there." We hesitate or don't go at all. Actually we are afraid God won't provide. So what's that? Is that freedom? No, it's not freedom. We are not free to go and do what God has said to do because of fear.

Here's another one that is a little bit different. God sends His love my way through a person. But I've been hurt in the past by someone who was supposed to love me. So, I don't receive the fullness of God's love through that person. I don't have *kheyrut*. I don't have true freedom. I'm bound by my past wounding.

Other spirits can also deceive us into these things that we don't think of as bondage, but they really are. They are holding us back:

Lust can bind us from fulfilling God's plan for us by destroying Godly relationships that we have. And again, how many times have we seen this with leaders in the Body? Over and over again, we've seen people fall into lust.

Greed can bind us from fulfilling God's will by compromising our handling of money. As I mentioned above, this is another reason people have fallen in the Body of Messiah when they start handling the money.

Unforgiveness can drag us into resentment, bitterness, and anger, and destroy relationships that God meant to prosper in our lives.

God's work, as I've seen in my life and in other's lives whom I know well and those I have counseled, is like peeling an onion one layer at a time. Each time a layer is peeled, you think it's over, but it's not. You soon find that God is going to peel off another layer. These are layers of things that have prevented us from doing and being what God has for us because the enemy has us bound in some way.

So I want to pray that this Pesakh, this season of *Z'man Kheyrutenu*—our liberation—that each of us would come into some fresh revelation of true freedom. May God reveal any bondages we have. Maybe we don't know what it is. Maybe we don't even know that we are bound by it right now. But it's there. Are you willing to pray for that? So let's pray for that because we all continually need further setting free so we can take our Promised Lands.

Prayer

Father, thank You for all the amazing prophesies that You fulfilled. Thank You that this passage in Malachi is so incredible how it predicts exactly what You did on the very same day that it was read in the synagogues all throughout Israel.

We thank You for giving us a calendar that celebrates, not only events in the Tanakh, but also events in the Brit Khadashah.

We thank You for being the unblemished lamb; that they couldn't find any blemish or sin in You. That's the reason why You were able to atone for all sin for all time.

Finally, Lord, we thank You for this season of liberation, of breaking bondages, of *kheyrut*, not *khofesh*.

You are the great liberator, so first of all, Lord, I pray for each one who is reading this that You would show us ways in which the enemy has still got us bound up, ways in which he keeps us from the fullness of what You have for us, Lord, that those things would be revealed to us, even if we've never seen them before. Then, Father, we pray that You would fulfill deeply being the great Liberator in our lives, and that You would break those bondages off of us.

We break fear in the Name of Yeshua. I pray, Father, that you would expose anywhere that this reader might have fear in their life. The Scriptures say, *"Fear not. I am with you."* We are not to be controlled by fear.

We rebuke the spirit of fear. We bind its power. Fear of man, fear of rejection, fear of lack of provision. We break the power of the spirit of fear over us, in the Name of Yeshua. We break the power of the spirit that keeps reminding us of past hurts so we can receive from God. We break the power of any wounding in our lives. We pray for healing, Oh God.

We break the power of lust, in the Name of Yeshua, and of greed. We break the power of unforgiveness and resentment and bitterness and anger. We thank You, Lord, that You are the great onion peeler, that You can peel these things off of us. Reveal any other things, Father, that are binding us up.

We receive, Father, that You said, that at the Name of Yeshua, every knee shall bow in heaven and on earth, and every tongue shall confess that You are Lord to the Glory of God the Father; that every spirit that You reveal, every thing that would try to keep us from all that You have, has no power against the power of Your Name. We declare that Your Name will be mighty in our lives to set us truly free. In the Name of Yeshua. Amein.

CHAPTER 10
THE UNBLEMISHED LAMB

We are in the season of Passover, the season of great deliverance. It is a joyous season and a solemn season.

For 1600 years, including the time when Yeshua was walking the earth, and the time of the New Covenant, up to the year 70 AD, the Jewish people obeyed the command to select an unblemished lamb on this Moad, on the 10th day of Nissan. Even though there was no plague coming to be protected from, they were to select an unblemished lamb and sacrifice it in remembrance of all this.

As we saw in the last chapter, Yeshua fulfilled this Moad for the day of selection of the lambs by choosing this day (Palm Sunday) to enter into Jerusalem. But here is something that maybe you haven't considered. Think about this: Yeshua would have obeyed this command for the tenth of Nissan all of His life. He would have obeyed it with his father as a child. They would have selected a lamb and that lamb would have become like a pet to Him and His brothers and sisters. And He obeyed it with His disciples every year of His ministry.

---

* Photo: Lambs, Pixabay.com, free.

Then we saw that Yeshua was being very dramatically examined for defects during those four days. While the lambs were being inspected, He was questioned—observed—*mishmerit* by the religious authorities—by the scribes, the Torah teachers, the Pharisees, and the lawyers—trying to prove that He was not *tami'im*, and so prove that He could not be the Messiah. But what happened? They failed. They failed in every attempt to confound Him in His Words. All of this was a prophetic fulfillment of the command that the Passover Lamb must be *tami'im*, be unblemished. Peter writes about this:

> I Peter 1:18-19 *You should be aware that the ransom paid to free you from the worthless way of life which your fathers passed on to you did not consist of anything perishable like silver or gold; 19 on the contrary, it was the costly bloody sacrificial death of the Messiah,* **as of a lamb without defect or spot.**

Now, did this mean that He didn't have any birthmarks or scars where He had cut Himself? No, Rabbi Sha'ul (Apostle Paul) explains it.

> *2 Cor. 5:21 God made this sinless man be a sin offering on our behalf, so that in union with him we might fully share in God's righteousness.*

The Mystery

So to be *tami'im* meant that Yeshua was what? Without sin! So I want to look into it now a little bit. Why? Why did they have to be *tami'im*? In the Torah, animal sacrifices were made by the Levitical priests. They were always made at the entrance of the Tabernacle and later the Temple. Those sacrifices, it is important to understand, covered the people's sins so that God could dwell in the midst of the people above the Mercy Seat in the Holy of Holies. I say "covered" because the Hebrew word for *atonement*, *kippur*, means *covering*. It is just like the kippa I wear. It means *covering*. It doesn't mean take away. It is covering my head. It is not taking my head away. ☺

> Hebrews 10:4 *For it is impossible that the blood of bulls and goats should take away sins.*

So that's what was happening in the Law of Moses, in the Torah, but God was planning to make a way for Him to dwell not in the Temple in the midst of the people, but where? Inside the people. He was going to make a way for Him to dwell in us, and that we could dwell with Him in the next life, in His presence in Heaven. Rabbi Sha'ul speaks about this.

> Colossians 1:27a (NKJV) *To them God willed to make known what are the riches of the glory of this mystery among the Gentiles....*

It had been a mystery up to the time of Rabbi Sha'ul. What is the mystery? Read this phrase in the last part of verse 27 that tells us what the mystery is:

> Colossians 1:27b (TLV) *—which is Messiah in you, the hope of glory!*

That was God's intention. The new plan was for the Messiah to be in you. Of course, the Messiah is One with God, so what is that saying? God in you, and the Spirit in you.

Now God is holy. He cannot dwell in the midst of sin. That's why the sins had to be covered over in the time of the Tabernacle and the Temple. But for God to dwell in you or I, our sins can't be covered over. They have to be removed. A more powerful sacrifice was needed to remove sin. So I'm going to go through some of the verses in Hebrews here.

> Hebrews 9:11 *But when the Messiah appeared as cohen gadol of the good things that are happening already, then, through the greater and more perfect Tent which is not man-made (that is, it is not of this created world),*

What's he talking about there? The throne room of God in Heaven.

> Hebrews 9:12 *he entered the Holiest Place once and for all. And he entered not by means of the*

blood of goats and calves, but by means of his own blood, thus setting people free forever.

So this offering, in the holiest place in Heaven in God's throne room, had to be *tami'im*. It had to be unblemished—pure enough to come into God's presence in Heaven. So I hope you can see that an animal sacrifice could never do that. It wasn't pure enough or of great enough value. Any other human being could not do that because all human beings have sin. We're not *tami'im*.

Only a sinless human being could make that offering. And if there had been any sin in Yeshua, He could not have accomplished this because ha-satan would actually have had a legal claim on Him to bring him down from there into hell. Yeshua would've had to offer a sacrifice for His own sin. In the Torah, before the High Priest could offer a sacrifice for the people, he had to offer a sacrifice for his own sin.

So Yeshua, if He hadn't been *tami'im*, if He hadn't been clean—we can't imagine such a thing—He would have had to come up to the presence of God in Heaven to bring a sacrifice for Himself. What could He have brought? What could have been clean enough? Nothing! Nothing!

So to go on in Hebrews, speaking for the Messiah, the author also writes:

> Hebrews 10:6-9 *No, you have not been pleased with burnt offerings and sin offerings. 7 Then I said* [This is the Messiah speaking], *'Look! In the scroll of the book it is written about me. I have come to do your will.'" 8 In saying first, "You neither willed nor were pleased with animal sacrifices, meal offerings, burnt offerings and sin offerings," things which are offered in accordance with the Torah; 9 and then, "Look, I have come to do your will"; he takes away the first system in order to set up the second.*

The first system was the system of animal sacrifices in the Levitical priesthood.

> Hebrews 10:10 *It is in connection with this will that we have been separated for God and made*

> holy, once and for all, through the offering of
> Yeshua the Messiah's body.

You can applaud! Thank you, God!

I just want to point out this *"being separated and made holy."* What does it mean? It means being separated out, set apart for God, and made holy enough for His Spirit to dwell in us.

> Hebrews 10:11-14 *Now every cohen stands every day doing his service, offering over and over the same sacrifices, which can never take away sins. 12 But this one, after he had offered for all time a single sacrifice for sins, sat down at the right hand of God, 13 from then on to wait until his enemies be made a footstool for his feet. 14 For by a single offering he has brought to the goal for all time those who are being set apart for God and made holy.*

Now the question is, what's the goal? The goal is to be set apart for God, so His Ruakh HaKodesh can dwell in you! That's the goal. After all, we call Him the HOLY Spirit. Right? Well, the Holy Spirit cannot be in an unholy place! So we need to be purified and set apart for that.

Born Under the Law

Now that we understand why Yeshua had to be without blemish, what did it mean for Him to be *tami'im*, to be unblemished? Well, in Galatians, Rabbi Sha'ul tells us this:

> Galatians 4:4 (NKJV) *But when the fullness of the time had come, God sent forth His Son, born of a woman, born under the law,*

What law would that be? The Torah, of course! He was born under the Laws of Moses. So what this means is that all the things that the Torah commanded to be done Yeshua did or as a child were done to Him. What were those things? He was circumcised. He had the *pidyon ha-ben*, which is the redemption of the firstborn done. And because His family kept kashrut (kosher) as commanded, He kept kosher from birth. And because His family kept the Moadim set by the Torah, He kept all the Moadim, from childhood, including since age 12, traveling to Jerusalem three times a year because that's a commandment. We read in the Gospels that He was in Jerusalem for Pesakh and for Sukkot.

As a child and as an adult, He never committed פשע *pesha* (**pay**-sha),[37] intentional transgression, breaking God's laws. He never lied. He never stole. He never murdered. He never used God's Name in a disrespectful way. He never broke any commandments.

In addition, He had no עון *avone* (ah-**vone**).[37] What is *avone*? Iniquity. He never entertained or dwelt on any ungodly thought or attitude. He never had any ungodly motivation. He was always led by the Ruakh HaKodesh, the Holy Spirit.

Now I personally believe that it wasn't that He didn't get any of those thoughts sent at Him by the enemy because otherwise, He wouldn't have been tempted like we are, but He was. By the Spirit of God, He was able to always, always resist those thoughts and renounce them.

And finally, He never committed חטאה *kha-tah'AH* (khah-tah-**ah**)[38] (also spelled chata'ah or hata'ah), missing the mark, meaning He never accidentally disobeyed a Law of God. He never forgetfully neglected to do something to keep a command of God. He brought a lamb to the Temple on Pesakh every year to sacrifice. He never ate any khametz (yeast or leaven) during the Feast of Unleavened Bread. He brought the firstfruits of His fields. I don't know if He had any fields. He was a carpenter. So He brought the firstfruits of His labor to the priests on the First Fruits. He went to Jerusalem to worship three times a year on Pesakh, Shavuot, and Sukkot.

If He neglected to do even one of these things that don't seem to be such a big deal, what would've happened? He wouldn't have qualified. He wouldn't have been *tami'im!* And He couldn't have been God's Lamb who takes away the sins of the world.

The other interesting thing about this is that in order to keep these things, He needed to be born into a nation where keeping the Torah was possible. Israel needed to be a nation with a functioning Temple and cohanim, priesthood, in order

---

[38] See page 225 for more on these three Hebrew words for sin.

for Him to be circumcised, to give 5 shekels to the cohanim for the פִּדְיוֹם הַבֵּן *pidyon ha-ben*, to keep the Moadim, to travel to Jerusalem. All that had to be in place. Yeshua could not have fulfilled the requirement to obey all of God's Laws unless Israel existed as a Torah-observant nation with a Temple and a priesthood.

This is why it was so critical that the Maccabees defeat the Greeks because what were the Greeks trying to do? They were trying to destroy the Jewish culture. They weren't trying to destroy the people, they were just attempting to prevent them from worshipping God in the Biblical way.

All of this so that Yeshua could be a fitting sacrifice to **take away—remove** the sins of all who would trust in Him. Not cover them over, but take them away. Why? So that this change could happen, as the writer of Hebrews says, so that the Ruakh could dwell in you. So after you have left this life you can dwell in God's presence in Heaven.

Application

Now let's make this personal. Let me ask you this question:

> I Corinthians 3:16 *Don't you know that you people are God's temple and that God's Spirit lives in you?*

Do you know that?! Come on! Say yes! Be excited about that! You are God's temple! God's Spirit lives in you! Why is the Spirit of God present during a worship service? Because He's in you. You bring Him! When you are late, you bring the Spirit late! ☺ Boy, some of my readers are going to feel convicted about that now. Right? ☺

If you have received Him, the same Spirit that was in Yeshua, is in you! Why? Because there's only one Holy Spirit. The wonderful thing about the Ruakh HaKodesh is that He can be in everybody at once. He's not bound. This is the radical difference between the Mosaic and the New Covenant. This is what Joel talked about.

> Joel 3:1a (2:28a in non-Jewish Bibles) *So it will be afterward, I will pour out My Ruach on all flesh:*

There were people who were filled with the Spirit in the Tanakh. Obviously Moses was filled with the Ruakh. Obviously Isaiah and David were also. But Joel is saying that all the people of God will be filled with the Spirit—the men, the women, the children—all people. That's the difference. This same Ruakh that healed unclean people who touched Yeshua is in you!! The same Spirit.

Now, how is this possible? How is it possible for God's Holy Spirit to dwell in us? Holy—Kadosh in Hebrew—means separate, separated from evil. How is it possible for God's Holy Spirit to dwell in my flesh and your flesh—mortal flesh? It is only possible because of Yeshua's sacrifice. He removed the sin. In Psalm 103, the psalmist saw this coming. It wasn't there when he wrote this. This is one of my favorite verses. It is also a song. Read it aloud.

> Psalm 103:12 *As far as the east is from the west, so far has He removed our transgressions from us.*

He uses the word *pesha*, transgressions. That's actually intentional breaking of God's commandments. That's the worst kind of sin. So that includes iniquity, *avone*, our inclination to sin, and *khatah'ah*, missing the mark, accidental sin. So He has removed even intentional sin.

If your are a geographer, let me ask you. How far is the east from the west? It's called infinity. If you leave this planet you keep going forever. If you leave and go west, you also would go on forever. It's infinity. If you stay on the planet and go east, you will always be going east, you will never be going west. It isn't the same for north and south. If you go north, you will eventually reach the north pole. If you keep going, you will then be going south.

Let me repeat. He didn't just cover our sins and iniquities and intentional sins, He removed them totally. Why? To enable His Ruakh, the Holy Spirit to dwell in us permanently and fill us to overflowing. That's the huge change. We call that a paradigm shift. But I really believe that most of us don't appreciate it. We don't grasp how incredible this is. It's what God did for us by coming to earth as a man. It's the only way this could happen. It changed everything.

This is the reason why Yeshua could give that Great Commission. He could command His disciples to go into all the world and turn people's hearts to the Lord by preaching the Gospel to them because the Holy Spirit will melt their hearts into conviction and repentance. This is why He could also command us to heal people by laying hands on the sick. Lay hands on the sick? I will become unclean! No! The Spirit will flow out of you so powerfully, He will protect you and heal them.

This has been very interesting historically. It's been the followers of Yeshua that have had the power to heal people supernaturally, but it is also followers of Yeshua that have gone to the sick even not supernaturally. For centuries, they've created hospitals and ministered to the sick. Most of the hospitals in the third world today were started by Christian organizations because they know they can go to the sick. God has commanded us to go to the sick.

So that's two things. I want to end here with seven more things that being filled with the Ruakh enables in you. Nine things altogether that were not possible before Yeshua's sacrifice and the giving of the Ruakh.

If you are filled with the Ruakh, if the Ruakh is overflowing from you:

1. Not only do you have the ability to touch sick people, you have the power to heal them by your touch, by anointing them with oil, and by your fervent prayer.
2. You have the ability, because there's a gift of the Spirit called discerning of spirits, to discern the spiritual forces behind the scenes. What's going on to cause these people to act this way. What's going on that's causing people to be the way they are. You see in the Tanakh, we don't see people discerning spirits and spiritual forces that are working against them. But you read through the Gospels, that's about 80% of what Yeshua did! He delivered people from spirits that were oppressing them. And in Acts we have

examples of the disciples also able to see into the spirit world.
3. Not only do you have the ability to discern spiritual forces, Yeshua said you have the authority over all of those spiritual forces.
4. You can understand God's Word and desire to obey it. Why? Because the Ruakh has put it, according to Jeremiah, has put it where? In your mind and in your heart! Who did that? The Ruakh in you put the Word in your mind and wrote it on your heart. So you can discern, and this is really critical because we have this phrase in our legal system, you can discern between the letter and the spirit of the law. There are many people who try to obey Torah by obeying the letter, but they always fail. We are to obey the spirit of the Torah.
5. You can be a witness for Messiah with boldness. When power comes upon you and me, He said we will be witnesses in Judea and Samaria and to the ends of the earth. You can proclaim the Good News because the Spirit in you can overcome that spirit of fear: fear of rejection, fear of man—that fear that we all get attacked with when there's an open door to share the Good News.
6. When you proclaim the Gospel, the Holy Spirit will cause the people's hearts to be drawn to the Messiah. He will open their minds and their hearts to want to receive Yeshua.
7. This is a wonderful one. We often have a great time of worship together in meetings. But you know what? Because the Spirit is in you, you can worship the Lord anywhere. You can worship in Spirit and in Truth, meaning you don't have to wait until you are with the congregation. You can worship Him right now wherever you are.
8. You can love your enemies and those who persecute you because the Scripture says, The Love of God has been shed abroad in our hearts by what? The Holy Spirit. It is the Spirit who gives you the ability to love your enemies and those who mistreat you.

9 This is a big one. You can come together as *mishpokhah* (family), in a Godly organization, a Godly *kehilah* (congregation), not motivated by the desire for power or recognition or fame or pride or greed. You can come together to seek the Kingdom of God because the pouring out of the Ruakh broke the curse of the Tower of Babel. That's one of the things that speaking in tongues was about: it broke the curse of us not understanding one another. So we can be together without being divided as the people were divided then.

Let's pray
Father, we thank You for Shabbat HaGadol!! Hallelujah! Thank You that we can remember that You were *tami'im*, unblemished—the Lamb of God—and that Your perfect sacrifice enabled You to dwell in us in the form of the Spirit. I pray that this reader will have a new sensation in their lives and actually experience being filled with the Spirit.

Thank You, Father, that we can be filled to overflowing! That rivers of Living Water can be flowing out of our inmost being because it's Your Spirit that has been poured into us. Thank You that that filling is not just for rabbis or pastors but for all of Your servants, young or old. We pray that our children will be filled, too. We believe that if we ask, You will fill us to overflowing because You want us to be filled to overflowing more than we do.

[If you've never been filled with the Spirit, or if you've had a filling, but you've never felt like it's been overflowing, we're going to pray right now. Maybe you know you've been filled, but we all need to be re-filled.

So lift your hands up to the Lord right now and pray this with me.]

Father, fill me to the overflowing. Fill me, Lord. Re-fill us, oh Lord! Re-fill us to overflowing again, Lord. We want all those things to be real in our lives. We want to see those things. And most of all we want to be filled because we want to be in Your presence. How much more can we be in Your presence than to have You in us!

It's great that we can look out into the universe and see stars a million miles away. But to know that You are in our every breath! That's the greatest thing! Every time we breathe in, Your Spirit is here.

[Take a deep breath.] Let it be Your Ruakh. Your breath that fills me. Fill me up, Father.

Father, I pray that You give us the discipline to spend time with You regularly, so You can fill us every day!

And, Father, give us the courage to go to the unclean. Bless those who do go to the unclean all the time, the homeless, etc. They're not afraid of anything happening to them because the Spirit is flowing out of them. May we bear much fruit among people. Really anyone who is not walking with the Lord is unclean, spiritually. Help us, Lord, to go to the unclean. May we have the boldness to witness and to overflow.

May the gifts of the Spirit manifest—tongues and prophecy, words of wisdom and knowledge, gifts of faith and healing, etc. May they all manifest in us. May we be able to discern spiritual forces of the evil one in all circumstances. May we not be like someone who is shadow boxing because we are trying to fight the unclean spirits in the natural, with our intellect or our good looks or talents. Give us discernment, oh God.

Give us the understanding that we have authority over all the forces of the evil one. That You weren't lying when You said: *"I give you authority over all the power of the enemy."*

And may we be able to love with God's Love, even those who persecute us or hate us, even those who have hurt us because Your Love is poured out in our hearts. May we have the desire to understand and to obey Your Word because it is written in our minds and in our hearts. And may we be able to be set free.

[Take authority in Yeshua's Name with me.]

I take authority in the Name of Yeshua over every spirit that has gotten authority over any reader reading this book right now. I ask that You, Heavenly Father, break the power of that spirit over that person. I ask You, Lord, to forgive that person if they've gone along with that spirit, if they've entertained it. For all those who are bound up and have repented, I just break the power of all spirits over them, over addiction. I break the power of every kind of addiction over them. I break the power of infirmity, every spirit of infirmity.

In the Name of Yeshua, I break the power of rejection from all those who have suffered from it. In the Name of Yeshua, I break the power of the spirit of poverty. Every occult spirit, in the Name of Yeshua, I break that power. In the Name of Yeshua, I break the power of fear. Fear is not going to have its field day anymore. We break its power. We break the power of the spirits of bitterness, anger, and unforgiveness, in the Name of Yeshua. Every spirit of self-condemnation, I break its power in Yeshua's Name. I break the power of self-bitterness, self-hatred. Every spirit of lust, in the Name of Yeshua, I break the power of lust. In the Name of Yeshua.

We thank You, Father, that it's Your Spirit that makes us one in the mishpokhah. Knit us together, Father. Cause us to forgive offenses, and take our minds off ourselves and love one another. We thank You, Father, in the awesome Name of the *tami'im*, the unblemished Lamb of God!! Amein. Amein!!

CHAPTER 11

YESHUA, THE PASSOVER LAMB: PARALLELS AND TRADITION

The Lord showed Moses that He had more purposes than just bringing the Israelites out of Egypt. He was also bringing judgment upon the Egyptians for the sins of Egypt. It was not just Pharaoh who had sinned. It was all the Egyptian people participating in the enslaving of the Israelites and also their idolatry. Rather than God doing something suddenly to bring the children of Israel out, He had a very elaborate plan. He hardened Pharaoh's heart to let the people go to demonstrate to the Egyptians that He is the true God and to turn them away from their idols.

That is God's ultimate goal still today, to turn the world from their sins and their idols and to turn to Him. That is why He sent Yeshua to be the Passover Lamb.

---

* Photo: Matzah for Passover with a metal tray and wine on the table, Shutterstock.com. Used by permission.

PARALLELS

In this chapter, we are going to look at some astounding parallels between Yeshua and the Passover lambs.

> Exodus 12:6b *Then the whole assembly of the congregation of Israel is to slaughter it at twilight.*

The first astounding parallel, which you already know, is that Yeshua's sacrificial death occurred at the exact same moment that the Passover lambs were being sacrificed at the Temple.

> Exodus 12:7 *They are to take the blood and put it on the two doorposts and on the crossbeam of the houses where they will eat it.*

They were to take the lamb with its blood back to their house and were to put the blood on the top of the door frame and on the two sides for their protection. Can anybody see what pattern the blood would make on the top of the doorposts and the two sides? It looks like a Cross because some of the blood would drip down to the ground and there would be some on the two sides and some on the top.

Also, if you think of the image of Yeshua on the Cross and you think of where the blood was on the Cross, it was at His head because He had a crown of thorns placed on His head so He was bleeding. Blood was on His hands because He was nailed to the Cross and it was at His feet which were nailed to the Cross. If you look at the pattern, it was the identical pattern to the blood that was on the doorposts of the houses.

The interesting thing is that the head of each household had to take that blood and put it on the doorposts, but Yeshua Himself put His Blood on the Cross by going to the Cross.

> Exodus 12:12-13 *For I will go through the land of Egypt on that night and strike down every firstborn, both men and animals, and I will execute judgments against all the gods of Egypt. I am ADONAI. 13 The blood will be a sign for you on the houses where you are. When I see the blood, I will pass over you. So there will be no plague*

among you to destroy you when I strike the land of Egypt.

What is interesting here is that God knew which ones were Israelites and which ones were not. So, why did they need to have this special sign? I believe it was because God was bringing a special judgment for sin upon the whole area and the Israelites were as much sinners as the Egyptians. (Just look at the golden calf incident.) They had to be protected because this plague that was going to wipe out all the firstborn would have wiped out the Israelites too. So the blood on the doorposts protected the Israelites from this death that was going to come into this area. It protected them and the death passed over them.

There is a tremendous parallel to the Blood of Yeshua. Yeshua's Blood was shed on this Cross. He died as a sacrifice in order to save people, according to the New Covenant, from eternal death. The Passover lamb saved the Israelites from the death of the plague, but Yeshua's sacrifice saves those who receive it from eternal death.

What is eternal death? The Bible uses the word "death" in several different ways. Eternal death in the Bible is not the same as physical death. Certainly all those who have trusted in Yeshua over the centuries have died a physical death. Eternal death means separation from God for all eternity. That is what Yeshua's Blood protects us from. It protects us from being separated from God and allows us to come into His presence.

That is really what "hell" is all about: Separation from God for all eternity. That is eternal death. We have the Passover lamb being sacrificed to keep the Israelites from this plague and we have Yeshua's sacrifice in the exact parallel to protect us from eternal death.

> Exodus 12:29-34 *So it came about at midnight that ADONAI struck down all the firstborn in the land of Egypt, from the firstborn of Pharaoh sitting on his throne to the firstborn of the captive who was in the dungeon, and all the firstborn cattle.*

Let's take a look at the imagery that I alluded to in here, the parallels between the Passover lamb and Yeshua as the Messiah. In the Brit Khadashah in two places, the authors actually call Him the Lamb of God. John calls Him the Lamb of God when He first sees Him (John 1:35), and Paul calls him our Passover Lamb (I Corinthians 5:7).

One of the things I have wondered about, especially since I have been a student of the Bible and a student of the Jewish holidays, is why was Yeshua associated with Passover and not Yom Kippur? For those of you who understand, His sacrifice was to save us from sin. Yom Kippur was the Moad in the fall when sins were atoned for. Passover was not for the atonement for sins. It was to save the people and bring them out of Egypt.

This really gives us a clue as the importance of Passover and what it teaches that I had never seen before. If you have studied it, you know that Yom Kippur is a Moad that was observed differently than it is today. At the time of the Temple in Jerusalem, sacrifices were made in the Temple to make atonement for sin for the entire nation. One of two animals were sacrificed by the high priest in the Temple to make atonement for the whole nation of Israel. Leviticus 16 has the instructions:

> Leviticus 16:34 *This will be an everlasting statute for you, to make atonement for Bnei-Yisrael once in the year because of all their sins." It was done as Adonai commanded Moses.*

What we have on Yom Kippur is an atonement—a sacrifice made once to atone, or cover over, or grant forgiveness for all the sins of all the Israelites. It didn't require any personal obedience to participate in Yom Kippur. The priests just did that. Whether you repented or were sorry for what you did wrong or not, you participated in that. What I understand from that is that there were sacrifices that were done all through the year when someone did something wrong to bring him forgiveness. But on Yom Kippur, the sacrifices were made for the ones that maybe forgot during the year or didn't realize they had done something wrong. Yom Kippur was substitutionary in that sense. The sacrifice was made by one person for everyone.

Passover, on the other hand, and this is so important, required obedience by each individual person in order for them to survive the plague that was coming.

> Exodus 12:3 ...*each man is to take a lamb for his family one lamb for the household.*

It was up to the head of each household to make this sacrifice. It was not just one person who did this for the whole nation.

> Exodus 12:22 ... *None of you may go out the door of his house until morning.*

Each individual person had to remain in their houses for protection. Even if your family was obedient and you weren't, you would not have survived this plague.

What we see here is a very big difference between Yom Kippur and Passover in terms of the personal responsibility that was required by God. Each individual had to demonstrate obedience to God's way.

What do you suppose would have happened if one of the Israelites had said to himself, "This is foolish, God knows that I'm an Israelite, I don't need to put blood on my doorposts"? What would have happened? His firstborn would have died. What do you think would have happened if a firstborn son would have said, "God knows I'm an Israelite. He won't harm me. I can go outside while this plague is going around." What do you think would have happened? He would have died. So there was this personal obedience necessary during this time of the Passover. They had to do exactly what God said. So, if you were a firstborn son, even if your father had put the blood on the doorposts and you decided to be disobedient and go out, you would have died. There had to be this perfect obedience.

So we see that this salvation from the tenth plague of the first Passover was through an individual act of faith and obedience. The parallel of that with the Messiah is that salvation through Yeshua is through an individual act of faith and obedience.

The reason this is so important is that this is a hard concept for Jewish people: that a person is not made right with God and brought into His presence through the Messiah because they are a part of some family, or congregation, or nation, or ethnic group. We are Jews because we were born Jews, and we kind of think that that is something special. And it *is* special. But what Passover teaches us as Jews, and this is so important, is that each of us has an individual responsibility before God to make our own peace with God. It *is* a Jewish concept—this individual responsibility—and it is demonstrated in this beautiful way at Passover because each person had to remain in the house and do it God's way.

You may ask, "What is God's way?" If you are a student of the Brit Khadashah, you know that God says some very astounding things. Yeshua Himself, in John 14:6 says, *"I am the way, the truth, and the life. No one comes to the Father except through Me."* That is a pretty astounding statement. I've heard people say, "I think Yeshua was a great teacher, a great prophet, and a great man, but I don't really believe in what He did." Well, I have a problem with people who say that. For Him to say things like this, He was either a liar or a lunatic or on some kind of power trip. He wasn't a great teacher unless what He said is true. We have to grapple with this. Either He is telling the truth here, or He was crazy, because that is an incredible thing to say.

The second thing He said, having to do with God's way, was to a Rabbi that came to ask Him some questions, *"I tell you the truth that no one can see the Kingdom of God unless he is born again"* (John 3:3).

Being born is something a person does by themselves. No one can do that with you, except the one giving you birth. Yeshua is saying that to enter into the Kingdom of God is an individual thing that we do with His help because He is the One giving us this new birth.

We will come back to this most important truth in a few pages. But first let's talk about traditions that Yeshua honored.

TRADITIONS

So those are a few parallels between the Passover Lamb and Yeshua. Anyone who has studied the Bible could have pulled out more parallels I'm sure. What I want to point out now is something a little bit more difficult to pull out. It has to do with the traditions that have grown up around God's instructions.

Of course we have to understand that traditions grow up because God's instructions don't always give us all the details on how to do certain things. So, people begin to do them in a certain way and after awhile that becomes a tradition. As you know if you have been to a Passover Seder, we drink four cups of wine (or grape juice) and yet there is no place in Scriptures that tells us to do that. But that became a custom, and now it is a tradition. What we are going to talk about is some of these traditions.

I'm fascinated that Yeshua not only fulfilled the commandments, but He used the traditions, which grew up around the commandments, to help us understand His message. I think that is amazing. It is also something you can't get unless you understand Jewish tradition. It is an area that Messianic Judaism has a monopoly on because we grew up with the traditions. We saw them in action as children. I am going to show you some really incredible things.

Personally, this is a big change for me because I am a person who doesn't like tradition. I would rather see things flowing in the Holy Spirit and not do anything twice. I used to think that if you do something and you do it again it's already "dead" a little bit because we should do everything as led by the Spirit.

But I've changed my mind and I'm really excited about how the Lord used these traditions. I've come to understand that traditions are necessary and we have a lot of traditions that we don't even really think of as traditions.

In order for you to help me get over this prejudice I have against traditions, I'm going to ask you to do something with me. Have you seen "Fiddler on the Roof"? Do you remember what Tevya, the dairyman said when this subject came up? "Tradition! Tradition!" I'm going to ask you to say that with me a few times.

The first tradition is that the Passover Seder itself and the way Jewish people do it is a tradition. I was amazed when I saw this Scripture of how the Lord thought it was so important to celebrate this Passover with His disciples before He went to the Cross.

Luke 22:15 (NKJV) *Then He said to them, "With fervent desire I have desired to eat this Passover with you before I suffer;*

Fervent desire. We are going to see why He had this fervent desire to celebrate this Passover with them, His last Passover. It was a ritual, covenantal meal that had so many traditions attached to it, all the traditions around the elements and the order, and the fact that there were two Seders.

Ever since I was a child—and many centuries before that—Jewish people celebrate how many Seders? Two. I remember when I first realized this I called my mother up because I wasn't sure. I hadn't been in a Messianic congregation yet at that time and I hadn't brushed up on these things. I asked her, "Do we celebrate two Seders always?"

She said, "Yes." I asked her why. She said, "Well I think it has something to do with the diaspora with the scattering of the Jewish people."

I said, "Oh, Okay. It didn't make too much sense to me. Later I began to study it out, which I explained before in an earlier chapter.

Why? Well, say it with me—Tradition!!

As we saw, because of this long term tradition of having two Seders, Yeshua was able to teach His disciples about the New Covenant with the Last Seder and still be able to be crucified the next day when the Passover lambs were being slaughtered. So, you have to see that tradition had a big part in this.

As I said, Jews today still celebrate two Passovers. At our Messianic synagogue, we have our public Passover Seder the second night because many of our people celebrate the Passover in their homes the first night.

Having a Haggadah for the Seder is—Tradition!! *Maxwell House Haggadah – Traditional Jewish Haggadah* is the one my family used.[40]

The Pesakh vigil that I referenced earlier that Yeshua fulfilled in Gat Shemanim (Gethsemane) was—say it—Tradition!!

---

40 Passover Haggadah, (Compliments of the Coffees of Maxwell House), Deluxe Edition Pamphlet – 1986

Here is another very important tradition:

> Deuteronomy 6:5-8 *Love ADONAI your God with all your heart and with all your soul and with all your strength. 6 These words, which I am commanding you today, are to be on your heart. 7 You are to teach them diligently to your children, and speak of them when you sit in your house, when you walk by the way, when you lie down and when you rise up. 8 Bind them as a sign on your hand, they are to be as frontlets between your eyes,*

This passage is called the v'ahavta because that is its first phrase, "and you shall love." This is recited by observant Jewish people every day of their lives, because of—say it—Tradition!! What other traditions have developed out of this? The tefillin or phylacteries are literally fulfilling this command. Also the "mezuzah"—on the doorposts of your house. These are two ways to literally fulfill this commandment. Say it again—Tradition!!

Obviously God meant more than just binding these on your hands and head and on your doorposts. I believe He meant that we are to keep the Law (Torah) and make it part of us. Of course, Yeshua would've also kept these traditions. He would have wrapped His tefillin (phylacteries), and He would have kissed the mezuzah as he entered a doorway. If not, they would've accused Him of breaking these commandments.

I want to describe a picture that I see when I visualize Yeshua on the Cross and I want to try to get it across to you so that you will see this picture. You are going to have to use your imagination. I'm sure you are familiar with the Scriptures that talk about Yeshua being the "Living Word."

> John 1:14 *The Word became a human being and lived with us, and we saw his Sh'khinah (Glory), the Sh'khinah of the Father's only Son, full of grace and truth.*

Certainly God's Word was in Yeshua's heart like the V'Ahavta commands us. He was the Word, so of course it was in His heart. When He was bleeding on the Cross, His Blood was going from His heart to His wounds and coming out. He was bleeding on the Cross and the Blood went from the place of the Word—His heart—out to His forearms (hands or wrists) and forehead. His Blood was flowing out to the places that are described in the V'ahavta.

So this is an incredible picture of what the Lord gives us through this "reverentially said" "tradition" of the tefillin and the mezuzah because that is how the Jewish people fulfilled it, by actually putting the actual Word on the forehead and forearms and "on the doorposts." Yeshua did it all. Isn't that amazing? It ties it all together.

When He was on the Cross, the Blood got on the Cross. He was placing the "Living Word" on the Cross—He was the "Living Word" and His Blood was being placed on the Cross. He was fulfilling the V'ahavta by placing the Living Word on the Cross. And as I pointed out, the Blood was in the same pattern as that on the doorposts. On the Cross, He was actually fulfilling that pattern by taking His Blood and putting it on the spiritual "doorpost."

We have this image—but what does it teach us about the Cross? The Cross is a picture of a doorpost. It doesn't look like a doorpost, but the Cross can be seen as the doorpost of God's house. We enter God's house through what? The doorway—the doorpost of the Cross. The Cross is how you enter into the Kingdom of God. Here we have this entryway into the Kingdom of God with the Blood. And not only is it in the place where the Passover lamb's blood was, but it is the Blood itself. It is the Word. This is absolutely amazing to me.

There are many images in Scripture of God's dwelling or Kingdom. *"In my Father's house are many dwellings"* (John 14:2). When we enter into His Kingdom, we are redeemed from eternal death just like those who entered into the house that had blood on it on the Passover were redeemed from being slain by the angel of death. Here's another verse that speaks powerfully to this:

> Hebrews 10:19 *So, brothers, we have confidence to use the way into the Holiest Place opened by the blood of Yeshua.*

We are entering into God's Kingdom through the veil, which is His flesh hanging there on the Cross and the Cross, which we never really see as an entry way, is really an entry way into God's Kingdom and His presence. We need that to enter the first time becoming born again through it. But I think we need to enter that over and over again as we mess up and sin and fall out of fellowship with God and we repent and we go back. We enter back through that same Cross where the Blood is. That is what buys us forgiveness of sin.

My wife, Dianne, had a vision one day. This is how she described it:

"I saw Yeshua standing as a very large figure and going up to Him was a road, and it was red for His Blood. What I realized was that we always say that Yeshua paid the price for us with His Blood so that we can be saved and can go to Heaven, but this road was that you had to walk that road and walk through Him to get to it, as if He were a wall you just walked through. And on the other side was the Glory."

So I just feel led to stop and pray before we go on.

So Father, we thank You that You invite us, You tell us to come boldly into the Holiest Place, into Your throne room. So that's our desire, Father, to enter into that Holiest Place into Your presence. Even when we are praying for people, Father, we want to pray in Your presence. We want to enter Your Throne. We want to put our prayers right at Your feet, knowing that You hear us.

So we thank You, Father, that You made a way to Your throne room through that Curtain. The Curtain was torn when You gave up Your Spirit. We thank You, Father, right now as we are looking into Your Word, we pray that we would do it in the Holiest Place, Father, right in Your presence, with Your Spirit speaking to us as we look into Your Word. We ask that You open our hearts and minds to understand, to receive, to be touched by You, however You want to touch us today. In Yeshua's mighty name. Amein

Wow! That is what the Cross is all about: to provide us the way into His presence in the Most Holy Place. Amazing! I am just in awe. I hope you are too. Hallelujah! Barukh haShem! Bless Adonai. Bless the Lord.

Let's move on. We also learn that this tradition of having cups of wine was already in place in the time of Yeshua.

> Luke 22:17-20 *Then, taking a cup of wine, he made the b'rakhah (blessing) and said, "Take this and share it among yourselves. 18 For I tell you that from now on, I will not drink the `fruit of the vine' until the Kingdom of God comes." 19 Also, taking a piece of matzah, he made the b'rakhah, broke it, gave it to them and said, "This is my body, which is being given for you; do this in memory of me." 20 He did the same with the cup after the meal, saying, "This cup is the New Covenant, ratified by my blood, which is being poured out for you.*

What you have there is multiple cups. So my inference here is that these multiple cups were already in place. Let me show you something else. In verse 17, it says, Yeshua made the *b'rakhah* (blessing). In English Bibles, it says He gave thanks. How do you think He would have given thanks?

Say it with me again, "Tradition!!"

It would have been the traditional blessing. Let's look at that traditional blessing. All the Jewish blessings start out the same. *"Barukh Ata Adonai Elohenu Melekh HaOlam"* "Blessed art Thou O Lord Our God the King of the Universe"

So when it says in English Bibles *and He took that bread and gave thanks,*[41] He would have said the beginning *"Barukh Ata Adonai Elohenu Melekh HaOlam....* This is different from what most of you think of as the blessing over the bread because this is actually the blessing over the matzah, which is said at Passover, not for the normal meal. So, there is a phrase that is added *"A-sher ki-d'-sha-nu b-mitz-vo-tav, v'-tzi-va-nu".* "who has sanctified us and commanded us..." That appears in many of these blessings. Then there are different endings—to eat the matzah (*al a-khilat ma-tzah*), to wash the hands, etc., —the different things people are commanded to do. For each cup of wine, the blessing ends in: *"boreh pri hagafen"* "who creates the fruit of the vine."

---

41 Of course it wasn't bread, because it was Passover. Even though the English translations say "bread," it was clearly Matzah.

Yeshua used the "Tradition!!" of these Cups of the Covenant to teach us about the Covenant He was about to give us, which is the New Covenant.

The four cups are based on four phrases in the verse Exodus 6:6 which we will learn all about in a later chapter. What I wanted you to see here is that Yeshua used the existing traditions of His culture. And it is amazing to see how far back this tradition goes. When I first started understanding Passover and its traditions, I thought that perhaps it went back a couple of hundred years, but it is pretty evident that they were doing multiple cups way back at the time of Yeshua and He used that to instruct us that His Covenant was going to include the things that were in the old Covenant, but in a new way.

The New Covenant provides a new level of sanctification that meant not just out from the Egyptians, but out from the world. A new level of deliverance. Not just from the bondage of slavery, but from the bondage of sin. And it provides a new kind of Kingdom, not just the kingdom that He had with the Israelites, but a new Kingdom with all who believe.

Let's Pray

We thank You, Yeshua, that Your body on that Cross is an entrance way into Your Kingdom. That it is the way to come through You, through the veil, through Your flesh to the presence of God.

And we thank You that with Your Blood on the doorposts—the Word on the doorposts—the living mezuzah on the door post—we are protected from Eternal death. We thank You for that image. We ask that You burn that into our minds and into our hearts that when we need to come back into Your presence, we would see that door welcoming us with the Blood, the Word, and Your flesh, bringing us in. We can never thank You enough.

CHAPTER 12
COSTLY AND SPOTLESS

Let's open this chapter with prayer.

Father, we thank You for Your Word. We just pray that you would open up our hearts and our minds to understand what You have for us today, that it would bear fruit in our lives. We come against any of the powers of the evil one that would try to keep us from what You have for us today. In Yeshua's Name. Amen.

The Parasha called "Tzahv," which means command or commanded (Leviticus 6:24 through 8:36), comes around the time of Passover. Leviticus chapters 1 through 7 detail all the sacrifices and what parts were to be given to the priests as food because this was their means of livelihood, etc.

In Leviticus chapter 8 and on into 9, we come to a big change in the instructions. These instructions are for the ordination of the cohanim, the priests. Part of the ordination instructions were that the sin of the cohanim needed to be atoned for. In other

---

* Photo: Lamb, Lightstock.com. Used by permission.

words, the sin of the priests themselves needed to be covered or dealt with before they could serve and come into His presence.

So what's so amazing is that, at the end of Exodus, we learn that the Tabernacle is set up on the first day of the month that Pesakh is in, Nissan.

Then the ordination, it says, happened during the first seven days, so from the 1st until the 7th. The atonement was accomplished for the ordination, of course, by the sacrifice of animals. But we also know that in Leviticus chapter 16, which talks about the instructions for Yom Kippur, that these atoning sacrifices for the nation and for the priests themselves had to be renewed every year. They had to go in and make the sacrifices for themselves before they could go in and make the sacrifices for the people.

We also have learned as we look through these offerings, that the sacrificed animals that were going to atone for the sin of the cohanim, any sacrifices, always had to be *unblemished*. Other words that were used were *spotless* and *without defect*. The Hebrew word for all these things is *tami'im* (pronounced *tah-mee-eem*). Remember that word? This was true for all the sacrifices. Only unblemished, *tami'im* animals were fitting for sacrifices.

So the first thing to see is that there's a spiritual principle here—a very important principle. Only the sacrifice of an unblemished animal could pay the price—atone for—the priest's sin or an individual's sin or the whole nation's sin.

So what we see is that in God's way of reckoning spiritually, an animal with defects could not pay the price to atone for or cover over humans' sin. And the reason should be pretty obvious because the sacrifice itself would be blemished. If the sacrifice itself has a defect, it can't pay the price to cover someone else's defects. Do you see that? There were no offerings to make a blemished sacrifice unblemished. Once an animal had a defect, there was no way you could make that animal clean and then make it be a sacrifice.

Why Were Unblemished Sacrifices Required?

So the question comes to our minds, why were these offerings necessary? What was going on here that they were required? Some people tend to think of it as God would be offended or injured somehow if priests came into His presence without the atonement—without their sin covered over. If he attempted to do his priestly duties in that way—un-atoned—that it would somehow hurt God.

But the reality in the Bible is that the person is the one that would be injured, not God. In fact, he would be seriously injured. He would die if he tried to come into God's presence without his sin being atoned for.

So we're going to look at where that principle is most clearly stated. It happens just after the people of Israel sinned with the idol worship of the golden calf. Moses is talking with the Lord.

> Exodus 33:5 *ADONAI said to Moses, "Say to Bnei-Yisrael, 'You are a stiff-necked people. If I were going up among you for one moment, I would consume you.'"*

So this means that if the presence of God were to come down amongst the people as He was intending, it would just be too hot. It would burn up the people. This is something that I believe most people haven't fully grasped. I know I haven't: The holiness of God, such that if He were to come into the presence of sinful people without their sin being covered, they would just like evaporate, they would burn up, be consumed.

So Moses understood this, that instead of God going with them, an angel would go with them into the Promised Land but not God Himself. See, an angel could come into their presence without their sin being covered, but not God. So Moses interceded for Israel in chapter 33. He begged God to go up with the people Himself. In fact he said, "if You're not going to go, I don't want to go."

> Exodus 33:14 *He* [ADONAI] *answered, "Set your mind at rest—my presence will go with you, after all."*

There's a really powerful message there in the power of prayer. Basically, Moses changed God's mind, it seems like, in this.

If we move on to chapter 34:10-27 and Leviticus chapters 1-7, God begins to state what the people need to do so that He can go up with them into the Promised Land. Basically, it's giving instruction to Moses on how to make atonement, so that He can come into the midst of Israel without burning up the people—without them being consumed. And the atonement for the priests was made, as it says in Leviticus chapter 8, in the ordination ceremony. It wasn't just a question of laying on of hands and praying for them, they actually had to sacrifice animals to make atonement for the priests, for their sins, and for their household sins, so that they could be the priests.

So let's go to Leviticus 9. We're actually moving into the next Parasha now.

> Leviticus 9:1 *On the eighth day, Moshe called Aharon, his sons and the leaders of Isra'el,*

Again, here we have this timeline: the 8th day of Nissan. We're just following right along here with this. So Moses calls Aaron and his sons.

> Leviticus 9:6 *Moshe said, "This is what ADONAI has ordered you to do, so that the glory of ADONAI will appear to you."*

So, in other words, this is what you have to do as priests in order for God's presence to come amongst the people of Israel

> Leviticus 9:7 *Moshe told Aharon, "Approach the altar, offer your sin offering and burnt offering, and make atonement for yourself and the people. Then present the offering of the people and make atonement for them, as ADONAI ordered."*

So this is in preparation for the presence of God coming down amongst the people so that they will not be consumed when He comes down. Then in verse 8-21, it is recorded that the priests do as they were commanded. It goes into detail of everything that they did. Then we have these wonderful three verses here.

> Leviticus 9:22-24 *Aharon raised his hands toward the people, blessed them and came down from offering the sin offering, the burnt offering and the peace offerings. 23 Moshe and Aharon*

> entered the tent of meeting, came out and blessed the people. Then the glory of ADONAI appeared to all the people! 24 Fire came forth from the presence of ADONAI, consuming the burnt offering and the fat on the altar. When all the people saw it, they shouted and fell on their faces.

Wow!! Wouldn't you like to have been there for that? Isn't that awesome? This was actually the first manifestation of the presence of God in response to what people did—in response to people obeying His instructions. Do this: set up a Tabernacle. I mean they had the whole Tabernacle to set up. It took about six months to make all the things that were needed. Then they made these offerings, and then God came down to be in their midst. I would love to have been there in the midst of that.

The Tabernacle was portable, so they could take God with them—all the way into the Promised Land where they set it up permanently. Of course, after a few hundred years, Solomon built the Temple where the same thing happened. You can read about when the Temple was finished and how the presence of God came and the priests couldn't even go in there—they couldn't even stand up—because the Glory cloud of the presence of God was so powerful.

So as time went on, even in that Temple, the high priest saw that Glory Cloud over the Ark of the Covenant when he went in once a year on Yom Kippur (the Day of Atonement) to make atonement for the people. So this was going on continually so that the presence of God could be present.

And I want you to get a grasp just how amazing this was because the presence of God was dwelling in the midst of Israel even though the people were still sinning. You can read through the books of Joshua and Judges and into Kings and Chronicles. There was still plenty of sin going on. The people were sinning. They were still stiff-necked just like before, but the presence of God was in their midst and they were not consumed or exterminated.

Of course, to have God's presence in their midst, that meant their enemies were not going to have victory over them. It meant there was going to be provision. It meant all of the things that the presence of God brings.

So the Spirit of God, as I was studying this, directed me to focus on the sacrifices for atonement having to be *tami'im*. This principle of an unblemished sacrifice was first brought forth in the instructions for the Passover lamb. So here's where the message goes from being about the Parasha to being about the approaching Passover.

As we have seen, it's important to realize that only an unblemished lamb's blood would have the power to protect them from the plague of death of the firstborn. If a person had taken a lamb with a defect and put its blood on the doorposts, what do you think would happen? They wouldn't be protected! So this is the part where we already learned about the whole value of the unblemished lamb.

Costly

The Passover lamb teaches us a second principal about the sacrifices, which is that the lamb had to be kept for four days in the household after it was selected, and so would become a pet. What this means is that it would've become a sacrifice of great value to them rather than just another animal from their flocks. It would become a costly sacrifice.

Do you see that, all you animal lovers? It seems kind of cruel, but this is obviously what would've happened. Their hearts would've been torn. "But, I have to sacrifice this to the Lord or else my firstborn will die." It was very hard now to sacrifice. It was not an easy thing to do.

So from this we see that the power of the sacrifice is proportional to its value to the sacrificer. That's what the English word sacrifice means, right? It means giving up something. In other words, the more it means to you, the more powerful it is as a sacrifice.

So now that we understand this as we've looked at the parasha, and as we've looked at the Passover, let's connect it to the New Covenant. In God's plan, Yeshua became our Cohane HaGadol, our Great High Priest. As the Levites were the priests of the Mosaic or the Sinai Covenant, Yeshua became the High Priest of the Brit Khadashah (New Covenant). This was predicted in Psalm 110.

> Psalm 110:4 *ADONAI has sworn, and will not change His mind: "You are a Kohen forever according to the order of* Melechizedek.

So Yeshua is to be this eternal priest. In Hebrews 8, we learn a little bit more about what He is like.

> Hebrews 8:1 *Here is the whole point of what we have been saying: we do have just such a cohen gadol as has been described. And he does sit at the right hand of HaG'dulah in heaven.*

That's the greatness in heaven.

> Hebrews 8:2 *There he serves in the Holy Place, that is, in the true Tent of Meeting, the one erected not by human beings but by ADONAI.*

So, this is God's throne room, basically, which Moses saw and made a model of. That's what the Tabernacle and the Temple were. So Yeshua, the Cohane HaGadol, the Great High Priest, serves directly in that throne room, not in the model here on earth.

Yeshua's Sacrifice Had to be Powerful Enough to Enable the Promises

So, let's think now about the sacrifice that this High Priest would bring because that's what a priest does. A priest brings sacrifices and they have to be unblemished and costly. And the power of the sacrifice is proportional to the value of the sacrifice. So, first of all, let's think about the sacrifice that Yeshua was going to bring. How powerful did it need to be? The New Covenant makes some promises, and the sacrifice had to be powerful enough to enable those promises.

So the one that we are probably most familiar with is the promise that people would be forgiven of their sins. So the sacrifice had to be powerful enough to forgive sins. The sacrifices in the Tabernacle had to be made by each person for their own sins. If they sinned again, they had to make another sacrifice. So

Yeshua's sacrifice has to be more powerful than that because it had to be once and for all.

In addition to that, it's not just that we're forgiven of our sins, the sacrifice has to be like the Passover Lamb. It has to cause the plague of what I like to call the eternal death to pass over us, so that we can have the gift of Eternal Life.

So there's a wonderful parallel there, to always remember, that when we have the Blood of the True Lamb of God on the doorposts of our heart, death passes over us, not physical death because most of us will die, but spiritual death. In other words, being separated from God and being in hell, that will pass over us because of the Blood of Yeshua's sacrifice.

But even beyond that, this has to be a pretty amazing sacrifice. Think about this. The sacrifice has to be powerful enough to make it possible for the Spirit of God to dwell in human beings like God's presence dwelt in the Tabernacle and the Temple. The Spirit of God has to dwell in humans whose very nature is inclined toward evil. We're iniquitous. We have a flesh that the Bible tells us we have to crucify daily. But we know it pops up again the next day.

So it's very important to get a grasp of this about how amazing it is that God says, "I'm going to put My Spirit in human beings." We're unclean, blemished, defective, sinful, stiff-necked, full of iniquity, and God says, "I'm going to live there." We know that He can't live any place where there's sin or what happens? He consumes the people! So are you grasping how incredible this is?

It is really an astonishing thing that I think people take for granted. They say, "Oh, yea, I received the Holy Spirit." Okay. Well, wow! That means the Spirit of God is living in a mortal human being, and that's an incredible miracle. Look at yourself right now. You are a miracle if you are filled with the Spirit. You are a walking miracle that the Spirit of God can live in you!

So are you beginning to grasp that this sacrifice had to be much greater than an animal sacrifice? But how about a person? Could a person go and sacrifice themselves and that would enable this? Well, I found this amazing passage in the Psalms. It's actually so Messianic. I never saw before how Messianic it is. Listen to this:

> Psalm 49:7-9 *No one can ever redeem his brother or give God a ransom for him, 8 because the price for him is too high (leave the idea completely alone!) 9 to have him live on eternally and never see the pit.*

Do you see what it is saying? No one can pay the price to have Eternal Life and not go to hell. Basically that's what it's saying. And that's in the Tanakh, the Old Testament! That's amazing! What it's saying is that someone who does this has to be beyond a human being. Right? This is the main sticking point between Judaism and Messianic Judaism is that the Messiah is divine. So we're going to get there. This is an amazing passage.

So to have enough power for the sacrifice of the New Covenant, it had to be something more valuable than an animal and something more valuable than a human being. So in God's amazing plan, Yeshua had to serve a dual role. He was the Cohane HaGadol and He was also the sacrifice, which when you think about it is mind-boggling. He has to sacrifice Himself and He is the Cohane HaGadol. Peter grasped this.

> I Peter 1:18-20 *You should be aware that the ransom paid to free you from the worthless way of life which your fathers passed on to you did not consist of anything perishable like silver or gold; 19 on the contrary, it was the costly bloody sacrificial death of the Messiah, as of a lamb without defect or spot.*

Peter got it. He understood what this was all about. Peter says Yeshua's sacrifice was costly. Why? Why was it costly? Well, it was costly because God Himself offered this sacrifice, and for it to have that much power, it had to be of great value to God.

What could be more valuable to God than His only begotten Son? That's one way to think about it. But, of course, the other way to think about it is that the Son was God Himself come as a man. So what could be more valuable to God than He Himself?! Right? God Himself sacrificed Himself! What could be more valuable than that? That's how valuable this sacrifice was.

To be the ultimate sacrifice, it had to be God Himself. No human could do it. No animal could do it. It had to be God Himself. And the priest who offered that sacrifice had to be God Himself also or else this could never have happened.

And it had to be perfectly unblemished.

We know that He was inspected for defects by His enemies during those four days after He entered Jerusalem on the day of the selection of the lambs (Nissan 10, Palm Sunday). And He passed all of those tests.

But I was thinking about this and I thought, "What is the hardest time for most of us not to sin?" I don't know about you, but for me, the hardest time is when I'm attacked. When someone comes at us with criticism or anger or accusation, those kinds of things, that's the time when we're really tested.

I thought we would also look, as we end here, at some of the trials that He endured after the four days without sinning, because if He had sinned, then He would not have been the unblemished Lamb of God. These trials happened after He was arrested and was brought before the Jewish and the Roman authorities.

> Matthew 27:12 *But when he was accused by the head cohanim* (priests) *and elders, he gave no answer. 13 Then Pilate said to him, "Don't you hear all these charges they are making against you?" 14 But to the governor's great amazement, he did not say a single word in reply to the accusations.*

So what was His response? Not even to defend Himself, to keep silent before both the Jewish and the Roman authorities. Then came the ultimate test—on the Cross.

> Luke 23:33 *When they came to the place called The Skull, they nailed him to a stake; and they nailed the criminals to stakes, one on the right and one on the left. 34 Yeshua said, "Father, forgive them; they don't understand what they are doing."*

This is the most amazing response to the most cruel attack imaginable. You can't imagine anything worse than being murdered by crucifixion. And rather than striking out or even trying to defend Himself, He prays for God to forgive His murderers, meaning really that He had already forgiven them. Even while they were killing Him, He was forgiving them.

So, why did He respond in this way? Well, He actually tells us. We can see by looking at what happened when His enemies to whom He had been betrayed, arrested Him. We have a little incident there that is kind of small, but is very significant. His disciples began to fight back. And if you know the incident, you know that one of His disciples, Peter, even wounded one of the soldiers. Yeshua put a stop to that and then He says this:

> Matthew 26:53 *Don't you know that I can ask my Father, and he will instantly provide more than a dozen armies of angels to help me? 54 But if I did that, how could the passages in the Tanakh be fulfilled that say it has to happen this way?"*

Do you see what's happening here? This is the reason He responded like He did. If He had defended Himself and stopped His accusers, God's plan would never have been completed. And so we see that there's a tremendous lesson here on how we respond to people who attack us. We do have to respond at times, but what's the key? We need to respond according to the will of God, not according to our own will which often times is to take revenge or get even. We can't make a rule to always be passive or never say anything. Some have made that the rule for believers for any kind of confrontation, but it's wrong. Sometimes we are supposed to respond, but only at the guidance of the Ruakh.

Interestingly, Yeshua is our example for this. In Matthew 23, immediately after He was attacked during those four days when they were trying to find defects, He says seven times, *"Woe to you, hypocritical Torah teachers and P'rushim! (Pharisees)...."* and *"Woe to you"* a total of eight times (Matthew 23:13-29).

He calls them blind guides, blind fools, blind men, blind Pharisees, white washed tombs, snakes, and sons of snakes to their faces. Okay? So it wasn't like He was saying we can never respond when we're attacked because, obviously, He responded here. And these statements were not sin!

He was speaking to their faces, not behind their backs. If you do it behind their backs, that isn't good. That would be gossip, which IS a sin. He was speaking to their faces. He was speaking the truth in love and He was speaking it forcefully. I don't think you could speak it any more forcefully than that. But that's not sin because when He said these things that's what God's Spirit was guiding Him to do.

So that's the challenge to all of us. How have you reacted when you were attacked? Can you remember a time when you didn't react so well? Yea, I've had some times, too. When you lose your temper, you can easily fall into sin.

I really think that attacks by other people are the ultimate test of our spiritual maturity. A real sign of maturity is to be under attack—somebody is saying bad things about me or to me, or maybe they're even physically doing something to me, attacking me—and in the midst of that to be able to follow the leading of the Spirit of God, that's difficult. That's maturity. That's what He was doing. And I believe that's the ultimate sign. It doesn't mean we are always supposed to be doormats to be stepped on, but that we need to be led by the Spirit when we're taking in shots. So that's a huge lesson out of that.

The second application that I want to wrap up with here has to do with our offerings. Yeshua gave Himself as the highest, most costly, sacrificial offering for our sins, once and for all. So we don't need to bring animals to be sacrificed anymore, but we do still need to offer gifts to God. Yeshua is our example for that. So, how and what do we give?

First we learned that offerings must be unblemished. Usually when we think of offerings, we think of money. That's the thing that comes to mind in our culture, right? So you might be thinking right now, "Well, how can money be unblemished? Some money unblemished and some blemished? That doesn't make any sense." Well, there are some ways. Certainly if you earn some money dishonestly, and then you offer it to the Lord, it's blemished.

Right? Another way is to be like Ananias and Sapphira (Acts 5) who were dishonest about what they gave, keeping some secretly for themselves. They gave a lot, but it was not pure.

Money is not the only thing that can be offered. Sometimes people give objects or items to the Lord, and they can be very much defective items. "I don't want this anymore, it's no good. I'll give it to the Lord." That would be defective.

But there's the really significant, good way to give to the Lord that doesn't involve material things or money. We can serve the Lord either by volunteering or through part of what we do for a living. We can give our time. We can give our energy. We can give whatever skills we have. We can give those things to the Lord as offerings in a sense.

And the lesson of the Passover Lamb is that to have spiritual power, those offerings should not be defective or blemished. When we do something to serve the Lord, it should be done to our best effort, and we need to do it with a Godly attitude, not grudgingly. That's why Paul says things like, *"Don't give grudgingly but give with a generous spirit."* He's talking about giving money.

We're talking about giving of our time and energy. So whether that's teaching the Bible like I'm doing right now through this book, or doing outreach, leading worship, cleaning the congregation building, fixing the plumbing, caring for the children, helping the sick or elderly or serving as a leader, we need to do all those things in an unblemished way, in other words, not in a way that's slipshod or half-hazard but with all of our heart and with all of our skill.

And the second thing we learn about these offerings is that the more valuable it is to us, the more power it has when it is offered to God. This, of course, holds true mathematically with offering money, but it holds true, I believe, in a different way of calculating than you or I would calculate. God values our monetary offerings not by how much they are but by the fraction that they are of what we have. We learn this from the story of the widow. (Remember that?) He counted the poor widow's penny of greater value than the large offerings of the rich people because it was all that she had.

So it also holds true when we talk about offering our time and energy and skills to God. If we willingly offer to God what's valuable to us, He sees it as valuable to Him.

I just want to encourage you because I think maybe you haven't gotten this. Maybe you have given much valuable money, or much valuable time, energy, your giftings, your skills to do things for your congregation, whether you're fixing something or leading worship, you're giving of your lives, which is your most valuable possession. I believe the Lord wants you to receive His Word to you today that He counts those offerings of great value. Don't think He takes those things lightly. When you give out of a good heart, when you give with a love for people, God sees that. No matter what it is, He rejoices at that. He wants to say thank you. So I'm ending with a thank you from Him. So thank you!

Let's pray.
Lord, we thank You that You gave the most costly sacrifice ever, but was necessary—Yourself--so that we can be washed pure to be able to come into Your presence. We are in awe of how much You had to suffer for us. We can never thank You enough. We want to give You our all every day to show our gratitude, but it will never be enough for what You deserve as thanks. We thank You, though, for what we see here that our giving pleases You, that You always notice and are delighted.

I pray that we would see our offerings the way You see them. I pray we would experience the joy that You experience when we give them. I pray that our offerings would be without blemish, that we will do it with joy. Help us to know that if we can't do it with a thankful, joyful heart, we shouldn't do it. So we pray that You will put that joyful attitude in us, Lord.

Father, we also ask for Your grace for the times when we are facing difficulties and personal attacks. Help us, Lord, to have the attitude You had. Help us to stay calm and to not seek revenge. Help us to be forgiving like You were even as You were being murdered. Help us to depend on You each day to give us the grace we need. Help us to abide in You and in Your Word to become more and more like You in all of this. In Yeshua's Name. Amein.

CHAPTER 13

SILENT AS A LAMB

We are going to continue on with looking at more "tests" Yeshua went through in the time before His death.

Sometimes in my personal reading time, I read the Bible according to something called a "chronological listing." So what that causes me to do is if there's an account that is recorded in all four Gospels, I'll read it over four times in Matthew, Mark, Luke, and John, in chronological order.

The Spirit let me to do that for the last days of Yeshua to draw from all four Gospels, to fill in all the details from each one. A lot of times we talk about what happened at the Last Supper at our Seder, and then the next day we talk about His Resurrection, but sometimes we miss what was in between there, which was really the dramatic and difficult part.

I will point out the fulfillments of prophecy as we go through the account. We are going to focus on how Yeshua reacted under the great stress of those last days. Mostly we're going to be reading directly from the Scriptures all that took place, although I will be skipping over some details because if we included every Scripture on it, this book would be really thick.

---

* Photo: Lambs, Shutterstock.com. Used by permission.

So let's begin with Yeshua and his disciples after they celebrated Passover and went to the Gat Shemanim (Garden of Gethsemane).

> Matthew 26:47-49 *While Yeshua was still speaking, Y'hudah [Judas] (one of the Twelve!) came, and with him a large crowd carrying swords and clubs, from the head cohanim [priests] and elders of the people. 48 The betrayer had arranged to give them a signal: "The man I kiss is the one you want—grab him!" 49 He went straight up to Yeshua, said, "Shalom, Rabbi!" and kissed him.*

Luke gives us a little bit further insight.

> Luke 22:48 *but Yeshua said to him, "Y'hudah, are you betraying the Son of Man with a kiss?"*

So, you know, if you've read the story before of the Last Supper, that Yeshua knew that Yehudah (Judas) was going to betray Him, but we can see His surprise and shock that He expresses here that he would betray Him with a show of affection, with a kiss. Yehudah was one of His closest friends, one of the twelve, and yet he betrayed Yeshua this way.

But this was the fulfillment of a prophecy.

> Psalms 41:10 (9 in non-Jewish translations) *Even my own close friend, whom I trusted, who ate my bread, has lifted up his heel against me.*

John adds some more details to this incident.

> John 18:4 *Yeshua, who knew everything that was going to happen to him, went out and asked them* ["them" being the crowd], *"Whom do you want?"*

He knew everything! This is a significant thing. He knew all that was going to happen to Him.

> John 18:5 *"Yeshua from Natzeret," they answered. He said to them, "I AM." Also standing with them was Y'hudah, the one who was betraying him. 6 When he said, "I AM," they went back ward from him and fell to the ground.*

Now Yeshua in saying, "I AM" used the special Name that God gave to Moses at the burning bush. And there was so much power when He spoke that Name! These people were not just anybody. These were soldiers! Soldiers are usually strong men! But they fell to the ground! They were knocked over!

As I was reading this, I realized that what Yeshua said and what He didn't say during these times was critically important to God's plan. Yeshua knew the prophecies that had to be fulfilled—the ones that predicted that He was in for a time of terrible suffering. That's why He struggled. If you read earlier in the Garden of Gethsemane, He struggled terribly in prayer there. But he also realized that He had a role to play in making those prophecies happen, in making them be fulfilled.

He could have said, "I AM! I AM! I AM!" over and over and just driven those guys away! They would've crawled away on their hands and knees! Or if you know other parts of the Gospels, He could've just walked right through the middle of the crowd and they wouldn't have touched Him. He could've been invisible. He did that in Nazareth.

So I believe He was tempted to do those things, and He resisted that temptation to do too much or too little to allow the plan to go forward.

> John 5:19 Therefore, Yeshua said this to them: "Yes, indeed! I tell you that the Son cannot do anything on his own, but only what he sees the Father doing; whatever the Father does, the Son does too.

So He did only what the Father was showing Him, and He only said what the Father was saying. He walked in the Spirit and was led by the Spirit, and was in complete obedience all the time.

John goes on in chapter 18 to describe this incident. He inquired of them once more after He had knocked them down by saying, "I AM."

> John 18:7 So he inquired of them once more, "Whom do you want?" and they said, "Yeshua from Natzeret." 8 "I told you, `I AM,'" answered

> Yeshua, "so if I'm the one you want, let these others go."

Now, He said, "I AM" again, but they didn't fall down this time. Did you notice that? So He must've realized, I can't be driving them away or they're not going to be able to do what they have to do. So even in this tone of His voice, in the volume of His voice, He was being obedient to the Lord, because the soldiers evidently remained standing at this point.

> *Matthew 26:50 Yeshua said to him* [to Yehudah], *"Friend, do what you came to do." Then they moved forward, laid hold of Yeshua and arrested him.*

So at this point He actually gave them permission to arrest Him. Then He gives a very interesting explanation.

> *Matthew 26:53 Don't you know that I can ask my Father, and he will instantly provide more than a dozen armies of angels to help me?"*

He wasn't making a false claim here, and He wasn't bragging. He could've done this. So why didn't He? Why didn't He just do this and get rid of these people who were evil and were trying to arrest Him? Well, He explains it in the next verse.

> *Matthew 26:54 "But if I did that, how could the passages in the Tanakh be fulfilled that say it has to happen this way?"*

So He was expecting all the prophecies about this part of His life to be fulfilled. He had struggled over this, but then He set His will in that garden, as He was praying, to submit to the terrible suffering that they predicted. Why? To obtain the wonderful promises that God had promised as the results of this.

Then Yeshua spoke to the crowd. He was talking to His disciples before.

> *Matthew 26:55 Then Yeshua addressed the crowd: "So you came out to take me with swords and clubs, the way you would the leader of a rebellion? Every day I sat in the Temple court, teaching; and you didn't seize me then.*

Now, up to this point, this verse included, it's almost like Yeshua is still a little bit defiant about what's going happen to Him. First He says, "I AM" which knocks them over, and here He says, "Why didn't you seize me then?" But then He says this:

> Matthew 26:56 *But all this has happened so that what the prophets wrote may be fulfilled." Then the talmidim* [disciples] *all deserted him and ran away.*

So here He explained to the crowd, not just His disciples, why He was going to submit to their arresting Him. He knew that from here on out, He needed to resist the temptation to defend Himself, and that He needed to actually be silent at times to allow His enemies to do what they wanted to do in order for this plan of God to move forward. He needed to be led by the Spirit in all that He said and did in obedience to the Father.

So the crowd took Yeshua to the religious leaders and they questioned Him.

> Matthew 26:59 *The head cohanim and the whole Sanhedrin looked for some false evidence against Yeshua, so that they might put him to death.*

And we know that they did that because they were envious of Him, basically, because the people were flocking to Him.

> Matthew 26:60 *But they didn't find any* [evidence], *even though many liars came forward to give testimony.*
>
> Matthew 26:62-63a *The cohen hagadol stood up and said, "Have you nothing to say to the accusation these men are making?" 63 Yeshua remained silent. ...*

The accusations were false, so He must've been sorely tempted to defend Himself, "No, that's not true. That's not true." But the Spirit of God was guiding Yeshua and He was being obedient to resist that temptation, and to not speak at all even to His defense, fulfilling this prophecy:

> Isaiah 53:7 *He was oppressed and He was afflicted yet He did not open His mouth. Like a*

lamb led to the slaughter, like a sheep before its shearers is silent, so He did not open His mouth.

If He had opened his mouth and given in to that temptation to defend Himself, He would've been disobedient to His Father. Not only would it have stopped the plan, it would've disqualified Him from being the spotless lamb because that would've been a sin, and He would not have been the fitting sacrifice.

> *Matthew 26:63b The cohen hagadol said to him, "I put you under oath! By the living God, tell us if you are the Mashiach, the Son of God!" 64 Yeshua said to him, "The words are your own. But I tell you that one day you will see the Son of Man sitting at the right hand of HaG'vurah* [the Power on High] *and coming on the clouds of heaven."*

Now this is a little confusing to some people, especially where it says, *the words are your own.* The literal translation of the Greek text that says *si ipos* is *you said it* or *you have said.* Most translators take it as a straight *yes,* like we say in English, "You said it!" meaning: "You're right!" But let's look at how Mark records Yeshua's answer, which is much more definitive.

> Mark 14:62 *"I AM," answered Yeshua. "Moreover, you will see the Son of Man sitting at the right hand of HaG'vurah and coming on the clouds of heaven."*

Here it says that Yeshua gave the straight answer, "I am."

So this was a key moment. He had not defended Himself and in complete obedience to the Father, He publicly identified Himself as the Messiah, the Son of God, which gave His accusers the ability to convict Him of blasphemy. In Mark, He used the very word God used to identify Himself to Moses at the burning bush when God said to Moses, "My Name is I AM WHO I AM" Not only did He affirm that He's the Messiah, the Son of God, but He hints to be identified with God Himself, that He is God come in the flesh.

Now, what would the temptation have been? I can just see Him doing this. He could've engaged these religious leaders in a theological debate about who the Messiah was supposed to be, and He was well able to prove that He was the Messiah. He had all the evidence, all the miracles, all the signs, but He was silent about that because if He convinced them that He was the Messiah, God's plan would not have gone forth. As a result of Yeshua declaring His identity, the next step in the drama happened.

> Matthew 26:65-66 At this, the cohen hagadol tore his robes. "Blasphemy!" he said. "Why do we still need witnesses? You heard him blaspheme! 66 What is your verdict?" "Guilty," they answered. "He deserves death!"

That was fulfilling another prophecy.

> Isaiah 53:8 Because of oppression and judgment He was taken away. As for His generation, who considered? For He was cut off from the land of the living [In other words, He was killed.], for the transgression of my people—the stroke was theirs.

There is much there in those little phrases. He was killed for *the transgressions of the people*, and the people who did it, were actually the people whose transgressions He was dying for. Amazing! This was written 600 years before the time of Yeshua and was recorded in the one book in the Bible that we have the most confidence in because this is the book that was found complete and whole among the Dead Sea Scrolls. Just absolutely amazing.

Now Israel was a colony of Rome at that time. Because the Roman government did not authorize the local Jewish authorities to execute anyone, they brought Him before the governor.

> Matthew 27:11 Meanwhile, Yeshua was brought before the governor, and the governor put this question to him: "Are you the King of the Jews?" Yeshua answered, "The words are yours."

We can interpret that the same way: "You said it." He's identifying Himself again now as the King of the Jews. Understand that this was another necessary step for Pilate to sentence Him, which we will see in a minute.

> Matthew 27:12 *But when he was accused by the head cohanim and elders, he gave no answer.*

He refused to rebut their accusations

> Matthew 27:13-14 *Then Pilate said to him, "Don't you hear all these charges they are making against you?" 14 But to the governor's great amazement, he did not say a single word in reply to the accusations.*

So he kept on refusing to defend Himself. He could've argued and forced them to release Him before sending Him to the governor. After all, He wrote the Law. So He could've debated the Law with them. He could've shown them that this was an illegal assembly because it was. They weren't supposed to meet in the middle of the night, for one thing. But He said nothing because this was the cup that He had to drink.

John adds some further detail here which gives us some insight into why He Identified Himself as the King of the Jews

> John 19:12 *On hearing this, Pilate tried to find a way to set him free; but the Judeans shouted, "If you set this man free, it means you're not a `Friend of the Emperor'! Everyone who claims to be a king is opposing the Emperor!"*

Do you see what they're manipulating here? These accusations that He was the king of the Jews were how the religious leaders forced Pilate to agree to their demands to execute Yeshua. "If you don't do it, you're not a friend of Caesar. Then we'll tell Caesar, and he'll remove you. He might kill you for this." So under pressure Pilate sent Yeshua to Herod. He wanted to get out from under this. He knew he shouldn't do this but he had to do it.

Yeshua was a Galilean from the Province of Galilee, and Herod ruled Galilee and he was in Jerusalem at the time.

> Luke 23:8-10 *Herod was delighted to see Yeshua, because he had heard about him and for a long time had been wanting to meet him; indeed, he hoped to see him perform some miracle. 9 He questioned him at great length, 10 but Yeshua made no reply. However, the head cohanim* [the priests] *and the Torah-teachers stood there, vehemently pressing their case against him.*

Again, before Herod, Yeshua resisted the temptation to defend Himself, and was silent. Pilate had given the case to Herod. He could've had His case thrown out. He could've performed a miracle, made Herod so happy, he might've said, "Hey, you guys, get out of here. I'm not going to let you execute this guy. He's a miracle-worker! I can use Him" But instead, this is what happened.

> Luke 23:11 Herod and his soldiers treated Yeshua with contempt and made fun of him.
> Then, dressing him in an elegant robe, they sent him back to Pilate.

Because He kept silent, refusing to say or do anything, He got sent back to Pilate.

> Matthew 27:26 *...after having him whipped, he handed over to be executed on a stake.*

This is fulfilling a prophecy again.

> Isaiah 53:5 *But He was pierced because of our transgressions, crushed because of our iniquities. The chastisement for our shalom was upon Him, and by His stripes we are healed.*

Stripes are the marks from the whipping. They were for our healing. The Roman soldiers abused Him in many other ways. They beat Him with their fists. They put a crown with sharp thorns on His head. They mocked Him. They spit on His face. They plucked out His beard.

> Matthew 27:21 *When they had finished ridiculing him, they took off the robe, put his own clothes*

back on him and led him away to be nailed to the execution-stake.

Through all this abuse, Yeshua not only was silent, but He submitted to it when He had all this incredible, supernatural power. He could've stopped it at any time.

Matthew 27:35 *After they had nailed him to the stake, they divided his clothes among them by throwing dice.*

It just always strikes me when I read through this that the authors say it so simply. Just a little phrase: *They nailed Him to a stake.* Just imagine being nailed to a stake, nails through your wrist, big, long nails, and through your ankles and hanging there. Just unbelievably cruel. It's the most cruel method of execution ever devised by human beings. The victim dies slowly over several hours. It took three hours for Yeshua to die. That was quick. The death is caused by dehydration, blood loss, suffocation, and then heart failure. And the Gospel writers just say, *they nailed Him to the stake.* Amazingly understated.

Of course this was a fulfillment of a prophecy. It is the most powerful one. It is one that has always spoken to me. Speaking of the people of Israel, it says:

Zechariah 12:10b *...they will look toward Me whom they pierced. They will mourn for him as one mourns for an only son and grieve bitterly for him, as one grieves for a firstborn.*

Psalm 22:19 *They divide my clothes among them, and cast lots for my garment.*

Luke 23:34b *They divided up his clothes by throwing dice.*

Everything keeps falling into place in these prophecies over and over again. While hanging on the Cross, Yeshua said this, the most amazing verse in the Bible, in my opinion.

Luke 23:34a *Yeshua said, "Father, forgive them; they don't understand what they are doing."*

And they didn't. They didn't understand that this was the Son of God, God come as a man, come to pay the price for them--the penalty for their sin. So this verse reveals Yeshua's amazing ability to forgive in the midst of extreme pain, extreme suffering; and His deep understanding of the power of human ignorance. That's what He's talking about here. When people are ignorant, how wrong they can be and what they can do.

> Matthew 27:36 *Then they sat down to keep watch over him there. 37 Above his head they placed the written notice stating the charge against him, THIS IS YESHUA THE KING OF THE JEWS.*

In the other Gospels, it says that they wrote it in three languages to make sure that everybody got it. And there He hung.

> Matthew 27:39-40 *People passing by hurled insults at him, shaking their heads 40 and saying, 40 "So you can destroy the Temple, can you, and rebuild it in three days? Save yourself, if you are the Son of God, and come down from the stake!"*

And of course, that was also a fulfilling of a prophecy.

> Psalm 22:8 *All who see me mock me. They curl their lips, shaking their heads:*

But also understand how Yeshua must have been resisting the temptation to do just what they were saying! In this terrible pain, with all of His supernatural powers, He could've made that Cross disappear. It would've been easily accomplished, but He stayed there for three hours.

> Matthew 27:45-46 *From noon until three o'clock in the afternoon, all the Land was covered with darkness* [while He hung on that Cross]. *46 At about three, Yeshua uttered a loud cry, "Eli! Eli! L'mah sh'vaktani? (My God! My God! Why have you deserted me?)"*

He was quoting from Psalm 22:2 *My God, my God, why have You forsaken me?* He was revealing something very significant here, even while experiencing the pain of being separated from God. He was revealing that all the sins of the world for all time, past, present, and future were being laid upon Him, so God could not be within Him anymore. It was the hour of His greatest need, His greatest pain, His greatest torture.

> Matthew 27:50 *But Yeshua, again crying out in a loud voice, yielded up his spirit.*

Other Gospel writers give us different details.

> Luke 23:46 *Crying out with a loud voice, Yeshua said, "Father! Into your hands I commit my spirit." With these words he gave up his spirit.*

> John 19:30 *After Yeshua had taken the wine, he said, "It is accomplished!" And, letting his head droop, he delivered up his spirit.*

We know that the phrase that He used in the Greek actually was what was stamped on receipts when someone paid their bill—paid in full. So what He was saying is, "I paid the price. Paid in full."

That gets us to what we should all be thinking. I hope you understand, because it's so important to make it clear. Why did He allow all this to happen to Him? I can remember when I was first reading this in the Bible. I didn't know how the story would end. I was on the edge of my seat wondering, "What's going to happen?!" And when He died, it was like, "Why?! Why?!" I couldn't understand.

Rabbi Sha'ul gives us, I believe, the most concise statement about this.

> 2 Corinthians 5:21 *God made this sinless man be a sin offering on our behalf, so that in union with him we might fully share in God's righteousness.*

So Yeshua was doing this so that you and I, even though we've sinned, can be forgiven and have right standing with God.

The other question is, "Why did He have to suffer so terribly to make this sin offering?" If you've heard or read some of my other teachings, you might know this already. In the Law of Moses, the sin offerings were humane. The animals are slaughtered in a very humane way when the Temple sacrifices were made. But they were for sin. Notice the word iniquity, *avone,* in this prophecy that Yeshua fulfilled.

> Isaiah 53:6 *We all like sheep have gone astray. Each of us turned to his own way. So ADONAI has laid on Him the iniquity of us all.*

So if you remember from Yom Kippur, the scapegoat bore Israel's iniquity, their *avone*. And remember the scapegoat did not die a humane death. The scapegoat died a painful death. So Yeshua had to die in this way to not only bear our sins, but our iniquity, which is, remember, our inclination to evil, our attitudes, our ungodly ways of thinking. It's not our acts or our words, but just our flesh, our carnal or worldly nature.

So in reading this whole account in all four Gospels, reading it over and over four times, what struck me, and I hope I communicated it well enough to you so it struck you, too, was how Yeshua resisted the temptation to defend Himself over and over. He was silent. Five times—it actually records five times in the Gospels that He remained silent.

I thought back to the story of Esther, and how we all puzzled, "Why did she wait?! Why was she silent when the king asked her what's wrong the first time? Why was she silent at the first banquet?" Well, just like Yeshua, she was following the leading of the Spirit of God.

As you read through this, it is so amazing that there were so many prophecies fulfilled. God was able to make them all come to pass with Yeshua being mostly silent. If He had spoken up in His defense, at those times, the prophecies would not have come to pass.

So the most amazing insight for me in this study was that Yeshua was led by the Ruakh, the Spirit, and was obedient even when He was being injured and abused and killed. Even when He was in terrible pain, when He was bleeding, dehydrating, being insulted and mocked and accused, He was still able to be obedient to the Spirit and not defend or rescue Himself.

SILENT AS A LAMB   217

So how does all of this apply to you and I? I mean, it's a powerful, powerful account. I saw three ways that it applies. First of all, it's really important to be reminded what terrible suffering Yeshua went through on His way to the Cross and on the Cross. It's important to understand that He did it for you! —for your atonement, for your forgiveness, so that you can become adopted as a child of God. He did it for all. This reminder fills me with gratitude. I hope it fills you with gratitude and love for Him.

It's also important to see all the prophesies that were fulfilled in His last days. This fulfillment of prophecies is a testimony to the truth of the New Covenant; to the truth of the Gospel; to the truth of what happened. It should strengthen your faith greatly to know those prophecies.

It's important, too, to understand that we as His followers, we are being conformed to His image. We are being made like Him. You and I are called to walk in the Spirit, too, even under pressure and stress. We don't face as much as He did, but we do face stress. We have experienced mockery, insults for our faith, accusations that were false, even abuse, certainly rejection and fear.

We've also suffered emotional and physical sickness that had nothing to do with our faith, as well as injury and pain. We've endured grief. Who hasn't grieved over something or someone? Hopelessness, depression, bitterness; many of us are enduring those kinds of things today, or we will in the future. We tend to lose our ability to behave in a Godly way when we're in the midst of that kind of pressure. We lose our ability to walk in the Spirit under difficult circumstances, in particular, the ability to hold our tongues. James speaks about this:

> James 3:8 *but the tongue no one can tame—it is an unstable and evil thing, full of death-dealing poison!*

Only God can tame our tongue. So what I can see is that it's hard to produce the fruits of the Spirit: love, joy, peace, patience... when we are being pressed on all sides, when we're in stressful circumstances. It's hard to resist the temptation to think, speak, or behave in a carnal or ungodly way when our flesh and our emotions are crying out, tempting us to sin. It's much easier when things are calm and we're not being stressed.

People usually think, "But Yeshua, He could do that. He had supernatural power, after all. He was the Son of God, right? I could never do that. I could never put up with things like that." But, you know, that's not what the Bible says. The Bible says that He was tempted in the same way that you and I are.

> Hebrews 4:15 *For we do not have a cohen gadol* [High Priest] *unable to empathize with our weaknesses; since in every respect he was tempted just as we are, the only difference being that he did not sin.*

We can see how He was tempted on that last day to save Himself and avoid suffering, but how did He manage to get to that place where He was strong enough to obey the Spirit under such terrible pressure? How did He get there?

Well, in Hebrews 12:2, we have some hints about this.

> Hebrews 12:2 *looking away to the Initiator and Completer of that trusting Yeshua—who, in exchange for obtaining the joy set before him, endured execution on a stake as a criminal, scorning the shame, and has sat down at the right hand of the throne of God.*

So what is this saying? It's saying that He was able to endure because He trusted that God was going to fulfill all His promises in the Bible, and would redeem and save all who will trust in Yeshua through His obedience. That was *the joy that was set before Him*. He was looking into the future and seeing you, and saying, "There's *(your name)* who is going to be one of my children! That's the joy that I'm doing this for. That's the joy of the future for which I can do this. I'm going to hang on because of that joy." To see those people come into the Kingdom and be right with God and be given access to Heaven rather than going to the place of darkness, hell. Because of His trust in what was set before Him by God, it says right there in Hebrews He was able to endure the pain and shame of the Cross, to resist the temptation to come down, or simply destroy His persecutors, or just destroy the Cross. He could've made it disappear, just like that, but He was able to resist doing that.

Now, here's another interesting thing that the author of Hebrews says. Where did that trust in God's promises come from? Did He just get born with it? Did it just come to Him just because He knew who He was? Hebrews 5:8 says this amazing thing:

> Hebrews 5:8 *Even though he was the Son, he learned obedience through his sufferings.*

Now this is not talking about His sufferings that He had on the last day because He already had the obedience by that time to get through those. He learned to trust God's promises through what He suffered during the 33 years of his life on earth. That obedience that He learned through His entire life enabled Him to resist temptation and to be obedient on that last important day.

So what did He suffer throughout this life? Well, first of all, He left glory to come to earth. Then He was in the womb for nine months. While in the womb, we know that the children actually experience what goes on around them. He was rejected in the womb by those who thought His mother was a fornicator and adulterous.

And then He was born, and it's not easy to be born. He went through the normal difficulties and struggles of childhood. We know He wasn't excused from them. He grew up with bigger kids who probably tried to bully Him and things like that.

He had the grief, which is not really talked about in the Scriptures, but you know, there's no mention of his father when He's an adult. So He had the grief by the age of 30 of the loss of His father. When He began His ministry, He was rejected by his family. They thought He was going crazy. Remember He went back to Nazareth where the people all knew Him. He was rejected by His neighbors! He was weary. It talks about Him having to go off and rest for a while. There were great demands on Him all the time by people. There were accusations and attempts to trap Him in His words by the religious leaders. He was abandoned by all but His closest disciples. And after He poured Himself out to them, He saw their unbelief and spiritual blindness, and their pride in wanting to be the greatest. And then He was betrayed by one of His closest friends.

He suffered things that you and I suffer. We've suffered some of those kinds of things, too. So here's the message that I see in this to all of us who have suffered, are suffering, or will suffer, which includes everyone. I know because people come into my office and tell me so. I'm not prophesying doom, it's just what life is like. We all have struggles. We will all be under pressure. We will all be stressed. So what's the point of all that? What are we to be thinking when we go through all that?

One of the fruits of our suffering is **to learn obedience through it**. God is working all things together for your good, the Scripture says. One of the things He's working on is for us to learn in the midst of suffering. It's easy to learn obedience when we're not suffering, but it is put to the test when we're struggling. Then you have to go before the Lord.

How do we learn it? Well, take every thought captive and focus on the joy set before you and I. What's the joy set before us? God's promises! The New Jerusalem. The golden streets. The marriage supper of the Lamb! We will be with Him! We will go up that red road and pass through Him to the Glory on the other side into the presence of God, as my wife saw. But not just that.

There are promises that He has for us for this life. I believe that He has a plan for every person, including you. He's going to fulfill that plan in our lives, and that plan includes bearing fruit—bearing the fruit in your life of love, joy, peace, patience, and kindness, and gentleness; and bearing fruit in the lives of other people, helping them, giving to them, and leading them into the Kingdom of God. That's the joy that we need to focus on.

We need to take every thought captive and say, "Yes, we're going through some big struggles right now, but I'm going to look at—I'm going to visualize, I'm going to imagine—what it's going to be like when we get to the other side of these struggles and then to the other side of life." In the midst of your struggles resist the temptation to give up.

When God instructs you in the midst of those struggles to do something, it's going to take faith and trust to step out and obey and do the thing that He has called you to do. I had that happen so many times—from little things to big things—like leaving my job at Xerox and stepping into ministry here. It seemed to me like an impossible thing. It seemed like I was giving up so much financially, giving up so much in terms of security. Now it has been decades, and I'm still going! And God has provided all through those times. Believe me, I struggled with taking that step, but I heard the voice of the Lord say, "Your supposed to do this now." I took that step and I learned obedience.

Sometimes it's just little steps. It's little things like you're short on money, I've heard this many times, and God says, "Give some away. Give some to this other person." Then all of a sudden you get the money for what you need. It happens. Right? We need to understand that that's what God is doing during all our struggles. He's teaching us obedience. So let's not get to that place where we cry out, "Oh no! I'm going through this struggle again! Oh, God, please! Please deliver me from this. Get me out of this! Why are you doing this to me, God? Oh I'm so miserable! I'm depressed. I have no hope." No! Instead we can say, "God, I'm going through this, but I can see the joy that You're setting before me, the joy of overcoming this, the joy of Your Word being fulfilled."

So, let's pray.

Father we're just so thankful today for Your coming as the Meshiakh (Messiah), the Son of the Living God; coming Yourself as a man, in the form of a man; for enduring so much suffering, so much pain for the joy of seeing a sinner like me set free from the bondage of sin, from the deception of our enemy, ha-satan; for not only atoning for our sins, but also painfully bearing our iniquity, so that You could dwell in us.

We thank You today. Give us the full measure of gratitude that we should have for You. Thank You for bearing the stripes of the Roman whip so that we could be healed. Thank You for allowing Yourself to be chastised, berated, insulted, as the Word says, so that we can have shalom, so we can have peace in the midst of trouble. Thank You for being obedient to the Ruakh's leading, so that You could be that sinless sacrifice, that spotless Lamb of God. Thank You for showing us, Lord, even by inspiring the words in Hebrews, that for You to do that You had to learn obedience through what You suffered all Your life. Help us to grasp that, Lord, that we have to learn obedience, too, that whatever I'm going through right now, suffering something painful or stressful, is for my good to learn obedience and become more like You.

In our congregation I asked people to raise their hands if they were going through something like that right now. Then I asked them to open their eyes and look around so they could see that they were not alone because everybody's hands were up. Everybody is going through struggles! Okay? Alright.

So you, personally, are probably going through a struggle right now. Why are you going through that struggle? To learn obedience. God is going to work good through those things. Can you thank Him?

Lord, I thank You for teaching me obedience in the midst of this trial. Thank You, Lord. Help me to learn to trust You. Increase my trust as I endure these trials. Father, one of the things that we understand is that for each thing that You call us to step out in faith, there can be greater stress to it, because You are always calling us to do greater things. Once we learn how to do something at one level, You call us to do something bigger. Lord, we see that. We understand that greater struggles will bring greater faith. It will increase our faith even more when we learn to obey and submit rather than resist. So help us, Lord, to overcome that temptation to give up. Help us to be obedient. In Yeshua's awesome Name. Amein.

Chapter 14
EVEN INTENTIONAL SIN

In the Torah, animal sacrifices were required to make atonement for people's sins. We are going to look at what sins were atoned for by these sacrifices and what sins were not. Then we will see if the Brit Khadashah (New Covenant) deals with the sins that were not atoned for in the Torah.

The sacrifice instructions are recorded in the Parasha reading called *Vayikra*, which is actually how you say Leviticus in Hebrew. It's the name of the book. In English we call it Leviticus because it has to do with the Levites, which is another word for priests. *Vayikra* which means *he called* is actually the first significant word in Leviticus. This Parasha is chapters 1 through 5 in Leviticus but it's a little confusing because if you have a Christian Bible, the numbering is different. So it's actually chapters 1 through chapter 6 verse 7. So the first seven verses in chapter 6 in the Christian Bible are in the end of chapter 5 in the Jewish Bible.

This section is really foundational to the laws of Moses. It details the primary task of the Levitical cohanim, and that is to participate in the animal sacrifices. I say "participate" because

---

* Photo: Lamb and shepherd, Shutterstock.com. Used by permission.

people think the cohanim did the sacrifices, but the people made the sacrifices themselves. The cohanim were there as they did them and they were the ones that would burn the sacrifice and would take the blood and sprinkle the blood around the altar, etc. But it was the sacrificer who was making the sacrifice. Sometimes the cohanim did sacrifices for themselves, but most of the time, they were overseeing the people's sacrifices.

Some would consider this dry reading because it isn't stories. I think many people have a misconception of the sacrifices. In chapters 1 through 3, there are the burnt offering, the grain offering, and the shalom (peace) offering. And these offerings were not for forgiveness of sins. They didn't have anything to do with sin.

They were the main form of worship in the times of the Temple. It's hard for us to imagine, but can you imagine? That's how people worshipped. They brought an animal from their flock, slaughtered it for the burnt offering, and burned it all up. For the shalom offering, they burned part of it, and then they ate part of it with the family. That was worship. You know, we just kind of gloss it over in our thinking. But that's really what it was. Okay?

We are going to focus on the sin offerings in Leviticus chapters 4-5. I just want you to grasp the monumental importance of the spiritual history of the world and the Kingdom of God here. What's happening here is that God is putting into His Law the forgiveness that had been modeled by Joseph toward his brothers and the forgiveness that God had spoken to Moses about when Moses asked Him to reveal Himself. God revealed, in Exodus 33, that His glory was His mercy and His forgiveness and that He would forgive sins. But here in Leviticus is where He actually put it into the Law that there would be forgiveness. There wasn't forgiveness before this for the people. There wasn't anything that they could look at and say, "God will forgive us." This is where it is. God explains here how to find atonement and forgiveness.

So as you know, we are called to be Yeshua's cohanim. And our primary task is to help people see this forgiveness from God and to know how to get this atonement that is available to us through the sacrifice that Yeshua made of His life.

So we're going to look at these. Specifically we're going to compare the power of these sacrifices made by the Levitical cohanim to the power of the sacrifice made by Yeshua our Cohane HaGadol.

But before we start, I want to review the three Hebrew words that I talked about before (on page 169) that are usually translated either sin or guilt or trespass. There are not many Bible translations that are consistent in how they translate these words. I have to say that the King James and new King James are, and also the Tree of Life Version, which I use a lot. These are three very different Hebrew words. Each one of them appears hundreds of times, and often times people just kind of lump them all together as sin.

The first one we will talk about is *avone*, which is *iniquity.*

עָוֹן *Avone* is our inclination to evil. In the New Covenant, it's called our flesh, our carnal nature, our carnal desires. It's our evil thoughts and attitudes.

No action or words are required to have *avone*. It can all be internal. It can just be bad heart attitudes. It's like a person who never actually grumbles or complains, but they have a grumbling or complaining heart. That's iniquity. That's the Hebrew word, *avone*.

The second Hebrew word is פֶּשַׁע *pesha*. It means *trespasses* or *transgressions,* which are violations of God's Law. So this is when people knowingly do something that breaks the Law that God has given. This is when you know something is wrong but you do it anyway. Or you know what is the right thing to do, but you refuse to do it. *Pesha* has the hint of rebellion in it. *Pesha* is sin that we do on purpose.

The third one is חַטָּאָה *khatah'AH*. It has that kh sound in it, the guttural sound in the back of your throat. This is best translated as *missing the mark,* but is usually translated as *sin,* which means *falling short*. In other words, when I'm supposed to do something, and I want to do it, but I don't.

The word *sin* is sometimes used for all three of these Hebrew words in some translations, so it can be very confusing. So keep that in mind. You got that down? You took notes? That's good.

We're going to start near the end of chapter 4 where it gets to the sin offerings for the individual people. It begins with the sacrifices for the congregation, for the leaders, and then for individuals.

> Leviticus 4:27a When anyone of the common people sins <u>unwittingly</u>

Here is another word I want you to learn. It's an awesome Hebrew word. It's so different. The word is *bishgaGAH*. Can you say that? It means *unintentionally*. So *khatah'AH bishgaGAH* is unintentional sin.

Notice it says, *"any one amongst the common people."* So this is not just for leaders. This is for all the people.

> Leviticus 4:27b by doing one of Adonai's mitzvot that are not to be done, then he is guilty.

The Hebrew word for *guilty* is another word that is very, very significant, that I want you to get. If a person does something unintentionally that is not supposed to be done, that is against the Torah commandments, he is *guilty*. This is the word: *ahsham* (pronounced ah-shahm). Sound familiar? It means *he is guilty* or *he is to be ashamed*.

> Leviticus 4:28a *When his sin that he committed is made known to him....*

In other words, when it is revealed to him.

> Leviticus 4:28b *... then he is to bring for his offering a goat, a female without blemish, for his sin that he committed.*

So again what is being spoken about here is a *falling short*, something caused by maybe ignorance of God's Law. A lot of this is talking about what offerings to bring. In verses 29 and 30, it gives more details how to do it. Then in verse 31, this is the key. It says so the cohane:

> Leviticus 4:31c *... So the kohen is to make atonement for him—and he will be forgiven.*

So these *khatah'ah bishgaGAH*, unintentional sins will be forgiven.

Let me give you an example of what unintentional sin is. Suppose you promised to meet someone somewhere and some emergency comes up, so you can't make it, and you're unable to contact the person you were supposed to meet, and it causes problems for that person. The promise you made to meet the person was still broken, but it wasn't intentional, so you don't feel guilty. Right? It was an emergency, but the other person was inconvenienced because you didn't show up. That is an unintentional type of sin.

So it's important to see that this atonement in verse 31 is only for unintentional sin *khatah'ah* and this offering is called a sin חטאה *khatah'ah* offering. All through this passage, if you look in the Hebrew, a sin offering is חטאה *khatah'ah*.

I struggled with this for a long time, trying to understand this. This is what I believe it means: this is for missing the mark when you don't even really feel guilty because there were extenuating circumstances as to why it happened. But you know something bad happened because of you because something came up. It wasn't your fault, so you don't really feel guilty, but you can make this offering and you can be forgiven. But this offering is not for *pesha*. It is not for intentional transgression of God's law, breaking God's law when you're well aware of what you are doing.

The text continues with speaking about this unintentional sin, but now it addresses sins that a person feels guilty about even though they're unintentional. It talks about touching unclean things being unaware that you touched them: unintentional; making an oath and then forgetting it: unintentional. But when the unintentional sinner realizes he's done something wrong, now that's the difference. In this sin, the person feels guilty. See in the earlier ones, they didn't feel guilty.

So here's an example. Suppose you promised to meet someone—this is the same example—an emergency arises, and you can't make it. But this time you are able to contact the person, but you don't. Now when that person encounters a problem because you didn't show up, you feel guilty. Right? We say, "Oh, I should have made that phone call. I could have made the phone call, I just I didn't." See the difference? So this is one that makes you feel guilty.

So for unintentional sins that causes a person to feel guilty, God commands a different kind of offering. There's even a different name for this offering, and it requires a different animal and a different method of offering. It took me a long time to figure this out, but this is the difference between this sin offering and what's called a guilt offering.

> Leviticus 5:6 *Then he is to bring his trespass offering* [some translations say guilt offering] *to Adonai for his sin that he committed: a female from the flock, a lamb or a goat, as a sin offering. So the kohen is to make atonement for him over his sin.*

Where it says *trespass* or *guilt* offering, it is actually the word *ahsham* offering. And if you haven't gotten it yet, from what I said before, we have an English word for this, and it's very clear. The English word *shame, to be ashamed* actually comes from the Hebrew word here, *ahsham*. This offering is for when you're guilty about something and you need to have that guilt taken away.

Have you ever felt ashamed about anything? Everybody has. Right? Chapter 5:2-19 gives the details of this guilt offering. Then in the rest of the chapter, there's this critically important further provision. Remember that if you are going to look this up in your Christian Bible, it will be in chapter 6 not in chapter 5.

> Leviticus 5:21-22 (English Bibles: 6:2-3) *"Suppose anyone sins and commits a faithless act against ADONAI by dealing falsely with his neighbor in a matter of a deposit or a pledge of hands, or through robbery, or has extorted from his neighbor, 22 or has found what was lost and lied about it, swearing falsely—so sinning in one of any of these things that a man may do.*

So this is a little different. This is dealing with extortion, stealing, lying, and finding something and not returning it. This is clearly not *bishgaGAH*. Right? This is intentional. You can't do those things unintentionally. Right? Do you agree? This is intentional sin. So now it gets interesting because everything else up to this point has dealt with unintentional sin.

> Leviticus 5:23-24 (English Bibles: 6:4-5) *Then it will be, when he has sinned and has become guilty, that he must restore what he took by robbery, or what he got by extortion, or the deposit that was committed to him, or what was lost that he found, 24 or any thing about which he has sworn falsely, he is to restore it in full, and add a fifth part more to it. He must give it to the one to whom it belongs on the day of presenting his trespass offering* [shame offering].

So there's an additional, critical provision here. Did you see what it is? The guilty person must restore what was lost or stolen or extorted and he must add one-fifth to it in order to be forgiven.

> Leviticus 5:25-26 (English Bibles: 6:6-7) *He is to bring his trespass offering to ADONAI, a ram without blemish from the flock, according to your value, for a trespass offering, to the kohen. 26 The kohen shall make atonement for him before ADONAI, and he will be forgiven concerning whatever he may have done to become guilty.*

So now what we are seeing here is that atonement, *kippur*, which is *covering*, required something more. Do you see what it is? Yes, restitution. It required restitution plus a fifth of the value in order for there to be atonement. Notice that all of these crimes are things for which restitution could be made.

So here's the conclusion the way I understood it. With restitution, repentance, and an offering, the Torah provides forgiveness even for some intentional sins or *transgressions* or *pesha*. Remember that was the other word, *pesha*—breaking God's law intentionally.

Here's the important point to grasp. No atonement is available for intentional transgressions when no restitution could be made. Grasp that. I think I heard you say, "Wow." No atonement could be made.

So what are some of the things that people might commit for which no restitution can be made? Let's just list some from the Ten Commandments. Idolatry. How can I make atonement for idolatry? Blasphemy, Shabbat breaking, disrespect of parents, adultery; murder obviously. How do you make restitution for those things? You can't.

This is a little known fact, I believe, that the Torah makes no provision for the forgiveness of those things. Most people don't realize that this was a limitation of the Mosaic Covenant.

Just so I can convince you that I'm not making this up—that this is actually true—let me show you from Scripture. (If you have read through the five books of Moses, you know this.) Think about the story of the man who broke the Shabbat (Numbers 15:32). What did they do to him? They executed him, right? Think about the man who blasphemed God's Name (Lev. 24:10). What did they do to him? They executed him by stoning.

In Deuteronomy 13:6, God instructs that idolaters must be completely destroyed, executed. We also know that adultery was punishable by execution (Lev. 20:10; Deut. 22:22). And, of course, murder must be punished by execution (Gen. 9:6; Ex. 21:12). So do you see what I'm saying here? These are all transgressions of God's laws for which no restitution could possibly be made. So the result of that was non-forgiveness.

So in the theocracy (government run by God) in ancient Israel, it really wouldn't have made sense for God to give laws, and then say that people could be forgiven of these laws if they just repented, unless they could make a restitution for what they had done. And if no restitution was possible for those crimes, there was no forgiveness. Another thing that was different from our culture is that imprisonment was not an option. You don't read about any prisoners or prisons in ancient Israel.

But we do know that God put another system in place, so that, for instance, if you robbed somebody of something and you sold what you robbed and spent the money, and then you felt guilty and repented and wanted forgiveness, you could actually sell yourself as a slave to that person to work it off. So that was kind of the equivalent of our prison system. These people would offer themselves up as slaves to work off what they owed them through restitution.

It's kind of amazing to really understand this about the Torah. This question came up in our Messianic Judaism class, and I realized that I didn't really understand it. So that's what caused me to dig in here to find out what could be forgiven in the Mosaic Covenant.

So how does this apply to us? Well, if we study how Yeshua interpreted the Ten Commandments, especially in the Sermon on the Mount, and if we can hear our consciences at all—if our hearts are just a little bit contrite—it will be obvious that we have all broken the laws of God.

We've all committed idolatry. How, you ask? We have loved things and people and activities and philosophies more than God. We have used God's Name in disrespectful ways. We have all failed to keep one day in seven holy all of our lives. Right?

We have committed murder by what? By holding hatred in our hearts. We have committed adultery by lusting after people, things, and positions. And we have also transgressed by disobeying God's command to forgive others. We have all had times when we couldn't forgive for awhile. Right?

And when we look at Yeshua's commands, we also find that He commands us not to fear, not to envy, not to promote ourselves, and not to harbor bitterness. How many can say they haven't done any of those things? So when we break these kinds of commands, do we do it *bishgaGAH,* unintentionally? Do you think it is unintentional? I didn't think so. Do we do it intentionally? Yes! How can we lust or hate or use His name in vain unintentionally? Impossible.

Now if we are ignorant of God's commands, we could claim we have done those things unintentionally. But I'm sorry to inform you that you just read his commands, so you can't claim that anymore.

Now in our society, because our government is not a theocracy, thankfully God doesn't punish us for all of these things. Can you imagine what that would be like? Only murder is punished by execution. Adultery, which used to be punished, is not punished by our legal system anymore. Our government certainly doesn't punish us for how Yeshua interprets the laws. Yeshua says hating is like murder, and lust is like adultery. Our government certainly doesn't punish us for that.

So since the government does not punish for these things, does this mean that we're not subject to any consequences for breaking these laws? Or do we still have consequences?

> Galatians 6:7-8 *Don't delude yourselves: no one makes a fool of God! A person reaps what he sows.*

A person reaps what? What they sow. They bring destruction upon themselves by sowing to the flesh. When we intentionally transgress God's Law there are consequences. So if we're honest enough, we all have to admit we are guilty—I am guilty, you are guilty—of intentional transgression of God's Law—*pesha*.

So we are destined, according to the God of justice, to reap the consequence we deserve for that *pesha*. I am. Are you? That really should be the case. We really all deserve punishment. So what hope is there for us. Everybody always answers, "Yeshua." That was your answer too, wasn't it? But look at this verse. You will find this really, really amazing. Yeshua says:

> Matthew 5:17 (TLV) *Do not think that I came to abolish the Torah or the Prophets! I did not come to abolish, but to fulfill.*

Everybody says amen to that. But if Yeshua came to fulfill the Torah and the Torah would not forgive us of our *pesha*, we have a problem here. For sins we can't make restitution for, the Torah doesn't provide forgiveness! So if Yeshua is fulfilling the Torah, we could not have forgiveness either. Uh-oh! Getting a little worried now, right? But wait a minute. When I saw this for the first time, I thought it was so awesome!

Notice the loophole. We missed *the prophets!* He came to fulfill the prophets. So what do the prophets say about *pesha*, about transgressions? Well, here's a verse that probably is dear to your heart. It's from the prophet, David. You can probably say it from memory.

> Psalms 103:12 *As far as the east is from the west, so far has He removed our transgressions from us.*

Now if you happen to know a little bit of Hebrew, you can go back and look and see what word that is in the Hebrew. It's actually the word *pesha*.

So what's happening here? This verse, which we just take so for granted, is actually dealing with the things that the Torah doesn't forgive. How far is the east from the west? It's infinity. It's immeasurable.

Now I used to think, and maybe you did too, that this verse was describing what the animal sacrifices did. But the animal sacrifices didn't deal with most intentional sin, with most *pesha*. Any *pesha* that could not be paid for in restitution could not be covered by animal sacrifices, which is a lot of them. So Psalm 103 is not referring to the animal sacrifices, it is prophesying the future. It is prophesying what is going to come in the future when even transgressions, *pesha*, when no restitution can be made, would be atoned for. That really covers most of the transgressions, so I will just call them transgressions from now on.

This prophesy and another prophecy in the book of Malachi that talks about our sins being carried into the depth of the sea are predictions of something coming in the future when *pesha* would be able to be atoned for. How? Well, another prophet gives us the details, in great detail. It is Isaiah. And again, if you've never seen this before, take note of the exact wording the prophet uses in Hebrew.

> Isaiah 53:5 *But He was pierced because of our transgressions* [pesha-enu (*enu* means our)], *crushed because of our iniquities. The chastisement for our shalom was upon Him, and by His stripes we are healed.*

There are four things in there, but I want to just focus on the one here. Isaiah is telling us how *pesha* will be atoned for. Someone would be what? Pierced! Someone would be pierced.

> Isaiah 53:8 *Because of oppression and judgment He was taken away. As for His generation, who considered? For He was cut off from the land of the living, for the transgression* [the *pesha*] *of my people—the stroke was theirs*

So now we've learned that this person that takes away *pesha* would be pierced and what else? He would die! *He was cut off from the land of the living.*

> Isaiah 53:10 *Yet it pleased Adonai to bruise Him. He caused Him to suffer. If He makes His soul a guilt offering,*

That's the same word *ahsham* right there. That's the key. So Yeshua was not just a *khatah'ah*, He was also an *ahsham* offering, a guilt offering. And then look at this.

> Isaiah 53:10b *He will see His offspring, He will prolong His days, and the will of ADONAI will succeed by His hand.*

So there's another amazing prediction about what this person would be like. Isaiah says this person would die, but also says he's going to see the fruit. So what's that talking about? The resurrection! He is going to die, but he's going to come back to life and see the fruit. He would be an *ahsham*, a guilt offering, and he would see the fruit.

So who was this someone? Isaiah gives us more clues. In verse 2 he would look disfigured; in verse 3 he would be despised and rejected, not esteemed or held in high regard; acquainted with grief; verse 4 he will be considered smitten by God—God was punishing him; verse 7, he would not defend himself; verse 9 he would be buried with the rich and the innocent; verse 11, he would see the fruit of his labor which ended in death, which again, can only mean that he would resurrect.

Now anyone who reads any one of the four accounts of the life of Yeshua would see that this is an exact description of who He was. And we need to only answer the question of why His sacrifice was powerful enough to accomplish this when the animal sacrifices could not accomplish it. They could not bring forgiveness for intentional sin.

And the answer is very simple. Isaiah 9 says that this man was God Himself, the almighty God, the everlasting Father, come as a man without any sin, the perfect sacrifice offered up to make atonement for even intentional sin, even if restitution could not be made.

> Leviticus 5:26 *The kohen shall make atonement (kippur)* for him before ADONAI, and he will be forgiven concerning whatever he may have done to become guilty.

Now this is another twist in here to understand when the animal sacrifices were made. *Kippur* means *covering*. The sins were covered over, but there was no covering over for intentional transgressions or *pesha*.

So how could this person in Isaiah remove them? Well, Hebrews tells us that Yeshua's sacrifice accomplished this removal. We're going to look at three passages.

> Hebrew 9:26b *But as it is, he has appeared once at the end of the ages in order to do away with sin through the sacrifice of himself.*

Not to cover over but *to do away with sin* because *pesha* can't be covered over. His sacrifice removed it as far as the east is from west.

So this is part of the power of Yeshua's sacrifice that I don't believe many people understand. But this is how, if you've ever wondered or marveled and thought that's not possible, even a murderer can receive forgiveness from God when he repents, even though he can't make restitution.[45] These are the stories you might have heard of people on death row turning to the Lord when someone shares the Gospel with them. God says even those will be forgiven.

It's also how we, you and I, who have transgressed in so many ways, can receive forgiveness, even for when we can't make restitution.

---

45 Not that people don't have to pay the price for their transgressions. Our legal system will prosecute you if you break the laws of the land, the civil laws.

But in addition to this, Hebrews tells us there is something more that happens here, and it has to do with that word, ashamed. There's something more to what Yeshua's shame or guilt offering did that the animal sacrifices couldn't accomplish.

> Hebrews 10:1 *For the Torah has in it a shadow of the good things to come, but not the actual manifestation of the originals. Therefore, it can never, by means of the same sacrifices repeated endlessly year after year, bring to the goal those who approach the Holy Place to offer them. 2 Otherwise, wouldn't the offering of those sacrifices have ceased? For if the people performing the service had been cleansed once and for all, they would no longer have sins on their conscience.*

So let's just look at a little detail on this. First of all, the word *sin* in the New Covenant includes all three types of sin. It is one Greek word *hamartia*. There is no distinction between *pesha*, *avone*, and *khatah'ah*. It's just one word.

The people performing the service that are referred to in verse one, *those who approach the Holy Place,* are the ones making the animal sacrifices, and the priests, the kohanim, help them with the sacrifices.

Now here's the question for you. Look at the passage again. What is the goal the animal sacrifices could not bring the people to? What is it? It's in verse 2: *they would no longer have sins on their conscience.*

So what is our conscience? It is a God-given part of us that knows right from wrong. It will constantly confront us when we do something wrong. It makes us feel guilty or ashamed. Right? See the connection here with the guilt or shame offering? It makes us feel ashamed, actually for our good, to bring conviction and repentance.

But sometimes our consciences can torment us, and keep on reminding us. Some people try to silence their conscience by keeping very busy. Or they try to seer it by indulging in evil constantly until it's overloaded. Other people try to drown their consciences with drugs or alcohol.

But God created our conscience to make itself heard so that no matter what you do to try to stop it, it will still pop up. Even in your dreams, it will show up.

So what this is saying here is that those offering animal sacrifices for their sins, according to Moses, still had sins on their conscience. Do you see that? They still had a guilty conscience. They had remorse. They had sorrow. They had guilt and shame for what they'd done that was wrong, especially if it was intentional, even if they did the sacrifice and made restitution and we're forgiven by God. They still carried around a load of guilt, of regrets, and of blame. Their consciences were not clean.

That's a big problem. Many people, even in synagogues and churches, are greatly burdened and tormented because their consciences are not cleansed once and for all. And we have learned over the years that many things that trouble us, like diseases or emotional problems or relational problems, can also be due to guilt and shame on our conscience. So the power of Yeshua's sacrifice to cleanse our consciences is clearly stated in Hebrews.

> Hebrews 9:14 (NIV) *How much more, then, will the blood of Christ, who through the eternal Spirit offered himself unblemished to God, cleanse our consciences from acts that lead to death, so that we may serve the living God!*

So when we confess our transgressions, our intentional sins, our *pesha* to God and ask Him to forgive us, and ask Him by the power of Yeshua's sacrifice to take away our sins, His sacrifice fulfills the prophecies of Psalm 103 and Isaiah 53. He removes our transgressions as far as the east is from the west.

And according to Hebrews, this means that we should have clean consciences. We should be set free from the shame for the wrongs we have done, even intentionally, and be able to go on with our lives without that awful burden of shame. And also, that cycle of reaping what we have sown is broken when we repent and Yeshua brings that forgiveness to us.

This is all part of what Yeshua paid for when He made His atoning sacrifice. Just like healing, just like deliverance, just like peace, just like the Holy Spirit, just like eternal life, a clear conscience is also part of our inheritance in Him, as is breaking that cycle of reaping what we've sown.

Here's the two applications for this for all of us. First of all, there are many people who have been exposed to that forgiveness offered by the New Covenant for a long time, maybe since they were little children. And I believe many people actually just take it for granted. The Spirit was saying to me, as I was studying this, "Don't take this lightly." Understand how amazing it is. It wasn't available to those in the times of the Temple with the animal sacrifices. And it is one of the reasons why Yeshua died the way He did. In fact, Yeshua said, "Many prophets and righteous men longed to see this day, but they never saw it." They never saw the day when their consciences could be cleared.

The second application is that there are some people who received Yeshua's sacrifice, but they still have a guilty conscience, oftentimes for good reason. They've sinned in some ways that they can't make restitution for. If it was murder, obviously you can't bring that person back. Or if you permenently injured someone physically, or you destroyed a relationship emotionally or relationally, and you can't get them back. Or maybe you want to apologize, but maybe the person has died.

So what happens is that there is a spirit that the enemy sends, one of his soldiers, one of his team, a spirit of unforgiveness, a spirit of shame, a spirit of guilt, and it deceives us into believing that we should live the rest of our lives in that shame. We can never get away from that. It comes up again and again. It keeps popping up, especially if it was something intentional, especially if we could've done something about it, but didn't. It deceives us, actually, into not forgiving ourselves when God has forgiven us

So if that's you, here's what we're going to do. We're going to pray. But first, here's what you have to do. Decide to do all you can to make restitution for anything that you can. Then receive the truth of what these verses say.

Receive the truth that Yeshua's atoning sacrifice is meant to cleanse your conscience of shame, of remorse, of sorrow, of guilt. That's why He was an *ahsham*, a guilt offering. Isn't that amazing that it's the same word?

We can break the power of that spirit of shame over us, that spirit of guilt, that spirit of remorse, that spirit of unforgiveness off ourselves by using those "R words": taking responsibility, repenting, and removing the spirit. Then we can also rejoice that this is an awesome, awesome thing, that we can be free.

But remember also, before we pray, that even though we can remove the spirit and break its power, we still have our flesh to deal with. And one thing that our flesh is, is habits of thought.

So if we remove this thing and tomorrow you get that shameful thought coming back up, that doesn't mean the spirit has gained access again or has control of you again. It means you've got this habit of thought about what you're ashamed of, and that habit has to be broken. And that takes time. You have to go over and over it again and say, "I'm not going to think that anymore." Instead what are you going to do? You've got to wash your mind by the water of the Word and replace those thoughts with God thoughts.

> Romans 12:2 ... *be ye transformed by the renewing of your mind....*

> Philippians 4:8 *Finally, brethren, whatsoever things are true, whatsoever things are honest, whatsoever things are just, whatsoever things are pure, whatsoever things are lovely, whatsoever things are of good report; if there be any virtue, and if there be any praise, think on these things.*

Replace those shame-filled thoughts with virtuous, lovely thoughts. Memorize the Word. Meditate on it. Sing Scripture to yourself, and eventually those thoughts will stop coming. You will have broken the habit.

Let's Pray

Father I just thank You for the revelation in this passage that is so amazing, such an amazing understanding of the greatness of what You have done as the Messiah, how far beyond what was there before. We are so thankful to be alive in this age.

[I just want to start by confessing that there are things in my life that I have done that I am ashamed of. How about you who are reading this book? Do you have things you are ashamed of?

In our congregation once, I asked everyone to close their eyes. Then I asked for everyone who had something in their life that they're ashamed of to raise their hand. And I can tell you that it was everybody in the room. So don't feel alone in this.

Take comfort from that and understand that this is part of the human condition. We all do things that we are ashamed of. We all have things that we wish we had not done.]

Pray this with me again now:

So, Father, we confess that we have intentionally transgressed and broken your Commandments. In Yeshua's Name we ask You to forgive us for anything we've ever done, anything we've said or thought that has been against Your will, or against Your laws. We look to Yeshua's sacrifice of His life, the life of the Son of God, of God Himself come as a man to pay the price for our transgressions, for our *pesha*.

We understand He made a guilt offering for our guilt and an *ahsham* offering for our shame. Show us, Lord, if we need to make restitution to someone.

We thank You today that You came not to cover our sins, but to **remove them as far as the east is from the west.** We also ask, Lord, that You would break that cycle of reaping what we have sown. Break that cycle, Lord.

And for those who feel shame, remorse, Father, even right now in this moment, fulfill Your promise to take away that burden. Set us free from it, Oh God. Cleanse our consciences, so we can come to You with a clean conscience.

You are our *ahsham* offering. You are our guilt offering. We received Your atoning sacrifice for our *pesha*, our transgressions, for our *khatah'ah*, our sins, for our *avone*, our iniquity and to cleanse our consciences.

Right now in the Name of Yeshua, I command every spirit of shame, every spirit of unforgiveness, of guilt, of remorse, of ungodly sorrow, everyone of those spirits, I break their power over the ones reading this book. In the Name of Yeshua, I break that power of shame. I break that power now by the mighty Name of Yeshua, who became a shame offering. I break that power. I command those spirits' power to be broken and for them to go into the dark places, in the Name of Yeshua.

Father, I pray for each of us that we would have the gift of discerning of spirits, that we could recognize when these things try to come back on us, and we would stand against them and refuse to allow them access to us.

And I also pray, Father, that You would help us renew our minds, to remove any habits of thought of being ashamed, of being guilty. Remove those habits of thought of unforgiveness of ourselves. Remove those habits of thought. Help us to replace those thoughts with patterns that You want us to think. Things that are true, that are noble, or righteous, lovable, admirable, virtuous, that are praise worthy, Oh God. Enable us to think Your thoughts, thoughts in the Word of God. We thank You for Your deliverance from this.

We rejoice together. We say, Hallelujah! We love You, Yeshua! Hallelujah! Thank You. Thank You, Lord, for Your great and awesome work. We rejoice in it. Amein

Chapter 15

WASHING FEET, SERVING

During the Passover Seder, there is a tradition of washing the hands called rachatz. Before the actual meal, there's a bowl of water that is passed around and everyone washes their hands. It's a ceremonial, ritual washing in preparation for eating the meal. We practice that at our Seders today.

Understand that Yeshua was keeping Passover on the night before He was crucified. He was keeping it with His disciples. They were going through the regular traditional things that go on in a Passover Seder.

I believe that rachatz became hand washing in more recent times. Before that it was probably just foot washing or both. In the culture of the Bible, people walked on dirt roads, not paved roads, and they wore sandals. Their feet were constantly in need of washing.

According to the people who understand the culture from this time, whenever you were welcomed into a home, the lowest servant—the one lowest on the totem pole—would be assigned

---
* Photo: Passover Seder Washing, 1939, Library of Congress.

to wash the guest's feet. This is how you were welcomed into the home. I believe this turned into just handwashing because people stopped wearing sandals and in other countries it was cold so they decided to just wash the hands.

Yeshua was building on the washing ceremony of the Passover Seder to show us something—to help us visually see something. Foot washing was in addition to the mikveh washing of the whole body, cleansing oneself before coming into the presence of God. Remember that people had to be ritually clean to enter the Temple. This is what happened at Mt. Sinai when they were told to wash themselves and all their clothes before coming to the mountain.

In this chapter, what we are going to focus on is the whole question of servanthood that Yeshua talked about in connection with the footwashing at the Passover Seder. First let's look at one of the laws about Pesakh.

> Exodus 12:11 *Also you are to eat it this way: with your loins girded, your shoes on your feet and your staff in your hand. You are to eat it in haste. It is ADONAI's Passover.*

I am amazed by this law. Have you ever eaten a Passover Seder in haste? People in my synagogue would be laughing because Seders usually take four hours! So, what has happened with this? Sometime after the first Passover, which is actually the escape from Egypt, the ancient Rabbis decided that we needed to obey this instruction while we were in Egypt, but once we were free people we could relax. We didn't need to eat in haste, and it is certainly not done in haste today. In fact the leader of the Seder always has a cushion or a pillow that he leans back on. This is to indicate that we are free people, so we can relax.

This is a very significant part of the Seder because if you remember the four questions that a child is supposed to ask, one of the questions is "Why do we recline at the Seder?" It is a little bit foreign to us in this culture because we sit up, but in the time of Romans, at the time of Yeshua, people reclined when they ate.

What is interesting here is that this tradition of reclining seems to go completely against what is commanded. At first I thought, "This is wrong! We should do what is commanded!" So in our household for a couple of years, we ate Passover standing with our shoes on and a staff in our hand to obey this commandment. Later I was praying about this and reading in the Scriptures to see how Yeshua celebrated it and I was surprised to find this verse:

> Matthew 26:20 *When evening came, Yeshua reclined with the twelve talmidim;*

It finally got through my thick head that He accepted that tradition. If He accepted it, it was good enough for me. The tradition of reclining pre-dates Yeshua and He honored it.

So, we are seeing in this book that Yeshua apparently honored all the traditions of Passover, including the important tradition of the lowest slave washing feet when guests arrived. It was especially important at the Passover Seder because they were reclining.

It is hard for me to imagine how they were eating while they were reclining—it is hard to do that. The only way I can conceive is that people laid on their side around a big table, perhaps on Roman couches. So if you were laying on your side so that you would have the food close to you, where would your feet be? They would be right near the nose of the person next to you. So, it was very important that they washed their feet. Besides that not only were the roads dusty, but this was also an agricultural society. We aren't used to that, but animal waste would have been all over the roads—I won't go there but—their feet could have been quite aromatic. ☺

I would like you to use your imagination and imagine that you are looking in through a window of the last Passover Seder that Yeshua celebrated.

Remember this room was miraculously given to Yeshua and His disciples to use for the Seder. I don't think it was actually somebody's home. I think that what was happening in Jerusalem was that because there were these pilgrimage feasts with so many people coming to Jerusalem for every feast, people would build a room onto their house that they could let out for guests from out of town to celebrate with their families. This was probably one of those rooms that was given to Yeshua. The Scriptures tell us that Peter and John went and made preparations while the rest of the disciples came a little bit later.

So now I would like you to imagine that all the preparations have been made. There is one of these low tables with cushions all around that all these people are going to recline on. Peter has been slaving in the kitchen there making food and getting it all ready. John's been setting the table, getting the Seder plate out, and all the traditional elements laid out there.

Finally, the group starts to arrive, but there is no servant on duty to wash feet. Maybe they hired one and he didn't show up, or maybe they just forgot to hire somebody. Just imagine what went through the mind of that first disciple as he walked through the door, and there was nobody there to wash feet.

Peter would have been like, "I just cooked this whole meal, I'm not going to go wash people's feet."

John would have thought, "I just set all this stuff out and put it all together. I'm not going to wash anybody's feet."

So, that first one that arrived had a decision point right there. It was, "Do I wash my own feet?" "Do I take off my robe and wash Peter and John's feet? Not me, that's not my job. I'm not a slave." So, he sat down at the table.

The second one arrives. "Nobody washed my feet. There's Thomas. He didn't wash my feet. I'm not gonna wash his feet!" So, he sat down at the table. This went on through all twelve of these disciples. They all laid down and made themselves comfortable and put their dirty feet up near the noses of their friends.

Last of all Yeshua enters. We know that this custom of foot washing was very important to Him. Remember when He was in the house of Shimon (Simon) the Parush (Pharisee)? He actually rebuked Shimon because he invited Him into his house and nobody washed His feet. It was such a strong custom, He took it as an insult.

So, Yeshua walks in and nobody washes His feet. He looks around. This is what I think He might have been thinking:

"Three years with them. Teaching after teaching about being a servant. Confronting them: Whoever wants to be a leader must be a servant. Whoever wants to be first must be your slave. The Son of Man did not come to be served but to serve and give His life as a ransom among you. The greatest among you must be a servant. Whoever promotes himself will be humbled and whoever humbles himself will be promoted. How many times do I have to say this?" It doesn't look good. "I'm about to leave and they still haven't gotten it. This is a fundamental principle of the Kingdom of God and they haven't gotten it." So Yeshua thought, "I'll give them another chance." He reclined at the table, thinking maybe someone will do it. I'll wait here a while." He waited for the meal—no one took the initiative. Then finally He couldn't take it any longer.

> John 13:4-5 *So he rose from the table, removed his outer garments and wrapped a towel around his waist. 5 Then he poured some water into a basin and began to wash the feet of the talmidim and wipe them off with the towel wrapped around him.*

Now I'd like you to imagine what was going on in the minds of those disciples at this point. Disbelief? Embarrassment? He came to Simon Peter who said, "Lord, you're washing my feet?" (See verse 6.)

Imagine what Peter felt as Yeshua, whom he had seen do all these incredible things, who had been leading him for three years, knelt in front of him to wash his feet. Embarrassment. Disbelief. Regret! "Why didn't I do this? What's wrong with me? How did I miss this? It's bad enough that I wasn't humble enough to wash my brother's feet, but I could have washed His feet! He's my Lord! How could I have been so stupid?"

Yeshua answered him and said: "You don't understand yet what I am doing, but in time you will understand." (See verse 7.) We will look at how they were all able to understand this in a minute.

"No", said Peter. "You'll never wash my feet!"

Yeshua answered him, *"If I don't wash you, you have no share with Me."* (See verse 8.) That was the part of this that stuck with me this time. It was so important that Peter had his feet washed. What Yeshua is saying here is, "Peter, if I don't wash your feet you are not going to be one of my disciples." Meaning – "You're not going to be in the Kingdom of God. You are not going to carry on My work. You will not be on My team. You will be off!" So, this is pretty important.

"Lord," Simon Peter replied. "Not only my feet, but my head and my hands too!" (See verse 9.) Peter expressed a great desire to be a follower of Yeshua, to be with Him.

> John 13:10-11 (TLV) *Yeshua said to him, "He who has bathed has no need to wash, except the feet; he is completely clean. And you all are clean, though not every one." 11 He knew who was betraying Him; for this reason, He said, "Not all of you are clean."*

Remember that each one of the disciples would have cleansed their whole body in a mikveh before they came so that they were ceremonially clean, as required for Pesakh. So, Yeshua would've been referring to that mikveh bathing. What He is saying here, spiritually, is that we are all cleansed by His atoning sacrifice, but we walk in the world, and as we walk in the world, we get dirty—spiritually. We do things we weren't supposed to do. We get defiled. We pick up things. Periodically, we need to be washed.

> John 13:12-15 *After he had washed their feet, taken back his clothes and returned to the table, he said to them, "Do you understand what I have done to you? 13 You call me `Rabbi' and `Lord,' and you are right, because I am. 14 Now if I, the Lord and Rabbi, have washed your feet, you also should wash each other's feet. 15 For I have set you an example, so that you may do as I have done to you.*

What we see here is that in His usual way, He took what was just a custom and made it much, much more. He was doing more than getting their feet clean. He was setting an example—a standard—for them and for us two thousand years later. If Peter had not allowed his feet to be washed, he would have missed the power of the example. It was important that Peter not just hear about it or see it, but that he experience it. What Yeshua was saying is "You cannot be my disciple unless you actually experience this."

> John 13:16-17 *Yes, indeed! I tell you, a slave is not greater than his master, nor is an emissary greater than the one who sent him. 17 If you know these things, you will be blessed if you do them.*

First of all, it is not a blessing to just know about it. That is significant right there. If you know important principles and don't do them, it is actually worse than if you don't know them. He says that if you know them and do them, you will be blessed. That is the wonderful part of this example. If we pick up the towel and serve one another we will be blessed. It will be a joy.

So, what is this? Why is it such a blessing to serve? Many of you would say that it is a blessing to serve. Why? Because things get done? Or the Kingdom of God advances? Yes, but there is so much opposition to this in our culture. Our culture teaches us the way to live a fulfilled life is to indulge yourself. "Fulfill your desires. Satiate your appetites. Pursue pleasure." I live in a place where there are a lot of hair salons. I like the one that says, "It's all about you!" That is what our culture teaches, "It all about me."

The Kingdom of God teaches just the opposite. We should realize that we're actually not happy when things go our way, although we might be for a little while. Having no problems or being healthy, etc., does not make us truly happy. Rather, real happiness is dependent on our finding fulfillment in this life, knowing our life has meaning and importance in the big picture.

Many people try to find fulfillment in natural ways. Acquiring things. "This will make me fulfilled." Gaining expertise. "I'll be the top in my field." Fame. "Everybody will know me." Power. "I will have control. They'll do it my way." All of these things Yeshua says don't work. None of them work.

We all want to get to the top in our fields, to be the best. It's the goal of everyone. "Be the top." But here is what Yeshua says, "If anyone wants to be first, he must make himself last of all and servant of all." That's totally upside down to the way our culture thinks. The way to come to the top is to be a faithful servant to the Father and a humble servant to each other.

Yeshua says, *"Whoever wants to save his life must lose it."* If you concentrate on making your own life good, you'll lose it. *"But whoever loses his life for my sake and for the sake of the good news will save it."* In other words, if you serve the Kingdom of God, your life will be saved. That means serving Him.

Why serve Him? Why devote ourselves to the Kingdom of God? Why do successful business people serve the Kingdom of God for nothing? There are people who are successful business people and yet they serve in my congregation. We don't pay them anything. Why do they do that? Why did I take a factor of two salary cut to leave Xerox and come serve at the synagogue? At Xerox I had a great job and great people to work with, wonderful environment, all the high tech stuff, but our motto was "We are making the world safe for laser printing." That is what we were doing. That is what I worked on: laser printers. I worked on them for years. I wondered, "Is that a high enough goal for my life when I'm done? Is that the motto I want on my epitaph?" There was no fulfillment in it.

I still remember the first time I experienced the fulfillment of servanthood. I had become a new believer and I had helped a friend with a roof on his house. I had spent the whole day on his roof, carrying heavy stuff. I was totally exhausted. I was so tired and so stiff when I got home that I decided I would take a bath. I was laying in the bathtub when I heard the Lord say in my mind, "Well done good and faithful servant. Enter into the joy of your master." I was like "Wow." That made the whole day worthwhile. It really did. Everything changed. Since that time I see all other rewards as vanity.

The one thing that is important is to serve Him. The thing that I've come to understand is this: God created us. He wired us this way. He designed us so that we would find fulfillment in serving. But we are so blinded to that by our culture.

John 10:10 *The thief comes only in order to steal, kill and destroy; I have come so that they may have life, life in its fullest measure.*

That fulfillment comes when we serve. That is the way to experience it.

How do we understand, like Yeshua promised Peter he would understand later? I have a book by Steve Sjogren, *Conspiracy of Kindness: A Unique Approach to Sharing the Love of Jesus.* He says this: "We love, serve, and care for others because that is normal behavior for people who are filled with God's Spirit. We are followers of the Messiah who was the ultimate Servant. We can't help but serve because the Spirit of the Servant has filled our hearts. When we serve, we are just being who we naturally are."[47]

I personally believe that it is a supernatural thing because we are not naturally that way, but I never saw that before, that the Ruakh that we all want to be filled with is the Spirit of the Servant! We talk about the Spirit being the Spirit of Truth, but He is also the Spirit of the Messiah who is the Servant. How would Peter understand later?

John 13:8b *"If I don't wash you, you have no share with me."*

I believe what happened is that when Yeshua put His hands on Peter's feet, somehow the Spirit of the Servant Messiah entered into Peter. It was supernatural. He understood the Kingdom principle: *"If you know these things you will be blessed if you do them."* It wasn't just in his head. He understood that a life of serving was a life that brings fulfillment. It is a life that is wonderful. He came to know those things and began to do them.

How do we wash each other's feet like Yeshua told us to? We can help each other physically when we are in need of help, fixing something or carrying something. We can help each other emotionally by just giving a hug or speaking comforting words; spiritually by caring and praying; financially by giving. We can pray for each other, encourage each other, and exhort each

---

47 Steve Sjogren, *Conspiracy of Kindness: A Unique Approach to Sharing the Love of Jesus,* Bethany House Publishers, Grand Rapids, Michigan, 1993.

other. We can serve the Kingdom of God by being part of a team that accomplishes things for the Kingdom of God. We can do more as a team. That is why we get together.

We have a worship team because they can do a better job at creating worshipful music than an individual can do. We have a Security Team because they can do a better job at keeping us safe than an individual can do. We have a Prayer Team because they can do a better job of encouraging prayer in the congregation than an individual can do. They inspire each other.

Also, I try to model servanthood in our congregation by being a servant to those whom I have delegated authority. When there is a workday, I come and serve our Facilities Manager who is in charge. When we have an Oneg, I serve the Oneg Coordinator by helping clean up. We receive donated groceries from local supermarkets to give to those in need, and I often serve as the person who picks up the groceries.

One year, I wanted to serve each one of my congregants in a special way. I wanted to demonstrate servanthood by doing something that everyone needed—clean their bathrooms? Do their grocery shopping? But then I woke up on Shabbat morning with the Lord telling me to wash their feet.

There was a supernatural impartation when Yeshua washed Peter's feet. Without that, the person can serve but have the wrong motives. Peter might not have experienced the complete fulfillment of serving.

So the Spirit said that I needed to wash feet during the service that morning. I trusted that the servant Spirit of Yeshua—the "I love to serve" spirit—would be imparted to them in a greater way. And it was a wonderful experience for me and for them. The Spirit of Yeshua was there in a powerful way. I encourage you to ask the Lord whose feet He would like you to wash and how He would like you to do it.

Chapter 16
WASHING FEET IN MINISTRY: FINDING FELT NEEDS

Now we are going to go into more depth about what foot washing means for our lives and ministries today. I gave you my idea of what the Seder scene might have looked like in that upper room. Now let's take a minute to look at it again from a little different angle, using only the Scripture this time.

> John 13:4-5 *So he rose from the table, removed his outer garments and wrapped a towel around his waist. 5 Then he poured some water into a basin and began to wash the feet of the talmidim and wipe them off with the towel wrapped around him.*

Notice that Yeshua got up to do this. The way I've always envisioned this is He would've gone to each disciple and knelt

---

* Photo: Passover Seder herbs, 1939, Library of Congress.

down, taken their feet in His hands and washed them and dried them off and then moved on to the next person.

> John 13:6-7 *He came to Shim`on Kefa [Simon Peter], who said to him, "Lord! You are washing my feet?" 7 Yeshua answered him, "You don't understand yet what I am doing, but in time you will understand."*

What Yeshua was saying is that His Kingdom is an upside down Kingdom. In the Kingdom of God, the leaders serve the people instead of the people serving the leaders. This is what this was all about. Leaders wash feet in this Kingdom.

> John 13:8 *"No!" said Kefa, "You will never wash my feet!" Yeshua answered him, "If I don't wash you, you have no share with me.*

Peter was still in the old kingdom. What he needed to realize here is that he had to let Yeshua wash his feet because Peter needed to be spiritually cleansed. He couldn't do that himself. Yeshua was the only one who could do that. That is the message to us as well. We can't cleanse ourselves and make ourselves fit to come into God's presence. God has to do that for us.

> John 13:9 *"Lord," Shim`on Kefa replied, "not only my feet, but my hands and head too!"*

Suddenly Peter got it. He was willing to be washed, not only his feet, but everywhere!

> John 13:10 *Yeshua said to him, "A man who has had a bath doesn't need to wash, except his feet—his body is already clean. And you people are clean, but not all of you."*

Yeshua explains further why they are clean in this verse:

> John 15:3 (TLV) *You are already clean because of the word I have spoken to you.*

Rabbi Sha'ul (Paul) refers to this cleansing.

> Ephesians 5:25-27 (TLV) *Husbands, love your wives just as Messiah also loved His community*

> and gave Himself up for her 26 to make her holy, **having cleansed her by immersion in the word.** 27 Messiah did this so that He might present to Himself His glorious community—not having stain or wrinkle or any such thing, but in order that she might be holy and blameless.

The Word of God—the Scriptures—cleanses us. Here is a beautiful picture of the man who was the Word of God kneeling at Peter's feet and washing him. The Word was literally cleansing Peter. When we receive the Word—when we let it be active in our hearts —when we are *immersed* in it daily—it cleanses us.

What He was saying here is that Peter had been bathed in the Word for almost three years because he had followed Yeshua for three years. But, his feet still got dirty. There is a lesson in that for us. We are cleansed by the power of the Spirit of God and the Word of God, but as we interact with this world, we get our "feet" dirty and we need to be cleansed again. We have to do that all the time because we are human and we slip into things of the world. I have to do it, too. For example, when I snap at someone, like the sound technicians when something isn't going right, I have to apologize to them.

> John 13:12-15 *After he had washed their feet, taken back his clothes and returned to the table, he said to them, "Do you understand what I have done to you? 13 You call me `Rabbi' and `Lord,' and you are right, because I am. 14 Now if I, the Lord and Rabbi, have washed your feet, you also should wash each other's feet. 15 For I have set you an example, so that you may do as I have done to you."*

A lot of times Yeshua taught in parables, but you get the sense here that He was being very, very clear. He was saying, "Don't mistake this. I did this as an example so that you will do this."

> John 13:16-17 *Yes, indeed! I tell you, a slave is not greater than his master, nor is an emissary greater than the one who sent him. 17 If you know these things, you will be blessed if you do them.*

Now, of course, it is certainly good to wash another person's feet. It is a wonderful sign of humility and love to do that. It can be a marvelous time in the presence of the Lord and can really minister to the person's spirit. But Yeshua is really not just talking about physically washing people's feet here. This is about serving each other and helping each other and praying for each other.

The example that is being given here is that Yeshua is the Son of God—when we look at Yeshua we see God. If we want to understand what God is like, He tells us. All we have to do is look at Yeshua. Look at what He did. Look at what He said. This is what God is like. When we see Yeshua's character, then we know God's character. So, what we can learn from this is that the Father expresses His love for us in the way Yeshua does. And Yeshua demonstrated God's Love by washing the disciples feet.

It's hard for us to comprehend the Love of God because it is so huge. There's this wonderful passage in Ephesians that I just love. Rabbi Sha'ul (Paul) is praying for all of us.

> Ephesians 3:18-19 *so that you, with all God's people, will be given strength to grasp the breadth, length, height and depth of the Messiah's love, 19 yes, to know it, even though it is beyond all knowing, so that you will be filled with all the fullness of God.*

I think what Paul is trying to say to us here is that it is like a drop of water compared to all the water that is in the oceans. That's how big the Love of God is compared to our human love. Yeshua demonstrated His Love by washing feet to help us grasp it because it is hard to grasp because it is so big.

So we know that love is shown when a person serves another person, especially if it costs them something, or if they have to humble themselves to do it. What we learn from this is that He took the role of the lowliest servant to serve each of those who were His followers. It is a message to us that we are to take those humble roles and to serve each other. We are to be His representatives. We are to let people see Him through our humbly serving them.

How do we wash each other's feet? By serving, helping, listening, praying for each other, forgiving each other, encouraging each other, exhorting each other. All of these are ways in which we "wash each other's feet" in a real way.

In the Kingdom of God, what's upside down is that those that are in leadership are called to serve. Yeshua tells us this very specifically in Mark 10:43 (NIV) ...*whoever wants to become great among you must be your servant.* It is upside down.

My Experience in Leadership

I want to share with you an experience that I learned from recently. I've been part of the leadership of a local group of ministers. We in the leadership have believed for several years that the true ministers of God—who are serving God—needed to be connected with each other to establish unity in order for God's Spirit to move upon our region.

When I started as president of this organization, we had the format that we would meet monthly for a luncheon. There would be announcements of what's going on and we would have fellowship and that was it. But we soon began to realize that this really wasn't accomplishing our goal. We had learned through many sources that the way this seems to be working in other places around the world—bringing pastors and ministers together—is through getting them to pray together regularly for each other and for the region.

So we changed the format of our meeting. We still had lunch, but we changed it to include forty-five minutes of prayer. We thought this would make a tremendous difference, and it did! It was overwhelming! The response was that people stayed away in droves! Attendance went down right away to about a third or a quarter of what we had before. Eventually, we went from around 300 pastors to just a small group. What we concluded was that we thought the pastors needed to come together to pray once a month, but evidently they didn't think so.

So we decided to try something else. We decided we would start an additional *weekly* meeting for pastors to get together to pray. We advertised it in our direct mailing to the 300 leaders. We chose a convenient location. We went for a year praying together. But again, we had the same reaction. Even more stayed away in droves! Soon it was down to only four pastors attending this. This was, as you can imagine, very discouraging. We thought pastors had this need, but they obviously didn't think so, and weren't coming.

So as we cried out to the Lord, and started to make a couple of changes, we noticed that if we happened to have a speaker at the monthly meetings who brought a message that the local ministers needed, our attendance rebounded. It would double!

So pastors did have needs that would bring them out, but the need for prayer, which we thought was crucial, was not one of them. So we began to invite what we call "resource people." We were doing subjects like pastoral burnout and how to deal with it, and persecuted believers around the world, and interaction with the media—how to interact with newspapers and radio stations, etc. And we turned a corner. Attendance picked up. People started coming!

We realized that now we were addressing a need that people felt like they had, whereas before we were addressing a need that *we* thought they should have. When we addressed what we thought was a need, no one came. But when we started addressing a need they actually had, things changed.

Then we had some interesting things happen with the weekly prayer meeting that I was really excited about. I knew someone who was leading one in another area. What he was doing was moving the meeting around, so every week it was in a different church. This was working very well for him, so I suggested it to our four regulars.

My strategy was this. And here you can guess how insightful I can be—or un-insightful. I thought lots of pastors would be willing to host the prayer meeting. I thought if I called them up, they would say, "Oh, sure!" I thought they would like it and then would come to another one. Sounds like a good strategy, right?

Well, it wasn't the Lord's strategy. I brought it up to our regular four, and one of the ladies (we will call her Laura) got the interpretation immediately of what it really was all about. She reminded me of what we had heard at a gathering of people who lead pastors' prayer groups like this.

The first speaker was a gentleman by the name of Joseph Materah, an author and an apostle, who is well known for having united the pastors in New York City. We were all expecting an inspiring message, and the first words were just what we wanted to hear. He said, "Many ask me how I brought together the pastors in New York City." There had been amazing things happening there back then. There was an awesome unity.

We were on the edge of our seats, wanting to learn about his method. But his next words were very hard to hear. He said, "I washed the pastors' feet."

We all sort of wilted, thinking, "Oh, you don't just go to prayer meeting? You mean we have to do more than that?" He said you have to wash pastors' feet, meaning you have to relate to them, help them, get to know them, befriend them. That sounded a little tougher than just organizing a prayer meeting and sending out a flyer.

So when I shared this about moving the prayer meeting around, it suddenly clicked in this Laura. She said, "You know, by doing this, we are going to fulfill what Joe Materah told us to do. As a group we're going to do this."

"What do you mean?" I asked.

"We're going to go and pray in these different ministries and churches. And when we're there, we're going to pray for that pastor or ministry leader, right?"

I said, "Yea! Sure we would!"

"So, we're going to be washing their feet and serving them!"

Finally, I started to get it. I began to realize that when Yeshua washed the disciples' feet at that Passover Seder, He didn't remain in His seat and say to each of His disciples, "Get up and come over here and put your foot up." No. He went to them to wash their feet.

So, we were going to go to the other pastors and "wash their feet." So, I called up about a dozen people who hadn't been coming, and just shared a little bit, and nine of them came! The other ones said they couldn't make it because they were going to be out of town, but they would come to the next one. I thought, "Wow! This is totally different!"

And immediately two of them said, "Could you come to my place next week? I want you to pray for our ministry!" One was

Teen Challenge. The other was a guy from Nigeria who had planted a church in our city. We had an anointed time of praying for him there and actually, literally washed his feet. One of the pastors felt led to do that. So I saw that there was something to learn in this—something to apply to any ministry, anywhere. I believe there is a key in this to make ministry more fruitful.

Let me define ministry first of all. What does it mean? Our culture has changed the meaning of that word. If someone says, "I went and ministered there," what do you think of? We think it means they brought a teaching or they lead worship. Right? Well, the actual definition of the word *minister* is *servant*. So to go minister somewhere means to serve.

We can see this change in our English language. The leader of Israel comes to see our president. What's his office called? The prime minister. Now to understand why it's called that, you have to go back in history to the time when there were monarchies, and there was a king, and he would have servants. One of his servants was always the number one servant—that was the "prime" minister. He was the number one servant of the king. He had oversight over many of the other servants. But with the demise of monarchies, the prime minister became like the king.

The prime minster in England now, for example, is much more powerful than the king. Other countries that adopted England's parliamentary system don't have a king, but they have a prime minister, and he's the boss. In our own country, we still have this also in our terminology concerning our political office holders. We call them "public servants." Right? We don't think of them that way, but we call them public servants because that is what they are supposed to be doing—serving the public.

I hear people say, "Someone came to our congregation and ministered to us." Have you ever used that phrase? What do you mean? Well, they came and spoke or they lead worship or something. But what would you say if someone came over to your house when you were sick and they washed your dishes? Would you say they came over to minister to you? You should, because that's the real meaning of it. That's actually the true meaning of the word.

Let's apply some of these principles, that I learned with the pastors, to reaching unbelievers because that is something we always struggle with. Now, we know that the people who don't know the Lord—their greatest need is to know Him and to obey Him. Right? That is a no-brainer. We all know that's their greatest need. But usually they don't feel that need at all, or else they would be believers.

If you were to say to someone, "I want you to come with me so you will come to know the Lord and then you can obey Him," they would say, "Well, I think I'd rather stay home and watch TV." Right? Because they don't realize that is what they need. Now the Bible tells us this in a verse you are probably familiar with:

> II Corinthians 4:4 *They do not come to trust because the god of the olam hazeh* (this world) *has blinded their minds, in order to prevent them from seeing the light shining from the Good News about the glory of the Messiah, who is the image of God.*

So, most people who are not believers feel their greatest needs are other things. Things like healing, food, and shelter. Maybe they are addicted to something and they need to be set free. Maybe they need peace in their life because they have a lot of conflict. They need joy. They're not happy. They need fulfillment. They need purpose. These are the needs people have. They would most likely mention one of those things if you would ask them, "What are your needs?"

The phrase I like to use for this is "people's felt needs." These are not the things that I think they need. These are the things that they *feel* they need. Do you see the parallel with the pastors? We in the leadership team thought the pastors needed a time to pray together, but the pastors didn't think that. So our trying to meet their needs by organizing a prayer time together didn't work. But when we said, "The pastors need a time to get their feet washed. Would you participate in that?" They said, "Oh yea, we do have that need. We'll do that."

We must try to understand what people's felt needs are. Addressing people's felt needs helps them see the Glory of God.

WASHING FEET IN MINISTRY

People won't show up for things that we organize to have their spiritual needs met because they don't realize they have them! But they will show up to have their felt needs met. I want to show you an example of this, so you know it's not totally out of the blue. We will look at a section of Scripture that you are probably familiar with. Maybe you will see it in a different way.

> John 2:2-3 *Yeshua too was invited to the wedding, along with his talmidim. 3 The wine ran out, and Yeshua's mother said to him, "They have no more wine."*

Miriam (Hebrew for *Mary*), His mother, was obviously concerned about this. Perhaps the host or the bride or the groom was a close friend or a close relative of hers. And she could see that it would be a great embarrassment—a disgrace—for the host and the bride and bridegroom to run out of wine in the middle of the wedding festivities.

My congregation can relate to this. One year during our Passover Seder, we ran out of food! Can you imagine how we felt? It was a disgrace. We were wanting to crawl under the rug!

So, there was a real need here in John 2. Do you see that? The real need was wine. And Miriam felt it.

> John 2:4 *Yeshua replied, "Mother, why should that concern me? — or you? My time hasn't come yet."*

Yeshua was obviously not concerned about them running out of wine. He did not feel their need. He knew their real need was to know Him and who He was, not to have more wine to drink so they could have a party. He might have even thought, "I don't want them to get any more drunk than they already are."

He also says, "It isn't time yet to reveal Myself—as to who I am." So He had no intention of meeting this need. Do you see that? He wasn't going to do it. Now I suspect that His mother knew that He was able to do this. Maybe He had done it at home. You know, maybe they ran out of wine one week for the upcoming Shabbat ceremony and he made some. Or maybe she had a word of knowledge here that this was His time because look at what happens in verse 5:

> John 2:5 *His mother said to the servants, "Do whatever he tells you."*

She did this in His hearing. Can you see what she was doing to Him here? She was putting Him on the spot. Right? I mean, this is a Jewish mother trick, putting someone on the spot! If you're Jewish, you know what I mean. I've heard that Italian mothers can be like this, too. Can you relate to this? It even worked with Yeshua!

> John 2:6 *Now six stone water-jars were standing there for the Jewish ceremonial washings, each with a capacity of twenty or thirty gallons.*

So Yeshua might have thought, "Oy!" It might have really made Him say to Himself, "What do I do?! My mother has gotten Me into this. I can't disgrace her. So I guess I've got to do something." So He says:

> John 2:7 *Yeshua told them, "Fill the jars with water," and they filled them to the brim.*

And something supernatural happened to the water.

> John 2:8-10 *He said, "Now draw some out, and take it to the man in charge of the banquet"; and they took it. 9 The man in charge tasted the water; it had now turned into wine! He did not know where it had come from, but the servants who had drawn the water knew. So he called the bride groom 10 and said to him, "Everyone else serves the good wine first and the poorer wine after people have drunk freely. But you have kept the good wine until now!"*

So we see a very interesting thing here that Yeshua didn't just make wine, He made good wine. Do you see that? Now wine doesn't seem like a very important need spiritually. But as Miriam saw, it was important because it was a felt need of the host of this banquet, and the bride and the groom, and probably the whole family. If they had run out, they would have been humiliated. And you can be sure that the host, the bridegroom and bride, and the servants who saw Him do it would all have sought out Yeshua very strongly after this experience, especially after He revealed Himself and began to teach all around the country.

> John 2:11 *This, the first of Yeshua's miraculous signs, he did at Kanah in the Galil; he manifested his glory, and his talmidim came to trust in him.*

And so His disciples began to believe in Him because He had done this! Yeshua always met the felt need of the people. If you look through the rest of the Gospels, you see that He dealt with things like healing. This was the felt need of the people. He didn't go to people and just say, "You need to repent because I am the Messiah." He first began to pray for people who were sick or people who needed deliverance. He fed the five thousand, and He forgave people who needed forgiving. Meeting the needs of people is what turned their hearts to the Lord.

And so, as we attempt to follow Yeshua, we need to see that to reach people with God's Love, we need to understand what their felt needs are. When we meet those felt needs, they will become open and will begin to be aware of their spiritual needs.

I think this is especially important in the American culture because as we fulfill our calling to be the light of the world like we are supposed to be, we are competing with a lot of other bright lights right now. They're false lights, but they're bright. You know, there's TV, there's movies, there's the internet—there's all these things that people can do rather than come to a meeting to listen to Bible teaching and worship the Lord. There are lots of other exciting things for them to do. If we don't meet people's needs, this is what I am learning, they'll find lots of other ways to fill them.

I want to share with you three different types of cases of meeting these felt needs. They're kind of like steps. Each case requires from us an increased step of faith.

The first type is felt needs of people that we can actually meet without much help from the Lord. If we meet someone and they're hungry, we can give them something to eat. That is just an example. There are lots of things we can do in our own "power" and our own abilities and resources. As we do that, it demonstrates God's Love directly through us. We will be shining His light.

> Matthew 5:16 *In the same way, let your light shine before people, so that they may see the good things you do and praise your Father in heaven.*

I love one person's comment on this, "We're not saved through good works—other people are." Isn't that beautiful? Of course, when we do this, we have to give the Lord credit for it. We have to say something like, "I'm doing this because the God that I serve calls me to love and help other people." Otherwise, it won't turn them to the Lord.

What about if we don't have the resources to meet their needs? That's the second type of case. Do we just say, how does James put it? "Be blessed! I'll see ya"? James doesn't speak too highly of doing that. (See James 2:15.) When we don't have the resources—when the needs are too big, then we need to begin to pray for the supplies to meet these needs that we can't do without God's help. When we do that, it gives God a chance to move, especially when we tell the people we're doing this: "I see your need. I can't help you, but I'm going to pray."

In our congregation's "Sharing Our Bread" ministry, we are feeding about 45 families every week through the work of about 30 people here. In just the first three years, we distributed 13,000 week's worth of groceries. We gave people 137,000 meals in those three years. Could we do that in our own strength? Of course not.

This demonstrates that when you begin to pray and move, God can move through you. We've got about 30-35 people working on this. We've got six grocery stores giving us food. We've got drivers and schleppers and administrators. And we're reaching Jewish people with this because most of the people who come are Russian Jewish immigrants who are elderly and very much in need of this, plus other people in the neighborhood.

These people have seen the power of God because we've looked at these people and said, "You know, we can't meet all these needs. But we'll pray to our God and He'll do it." And He did it! And He's still doing it, and He will keep on doing it!

So the first case is that we can meet the need. The second is a case when there is no way, but with God we can meet that need.

The third case is when we see someone who has a felt need, but we can't meet that need in any way possible. What do I mean by that? Well, what if a person needs a healing? I can't heal them. You can't heal them. What if they are addicted to something? I can't get them free from that addiction. What if they need a relationship restored? I can't do that either.

But I can say to them, "I see you need a healing, can I pray for you?" When we do that, it opens up a door for God to work because now God can move, and the person can see that it's the God of Israel, Yeshua the Messiah, that has brought this healing in their lives. That is an awesome way for God's power to be demonstrated. So when we find those needs and we pray for the person and we tell them we are praying to God for them, miracles can happen.

We saw a tremendous testimony of this from one of our Russian-speaking friends. Our administrator was interviewing him and asked him, "Do you believe in God?"

He said, "Yes, I do!"

"But you come from Russia, lived there most of your life, where they didn't allow you to believe in God. So when did you start believing?"

"While I was living in Russia, I got very sick, and the doctors couldn't heal me. I prayed to God. There was nothing else I could do. And I got better! So I believed in God!"

"Do you believe in Yeshua?"

"Well, I didn't believe in Yeshua then. But when I came to America, after I started coming here for food, I got sick again. And people prayed for me in the Name of Yeshua and I got well! And now I believe in Yeshua!" How could it be more simple?!

You know, what I see is when we begin to move in this, where we see a need and we meet it, that is when we enter the area of our anointing. There is an anointing there because God can move through that.

So what kinds of needs do people have? I made a little list here. It might make you see that these things are not so foreign.

Physical needs – food, clothing, shelter, transportation. That's a good one because many people would like to come to services, but they can't because they don't have a car.

Health needs – healing, medical treatment, preventative knowledge or resources to keep them from getting sick or from suffering all the time.

Intellectual needs – language skills. That's what we are helping some of the Russian people with. Many people want to learn Hebrew, so there's another need. Some people need to learn about computers. People need wisdom. These Russian people were raised without any knowledge of Judaism. They need to learn about their Jewish background.

Emotional needs – counseling and prayer ministry

Social needs – fellowship, nurturing relationships, healthy relationships

Relational needs – parenting instructions, how to care for elderly parents, marriage counseling.

Spiritual needs – forgiveness, deliverance. They need the Lord.

We have to start with what they think is their need, or else they're just not interested. So how do we find out what people's needs are? Well, you ask them! Yes! You know the answer to that. Or you know, sometimes people don't realize what their needs are, or they're too proud to say what their needs are. So, we can ask God. And God, through the gifts of the Spirit, can show us what people's needs are.

Now Sharing Our Bread, our food ministry, started by meeting people's physical need for food. And it's been amazing how this has expanded because now we're meeting their intellectual need. They needed to learn about their Jewish heritage, so we're teaching them about Judaism as well as the Gospel and the New Covenant.

They need language. A lot of them don't speak English very well. This has been so awesome. We hooked up with a local Bible College (Elim). They have a class on how to teach English as a second language and they have been using our Russian-speaking friends as their subjects to learn from! They have a requirement in those courses to go out and actually practice. They spend an hour and a half in the Russian people's apartment complex teaching them conversational English! It's awesome!

We are also meeting their social needs because we are inviting them to come and fellowship. They're coming and talking. And we're meeting their real need—the thing that we know is their real need—to know and obey the Lord.

There's another testimony from this group. There's a gentleman there who's a very strong man. His name is Sasha. He was a top surgeon in Russia—a very strong personality. He doesn't speak much English. His wife whose name is Levonda, a beautiful name, speaks very good English, and she has known the Lord since she was a teenager. He has come to know the Lord through what has been going on here. And one day, as soon as he came through the door, he grabbed my arm and took me over to sit down and in his broken English said, "Levonda said I have to come tell you this."

"Okay. What is it?"

He was trying to get this out. He said, "We have a son. And this son is in residency. He's a doctor. And he just passed his residency exam. And Levonda wanted me to tell you that it's because we prayed to Yeshua!" So he was getting it. He was giving the glory to the Lord because he was seeing those needs getting met.

So, I want to get this across that as we try to reach out, we don't need to go out with our own agendas of what we think people need. We need to find out what their needs are and then meet them.

If we're thinking of doing something in ministry, the question we need to ask is: whose needs are really being met? The people we want to reach or my need? Here's a pit that we often fall into. Is it my need for fulfillment or recognition, or is it their need?

I had an example of this with the Sharing Our Bread folks, too. After they started coming here, I started to try to get them to come to Shabbat morning services. After all, that's our main service, and we should get them here. We will get an interpreter to come. They need to be here so the numbers in our congregation can grow and we can see that more people are coming because of all this stuff.

But they didn't seem to want to come! They were coming Tuesday night to get food, and we had a Bible study for them, but I got frustrated. So, I went before the Lord. And the Lord said, "They're coming Tuesday night. Meet their needs Tuesday night! They don't need to come Saturday for your sake! They're coming when it's good for them to come. We supply their groceries. That's a good reason to come. So they're coming! Meet their needs then! Don't try to get them to do what you want them to do." And so I stopped pushing them.

So what happened is we turned the forty-five minutes before we give out the food into a mini service. We have music. We have a teaching and a time of prayer. Then afterwards when people are going up to get the food, we share with the people. We get to talk and have fellowship with them.

Here's the bottom line. Meeting people's felt needs will draw them to the Lord more powerfully, I believe, than trying to preach at them or trying to teach them when they are not open. It's even better than trying to even reach them through music or drama, although all those things are good.

Once you get them connected with you through meeting their felt need, then you can begin to reach them through example and teaching and demonstration and prayer. But first, you have to meet their felt needs. After their needs are being met and they're connecting with you, that's when the teaching, preaching, drama, and music come in. All those things are needed to disciple them and to help them learn about the spiritual things they need.

This has been actually a pattern in our congregation. I want to encourage others to move in this direction. We have a women's group called "Women of Influence." This is really interesting. It seems women have a need to participate in some humanitarian aid projects! So there's a bunch of women, half of them nonbelievers who are coming regularly to participate in helping out folks over in the Ukraine—women who are very poor and are struggling over there. They're collecting things—clothes and money and stuff—and they're sending them over. And people are really excited about doing this. They have a need to participate in something good that isn't just sending money in an envelope, but where there's fellowship and connection involved.

We want to have an interfaith marriage group. Many of us are in interfaith marriages. We know the struggles that go with trying to blend two cultures that are pulling both ways. We know that Yeshua is the answer to that because He puts it all together. We believe there's a need out there, so we want to get the word out to intermarried couples that we have something that can help you.

The last thing I want to say here is that when we do things like this, everybody needs to understand that meeting needs is kind of just the beginning. There needs to be a real strong follow through. If you put on an event that meets somebody's needs, for example, they come and watch a movie or video and then they say, "Oh, that was very nice. Bye." And they're gone. Then it didn't work. It failed because there was no strong follow up. There needs to be some way to connect with these people in order for it to bear fruit—real fruit—amongst them.

So we need dedicated ministers—dedicated servants. The Sharing Our Bread takes 30-35 people to make that thing happen every week. And for everyone of them, it's a lot of hard work—a lot of back-breaking work. But it's worth it because we're seeing fruit.

Every one of these kinds of ministries is work. The leaders need helpers to come along side them to help relate directly to all the people. It takes teams. It takes people who are willing to take long term responsibility. These are not short-term kinds of ministries.

This is the Father's upside down Kingdom. The way in which His Kingdom expands is not by us going out and conquering or showing that we have the best ideas or us going out and blowing them away with music that overwhelms them or preaching styles that grab them. I have seen those things totally not work unless people are open. But I have seen that when we meet their needs, it opens their hearts.

So, I pray the Lord will help us understand this, so that we can begin to be fruitful in finding out what others need and begin to minister in those areas, especially amongst those who don't believe—especially in the Jewish community—in the way in which Yeshua can move to bring His Love into their lives. May the Lord help us be willing to serve.

How are we able to do this—to meet others' needs? There is only one way. We are only able to meet other people's needs when we have faith that God will meet our needs. When we trust in His Love—that Love we talk about that is so big that it's incomprehensible. When we can trust that He loves us and trust that He will take care of us when we go out to help other people, that is when it will make us fruitful ministers—disciples. If you need your faith turned up, come to the Lord and ask Him to give you more of a servant heart. Who knows what you will accomplish through the Lord. The Bible says we will do greater things than Yeshua did.

So I want to challenge you to see that there are ways that the Kingdom of God can expand in our culture, in the world, and in the Jewish community. It's not easy. It takes work. I want to challenge you because this is the great calling that we are all called to. There's nothing higher than this calling of the Great Commission. The Lord calls us to lay down our lives for this. The rewards are very great, but the calling and the price is high.

Let's pray.

I pray, Father, turn up this reader's faith, God. Increase their faith, Father, that they know that You are going to meet their needs as they reach out to those around them. I believe You're going to do it, Father. Your Word says they are going to do *great exploits*, Oh God. Your Word says that those who lead others to You *will shine as the stars in heaven.*

I pray, Lord, that not only would You turn up their faith, I also pray that You will show them where and how. Who are those they can reach out to? Maybe it's a neighbor or a relative or a co-worker that they can reach out and meet a need and can give You the glory for doing it, and just watch as You do it. I pray for testimonies of how You work through them. We pray that we will see ever increasing fruit, Lord.

We pray for American Jewish people, Father, who seem to have no needs. They have money. They have good jobs and kids who are becoming doctors. What needs could they have? But You know, Lord, that many of them are lonely. Many are addicted. Many are without purpose. Some are dealing with personality problems and relationship problems that they can't handle. Show us, Lord. Show us how to meet their needs. In Yeshua's Name, I pray. Amein.

CHAPTER 17

COVENANT MEAL, RENEWING THE OLD ESTABLISHING THE NEW

The Lord spoke to me a few years ago that Passover is a Covenant Meal. It is the Covenant Meal of the Mosaic Covenant. I know I have mentioned this a few times in this book already, but in this chapter I want to go into all the amazing things this means.

First let me clarify what a covenant is. The Bible is The Covenant. It says "Testament" but really it means "Covenant". The New Covenant and the Old Covenant. A covenant by definition is a legally binding agreement between God and His people. It is not a contract, because a contract is based on distrust. There are all kinds of ways that the two parties can cheat each other, so they set up legally binding terms to rule all that out. That is an agreement based on distrust. A covenant

---

* Photo: Passover Meal, Der Oster-Abend, Moritz Daniel Oppenheim, 1867, theJewishMuseum.org, public domain.

is based on trust. Both parties bind themselves with specified obligations. God, who initiates the Covenant, binds Himself to keep the Words that He has spoken.

The Hebrew word for Covenant has been misunderstood because there are three pronunciations. There is "brit," the modern Israeli Hebrew pronunciation of Covenant. "B'reet" is a little bit older. Then if you are Ashkenazi it is "bris" with an "s." When Ashkenazi people talk about circumcision they say "Bris." It's just the accent "y'all." We have them, too.

In the Bible I can think of six Covenants.

    Adamic
    Noahide
    Mosaic
    Abrahamic
    Davidic
    New

These are the major ones. We will just be touching on them here a little bit. In the next chapter, we will look at the Scriptures that go with each one and learn more about them. Covenants have a common structure. They have promises or rewards for compliance, with "rules" and "curses" for non-compliance. There are conditions that if you comply with these expectations of the Covenant maker, you will be blessed.

Covenants often have signs, or visible reminders of the Covenant. What is the sign of the Abrahamic Covenant? Circumcision. The sign of the Noahide Covenant is the rainbow. The sign of the Mosaic Covenant is Shabbat. Covenants have remembrances or ceremonies to remember the Covenant by. Often times those remembrances are meals.

In the Bible there are several examples of covenant meals. There was a meal between Abraham and Abimelech when they made a peace treaty. There was a meal between Jacob and Esau when they made a peace treaty. When the children of Israel went to Mt. Sinai, the seventy elders went up on the mountain and had a meal in the presence of God. If you read there, it says they saw the Glory of the Lord and they ate before Him. (We will look at this in Scripture in the next chapter.)

A meal was usually part of the covenant. The reason is that culturally when two people made a peace agreement, they would sit down and have a meal together. If you think about this, it is a vulnerable thing to do with somebody: to sit down to a meal with them. You don't sit down to a meal with somebody you are afraid is going to attack you. I have noticed that even animals will not eat together unless they trust each other.

Covenants are kept in the open. I was thinking about our own culture. Thanksgiving is a covenant meal. It commemorates our covenant that says we are a nation under God and thanks Him for His provision. July 4th is also a day we do barbeques celebrating our independence when we renew our covenant to be one nation under God. It is a covenant meal. It's not official but this is what we do. In Christianity, Christmas dinner and Easter dinner are Covenant Meals. The whole family gets together. How about birthdays? People have a dinner. How about weddings? Did you ever have a wedding without a meal? How about anniversaries? There's usually a meal. At Bar Mitzvahs and Bat Mitzvahs, you always have a meal. So it is not that foreign to us that when we want to covenant with somebody, we have a meal together.

One of the stipulations of the Mosaic Covenant that I hadn't focused on until the Lord spoke to me a few years ago, is that the Covenant must be renewed yearly. The meal renews the Covenant. That is what the Passover Seder is: A Covenant Renewal Meal of the Mosaic Covenant.

Remember *Seder* means the *order* of all the rituals during the ceremony. We celebrate it in homes, generally. It is a time of joy and celebration especially aimed at children. Of course, it focuses on the telling of the Exodus story. One of the most important things about a covenant is that there must be a way of passing it down to the next generation or else it dies with that generation. Somehow in the traditions of the Seder, it has gotten lost that we are actually eating the Covenant Meal to renew the Mosaic Covenant.

Since the year 70 AD when the Temple was destroyed, Jewish people do not eat lamb on the Passover. Instead there is a little bone of a lamb on the Seder plate to remind us of that. What has happened, as I mentioned before, is that a broken piece of Matzah called the "Afikomen" has become the symbol of the lamb. It has replaced the lamb as the Covenant food.

There are two other parts to the Covenant Meal. There are the bitter herbs—the Maror—which is symbolic of the bitterness of slavery. Another very important part is there are four cups that we drink that are symbolic—the wine or the grape juice—of the blood of the lamb that was sacrificed at Passover. These cups are not commanded in Scripture, but have become an ingrained tradition that we can see was already solidly in place at the time of Yeshua.

This is kind of interesting. Looking at this as a Covenant Meal, I was reminded of the story of King Hizkiyahu (Hezekiah), which starts in II Chronicles 29. As soon as he started his reign as king, he realized that evil was coming upon the nation because they had strayed from God's Covenant. They decided as a nation to renew the Mosaic Covenant with God. They began by cleansing the Temple that was still standing at that time. Then they restored the worship and the priesthood. This was about 700 years before Yeshua. It says that they finished on the 16th day of Nissan, two days after Passover.

Because they had missed the day to select the lambs, they decided to keep Passover in the second month. That means the Passover was pretty important with the whole concept here of renewing the Covenant. They didn't say, "Oh well, we'll just have to wait until next year." They said, "We are going to keep it in the second month." It doesn't say this in Chronicles, but provision was made in the Torah for them to do this.

> Numbers 9:10-12 *Say to Bnei-Yisrael saying: If any man, whether you or your descendants, becomes unclean because of a dead body, or is away on a long journey, he may yet observe ADONAI's Passover. 11 They are to celebrate it at twilight on the fourteenth day of the second month. With matzot and bitter herbs they are to eat it. 12 They are not to leave any of it until morning, or break any bones. When they celebrate Passover they are to observe all its regulations.*

Here we see the three items that are part of the Covenant Meal: the lamb, the bitter herbs, and the matzah. At one point in the Seder, the tradition was to eat the three items together (until 70 AD). This is what we call the "Hillel sandwich" because it is attributed to the famous Jewish sage who lived from 110 BC to 10 AD. Since in our congregation we do have lamb on our Seder tables, we do go ahead and enjoy that tasty "sandwich."

> Numbers 9:13 *But the person who is clean and not away on a journey, yet neglects to celebrate Passover, that soul shall be cut off from his people because that person did not present ADONAI's offering at the appointed time. That man will bear his sin.*

I want you to grasp the importance here This is saying that for all those years, anyone who did not keep the Passover was cut off from His people. If they could do it and they didn't, they were cut off.

What this says to me is that Passover is more than just a holiday. It is more than just a time of celebration. It has spiritual significance. The significance is that it was part of the Mosaic Covenant and was required in order to renew the Covenant once a year. God knew that we as people would forget what the Covenant was and would forget to renew it every year.

For those of you who were not born Jewish:

> Numbers 9:14 *If an outsider living among you would celebrate Passover to Adonai according to the requirement, so he should do. There will be for you the same regulation for the outsider and the native of the land.*

This indicates that for those of you who aren't Jewish who have chosen to do the Passover and attend a Passover Seder, it is right of you to do so.

> Exodus 12:48 *But if an outsider dwells with you, who would keep the Passover for Adonai, all his males must be circumcised. Then let him draw near and keep it. He will be like one who is native*

> to the land. But no uncircumcised person may eat from it.

Some of you who may be non-Jewish and not circumcised may think you cannot eat the Passover. However the New Covenant teaches that circumcision is of the heart. When you become a follower of Yeshua, when you are born again and become part of His Kingdom, your heart is circumcised. So, you don't have to go out and get circumcised to celebrate the Passover. You have a circumcised heart. That should encourage you. If you are, as it says here, "an alien," but are a disciple of the Messiah, you are welcome to eat the Passover.

The story of Hezekiah ends in an incredible way. What was happening at this time was that the kingdom had been divided for a couple of hundred years already between north and south, Israel and Judah. Hezekiah was the king over Judah. Israel, the northern kingdom, right around this time was conquered by Assyria. All the people were deported and taken into exile.

Then that same Assyrian king came against Judah. That is when Hezekiah and the people said, "We have to get back to the Covenant." They recognized that there was protection by being in a Covenant with God and they were vulnerable if they were not.

The end of the story is incredible. They kept the Passover. Then Hezekiah consulted with Isaiah the prophet. They prayed together and Isaiah prophesied deliverance, and there wasn't even a battle. It says the angel of the Lord came and wiped out all the mighty men of the Assyrians, and the King of Assyria fled to his own country. And when he got home, he was assassinated by his own sons. What a violent, wicked nation Assyria was.

But for Israel, what a victory! Decisive. This is a confirmation of the power of being a partaker of the Covenant. It is so very clear here. The point is that they had to actually do what God had commanded them to do.

Yeshua kept the Passover before He went to the Cross. Why did He keep it? He was an Israelite, and it would certainly not have been fitting if He was cut off from His people the day before He went to the Cross, right? He had to keep the Passover to remain the sinless Son of God. And He did.

There are more chapters in the New Testament devoted to the Passover than to any other event. There is a reason for that. The reason is that Yeshua did something more during that Passover than simply renewing the Mosaic Covenant. What did He do? He gave us the New Covenant at the meal that was the memorial for the Old Covenant.

What is the New Covenant? Where do you find it? You find it in John chapters 13 through 17. It is laid out exactly like all the other Covenants.

There are promises. What are some of those promises?
- Eternal life
- The sending of the Holy Spirit
- Preparing a place for us in Heaven
- Answered prayer
- Peace in the midst of tribulation
- Fullness of Joy
- The resurrection

There are also conditions in there. What are some of the conditions?
- Keep His commandments.

What are the key commandments?
- Love one another
- Abide in the vine

Then there are ceremonies that commemorate the keeping of that Covenant. What are the ceremonies?
- Communion
- Foot washing

He gave us the New Covenant at the Passover that was the Covenant Renewal Meal of the Mosaic Covenant. Why did He choose this particular event to do it? I do not believe that He did it just to show the congruency between the two Covenants. I now believe the correct answer is.... Hang on to your seats! I believe He made the Passover the Covenant Meal of the New Covenant, building it right into and continuing the Old Covenant. So, the Passover Seder plus the things He added into it became the Covenant Meal of the New Covenant, which builds on, continues, and renews the Old.

I know this is controversial. Let me dig into this.

As the Covenant Meal of the New Covenant, I believe it has the same weight for those who participate in the New Covenant as it had amongst those who participated in the Mosaic Covenant. What do I mean by that?

Let me point out something different about this Covenant Meal compared to all the other Covenant Meals. The Covenant Maker actually ate it with the people! You see that difference? When the elders ate before God, it doesn't say that God ate with them. But in this Covenant Meal, the Lord ate it. He broke the bread and passed it around. He dipped the matzah. He passed around the wine. He ate the meal with those He was making the Covenant with. In an important way, this is more powerful than any other Covenant because the Covenant Maker participated in it Himself.

Let me get back to the controversial part. I believe He made the Passover, not just Communion but the whole Passover Seder, the Covenant Meal of the New Covenant.

The first thing to ask is, "After the pouring out of the Ruakh, the Spirit, you have the early congregations that were all Jewish. Did they continue to keep Passover?" Yes! Of course they kept Passover.

> I Corinthians 5:7-8 *Get rid of the old hametz, so that you can be a new batch of dough, because in reality you are unleavened. For our Pesach lamb, the Messiah, has been sacrificed. 8 So let us celebrate the Seder not with leftover hametz, the hametz of wickedness and evil, but with the matzah of purity and truth.*

To me, that sounds like Rabbi Sha'ul is saying, "We should still be celebrating the Passover." Not only that, but he is saying that we are to celebrate it while looking to Yeshua as the Passover Lamb. It wasn't disconnected at all.

So, how would the Jewish followers have kept it in those days before the Temple was destroyed? I believe they would have had a traditional Seder. When you study what happened in John 13 through 17 and the other Gospels concerning the Last

Supper, it is very clear that it was a traditional Seder. They were doing things that are almost identical to what we do today in a Seder.

The Jewish Believers would have kept a traditional Seder, and they would have remembered the Mosaic Covenant. But at the third cup, the cup of redemption, they would have reminded each other of what Yeshua told them to say. *"This is the cup of the New Covenant in my blood poured out for the forgiveness of sins."* Then when they ate the Passover lamb, because they were still eating lamb, they would have said something like, *"This lamb represents the Lamb of God who was slain to take away the sin of the world"* (John 1:29). When they would have eaten the Matzah, they would have said, *"This is the body of Messiah broken for you."*

Then later, after the year 70 when they no longer had the lamb, they would have taken the Matzah and said, *"This is the body of Messiah, broken for you. Take eat in remembrance of Him."*

This Passover Seder that they would have kept would have been the New Covenant Meal. Do you see that? Once a year the Apostles and the new followers would have kept Passover and it would have been the New Covenant Passover, which included and continued the Old Covenant. You see, they didn't throw it out. They just built on it.

I believe at that New Covenant Passover, they would have remembered, not only the Exodus story, but they would have also recalled, especially for the children, the story of Yeshua and the crucifixion, not to replace the Exodus story, but as a continuation of it. In addition, I believe they would have stated some of the conditions of the New Covenant, like love one another and obey His commandments.

Perhaps they would have recalled the betrayal in the eating of the Maror (bitter herbs) because we read in the Gospels that Yeshua took the Matzah and He dipped it and gave it to Judas. He gave it to the man whom He knew was about to betray Him.

Which of His commandments does that speak of? *Love your enemies.* Another even more beautiful picture of loving your enemies is at the crucifixion when Yeshua said, *"Father forgive them they know not what they do."*

Let's look now at the ceremony of Communion.

> I Corinthians 11:23-25 *For what I received from the Lord is just what I passed on to you — that the Lord Yeshua, on the night he was betrayed, took bread; 24 and after he had made the b'rakhah he broke it and said, "This is my body, which is for you. Do this as a memorial to me"; 25 likewise also the cup after the meal, saying, "This cup is the New Covenant effected by my blood; do this, as often as you drink it, as a memorial to me."*

What is the memorial? To eat the Matzah and drink the cup. But notice that it says something about a meal. He says, "*…the cup after the meal.*" The other thing that is interesting and is somewhat of a mystery here is that it says, "*…as often as you do this.*" So, how often is this?

People have several different opinions on that. Some say it means every time you eat something. That is one extreme. The other extreme is that it means only once a year at the Passover Seder. There are many ideas in between, like once a week using the traditional wine and bread that is lifted and blessed at the Shabbat meal. Catholics do Communion once a week. Some do it every day. Notice also He says it is the cup after the meal. Today we sort of expect that Communion is a little bit of grape juice and a little bit of Matzah, but what about the meal? Look at how Rabbi Sha'ul says it;

> I Corinthians 11:20-21 *Thus, when you gather together, it is not to eat a meal of the Lord; 21 because as you eat your meal, each one goes ahead on his own; so that one stays hungry while another is already drunk!*

You don't get drunk on that tiny cup of wine at a Communion, do you? You don't have one person hungry and another not because you ate a little piece of Matzah, right? They were actually eating a meal at this time.

> I Corinthians 11:33 *So then, my brothers, when you gather together to eat, wait for one another.*

We see this in the Passover Haggadah, that people want to read through it as fast as they can because they want to get to the meal. They are hungry! That is why Sha'ul is saying, "Don't do that. Eat a little bit before so that you are not dying of hunger."

Let us think a little bit why some of these things might have changed. We have learned that in the year 325 CE something drastic happened in the church: it cut itself off from its Jewish roots. A big part of that is that Passover was forbidden. If you got caught celebrating Passover, you were excommunicated from the Church. The meal was outlawed.

So what did they do? They kept the cup and the matzah and got rid of the meal. They made the Communion or the "Eucharist" as it is called, the meal. Out of that came Replacement Theology and all that that means, which led to some very terrible things.

My question is this, "Is that really what it was like in the first century?" I don't think so. I think it was actually the Passover meal. Why? Because the believers understood that it was building on the Mosaic Covenant, not replacing it. But what the enemy meant for evil, God used for good in that believers over the centuries still had Communion and all that it symbolizes.

Communion is *symbolic* of the Passover meal. It is a wonderful tradition. It is important that we periodically focus on renewing the New Covenant. I'm not suggesting that we only do it once a year because we need to search our souls and seek God's cleansing more often than that. But the Communion that we keep is a symbolic meal and the Passover is a real meal. There is a difference. That is where I am going with this. And now that you understand this, we will take Communion together at the end of the next chapter. I hope it will be very meaningful to you.

During our Passover Seders when we get to the breaking of the Afikomen and the drinking of the cup after the meal, we actually say that this is the Blood of the Lord and the body of the Lord, and I speak about it. I have experienced it as an incredibly powerful time—much more powerful than any other time when we speak of the Lord's Blood and body.

When we first began to do Messianic Passover Seders, we didn't do that. We did it in the regular Jewish way, and then we began to understand this and started saying that this is where Yeshua said, *This is My body* and *This is My blood*. Some people said, "I don't know if you can do that. It is such a 'church' thing. Can you really put that into a Jewish thing?" Should we really have that problem—that we can't put that in? Isn't Yeshua's sacrifice what we are all about?

I want to wrap up by going to something else that has been happening in our modern day. It seems that what we learned about Hezekiah has been repeating itself in the Middle East. Israel became a state after 1829 years of being in exile, and yet for many years, most of the Jewish people there had not been seeking God. Most of them, maybe even up to 80%, were secular. They didn't attend services. Even the religious people, the orthodox who seemed to be seeking God—in most of our eyes—were actually getting caught up in traditions and rituals and laws instead of really seeking God, especially in rejecting that Yeshua is the Messiah. We saw that country experiencing terrible suffering from their enemies.

But then, recently, we have seen the religious leaders of the land begin to call the people back to God, just as Hezekiah did. The timing is absolutely amazing. Many organizations have been working hard to reach Israelis, including the Orthodox, for Messiah and we are seeing the fruit. The number of Messianic congregations is increasing every year.

In 2002, the call back to God came exactly two weeks before Passover, which is great because even non-religious Jews keep Passover—even my atheistic family would always keep the Passover. It is such a strong family tradition, even for those who are not religious. It is such an historically great event of the freeing of the people from slavery that it is hard for anyone to say that we should not remember that.

All Israeli people will be keeping the Passover this year too. What will be happening in their hearts this Passover with what they have been going through in the Land? It would be hard to see the Israelis not seeing the need to turn to God in this time.

> Deuteronomy 4:30-31 *When you are in distress and all these things have come on you, in the latter days you will return to ADONAI your God*

and listen to His voice. 31 For ADONAI your God is a merciful God. He will not abandon you or destroy you, or forget the covenant with your fathers that He swore to them.

Let's Pray

Father, we thank You for Your Covenants. We thank You that You are a Covenant keeping God and that You will not forget Your Covenants with our fathers. We are all children of Abraham, including those who have received the Messiah. We thank You, Lord, that those Covenants are not based on us, they are based on Your faithfulness.

We thank You that in the Passover Seder we can renew the Mosaic Covenant. Those of us who are Jewish are going to do that and those of us who are "strangers in the land" are going to do that, too. We thank You that there is power in the renewal of the Covenant.

I thank You for what I am seeing in this, that this renewing of the Mosaic Covenant is also the renewing of the New Covenant. As we lift up the cup that represents Your blood and the Matzah that represents Your body, that is what You meant for us to do to renew that New Covenant too.

We thank You, Lord that You actually ate that Covenant Meal with us, with our forebearers in Jerusalem. I pray that when we do this, the renewal in ourselves would be genuine. That renewal of ourselves being consecrated and set apart for You, of our willingness to obey Your commandments and to serve You. I pray, Lord, that it would not just be a ritual or a ceremony but it would be a true renewal.

And Father, we pray that Passover time in Israel this year will be a special time for all Israelis. We pray that You will reveal Yourself to them. We pray that their eyes will be opened to see that the Seder points to Yeshua as the Messiah, the Passover Lamb. We pray they will see and believe and receive Your New Covenant.

We also pray for Your protection over the whole land of Israel. Protect them from their enemies. We pray that very soon the whole nation of Israel will call out to Yeshua their Messiah, saying, *"Barukh haba b'Shem Adonai."* We ask all this in the mighty Name of Yeshua. Amein.

Chapter 18
Renewing The New: Promises and Conditions

The Covenant that was made at Mt. Sinai was the founding Covenant of the Nation of Israel. God told Moses:

> Exodus 12:14 *This day is to be a memorial for you. You are to keep it as a feast to ADONAI. Throughout your generations you are to keep it as an eternal ordinance.*

Right there is the commandment to keep this ceremony, this Seder, as the yearly renewal of the Mosaic Covenant. Again, it's a Covenant renewal meal where we eat and drink things that remind us of what God did and all about the Covenant—really to renew the Covenant—to make it alive, to give it life.

I have to say, it's one of the amazing testimonies to me of the wisdom of God that He would say, "This is how you will keep it alive." He told us 3500 years ago to do this, and we're still doing it! It's a still alive! So it worked. God knows what He is doing!

---

* Photo: Kurdish Jews in Israel, 1953, @TheRasti on Twitter, 11:25 AM - 9 Sep 2016, https://twitter.com/TheRasti/status/774282655974260736. Unable to find the original or photographer.

So, in this chapter, I felt led to take a closer look at the covenants God has made with us. Do you remember the definition of a covenant? Again, the best one I've heard is that it's simply an agreement between two parties based on trust, as opposed to a contract, which is an agreement between two parties based on distrust. In a contract, you try to cover all the bases of what could go wrong or how you could cheat each other. But a covenant is based on trust.

A covenant can be absolute. In other words, God can make a covenant for which it doesn't matter what the people do. Or a covenant can be conditional, dependent on the people fulfilling the conditions of the covenant. The core of the covenant is God's promises—what He is covenanting to do—and the conditions for receiving those promises, but also the warnings of what will happen if those conditions are not met. That's the heart of God's covenants.

Now God made several covenants with people in the Bible. Some of them have renewal ceremonies or meals and signs, and every covenant also includes a narrative. The narrative is the story of what the relationship between the covenanting parties was—the relationship between God and the people up to that point in time.

So let me just remind you that in Genesis 3, God made a covenant with Adam, and the narrative for that covenant is the story of creation, the fall of man, and the curse.

In Genesis 9, God made a covenant with Noah. We call it the Noahide Covenant. The narrative is the story of the flood. What's the sign of the Noahide covenant? The rainbow!

And then God made a covenant with Abraham in chapters 12-24 in Genesis. The narrative is the story of Abraham's call, his wanderings, his struggle to have children, and his testing. What's the sign of the Abrahamic covenant? Circumcision!

Then there's the Mosaic covenant, which is the fourth one. And, of course, the narrative of the Mosaic covenant is the whole story of the Exodus up to that point. Then later other parts of the history were added in to the narrative: the taking of the land, the starting of the monarchy, the sin of the people, the exile, and the return.

The renewal meal or ceremony of the Mosaic Covenant is the Passover Seder. And what is the sign? Shabbat! Shabbat is the sign of the Mosaic Covenant. And it's very significant because everywhere Jewish people have lived and had a community, how does the rest of the city know that there are Jewish people there? They see them out walking on Shabbat and having their businesses closed. So that's the sign of the Mosaic Covenant.

There is the Davidic Covenant made with David in II Samuel 7 where God promised the kingship to him and that it would be passed on down to his sons.

And finally, there is the New Covenant, the Brit Khadashah. It is foretold in Jeremiah 31, and then it is given in detail in the back part of the Book. The back part of the book is sometimes called New Testament, but I will always call it the New Covenant because that's what it is.

So let's start out by looking at the cutting, as God puts it, or the establishing of the Mosaic Covenant. It's described in Exodus 24. It was just after God had spoken the Ten Commandments in Exodus 20. He gives some other instructions there, and in chapter 24, He says this:

> Exodus 24:4-5 *So Moses wrote down all the words of ADONAI, then rose up early in the morning, and built an altar below the mountain, along with twelve pillars for the twelve tribes of Israel. 5 He then sent out young men of Bnei-Yisrael, who sacrificed burnt offerings and fellowship offerings of oxen to ADONAI.*

Now this is interesting. Notice that it wasn't the Levites or the Priests that He sent out because He hadn't appointed them yet. This was just the young men of Israel who made the offerings.

> Exodus 24:6-7 *Then Moses took half of the blood* [from the sacrificed animals] *and put it in basins and the other half he poured out against the altar. 7 He took the Scroll of the Covenant and read it in the hearing of the people. Again they said, "All that ADONAI has spoken, we will do and obey."*

Now at this point, understand that the stone tablets had not yet been given. So Moses wrote down all that God had said, including the Ten Commandments and chapters 21 through 23 which are called ordinances, but other instructions for the people. If you ever get into a discussion with Orthodox Jewish people, this is a very interesting verse to point out because, as you might be aware, Orthodox Judaism claims that God gave Moses an oral Torah on the mountain. They say Moses wrote down the written part, but he passed down another large section of instructions from God in oral form. They say it got passed down orally, and didn't get written down until like eighteen hundred years later in the Talmud. But look at what a couple of verses before this said:

> Exodus 24:4 *Moses wrote down all the words of ADONAI.*

Moses wrote everything down. He didn't transmit it orally. He didn't trust it to that. He wrote down everything.

> Exodus 24:8 *Then Moses took the blood, sprinkled it on the people....*

I want you to get the picture of this. This is something really incredible. He sprinkled it on who? On the people!

> Exodus 24:8b *...and said, "Behold the blood of the covenant, which ADONAI has cut with you, in agreement with all these words."*

Now I understand there were three million people. They must have passed before Moses and he sprinkled the blood on them. It must have taken a lot of blood! It must have been a lot of animals that they sacrificed! Plus he sprinkled it on the altar, and the book of Hebrews says he sprinkled the scroll. And this is how the Covenant was established:

> Exodus 24:9-11 *... Then Moses and Aaron, Nadab and Abihu, and seventy of the elders of Israel went up. 10 They saw the God of Israel, and under His feet was something like a pavement of sapphire, as clear as the very heavens. 11 yet he*

> [God] *did not raise his hand against the nobles of b'nei Yisrael,* [the sons of Israel] *so they beheld God and they ate and they drank.*

This eating and drinking is a prophetic picture of the Passover Seder—this eating and drinking to confirm the Covenant.

> Exodus 24:12 *Then ADONAI said to Moses, "Come up to Me on the mountain and stay there, and I will give you the tablets of stone with the Torah and the mitzvot* [the commandments], *which I have written so that you may instruct them.*

Again we see things written down.

And Moses remained by himself on the mountain for forty days. That was when God gave him more of the Torah, including the plans for the Temple. The next few chapters is where the plans for the ark and the Menorah and the table and the vessels, etc., are detailed, and where God promises them workers. All those things were shown in detail by God to Moses as he was up on the mountain. So really this is the beginning of the Bible. This is God giving the Scriptures to us.

So we see, the words on the scroll that Moses wrote included the core of the Covenant: God's promises and conditions and commands. And there were promises. Let's just name a few of them here: the land, the blessings, healing was one of the main promises, prosperity, increase, multiplication, victory over their enemies, and many other promises from God to the people of Israel.

But there were conditions for those promises, which are also very significant. The conditions were very simple: obey My commands. And, of course, we have the Ten commands, but also there are another 603 commands that God gave in the Tanakh that the people are to keep.

So this is the Covenant that God gave at Mt. Sinai, but later, if you read through the prophets, you find that the prophets are adding greater understanding to the Covenant. They are giving greater insight.

For instance, God says, "Keep the Shabbat. Keep it holy to Me. Don't work. Rest and have a holy convocation." That's what

God says about the Shabbat. But Isaiah gives us this amazing insight that Shabbat should be a delight.

> Isaiah 58:13-14 *If you turn back your foot from Shabbat, from doing your pleasure on My holy day, and call Shabbat a delight, the holy day of ADONAI honorable, If you honor it, not going your own ways, not seeking your own pleasure, nor speaking your usual speech, 14 then You will delight yourself in ADONAI, and I will let you ride over the heights of the earth, I will feed you with the heritage of your father Jacob." For the mouth of ADONAI has spoken.*

See how that changes everything. It's not to be a burden. It's to be a delight.

Now, God's plan for Yeshua was that a Passover Seder was supposed to be His last meal with his disciples. All four Gospels record this Seder, but John devotes five chapters to it. I just want to point out a couple of things here because some people think he only devotes two chapters to it, chapters 13 and 14 because at the end of 14 in verse 31, it ends with the words *"Get up. Let's get going!"* So people think they ended the Seder there, but then in the beginning of chapter 18, look at what it says:

> John 18:1 *After Yeshua had said all this, he went out with his talmidim across the stream that flows in winter through the Vadi Kidron, to a spot where there was a grove of trees; and he and his talmidim went into it.*

Do you see what it says in the beginning of this verse? He might have said, "Let's get going" at the end of chapter 14, but they didn't actually leave until the beginning of chapter 18. So actually chapters 13 through 17 are all happening at the Last Seder with His disciples.

That's why I said that more verses of the Gospels are devoted to this event than anything else in the entire four Gospels: more than His birth, more than His death, more than the Sermon on the Mount, more than His Resurrection, more than any of those things. So why is so much devoted to this? Why five chapters?

I think it is because at His Last Seder, Yeshua actually gave the heart of the New Covenant, and He gave the renewal ceremony, actually two renewal ceremonies, of the Covenant.

So now understand that we refer to the entire back of the book as the New Covenant. Right? But when you read through it, you see that a lot of it is narrative. That's not the heart of the Covenant. Right? Then there's the history of the followers of Yeshua, of how they walked it out, in the Book of Acts.

Then there are letters of instruction to different congregations, which are all a part of giving more insight into it. But the incredible promises of the New Covenant are recorded in John 13-17, and the conditions are there, too.

One question that occurred to me as I was looking at this was: Why did God choose to use a traditional Passover Seder as the occasion to give us the New Covenant? And I see a couple of answers. I'll give you one now and one later.

I believe He gave the new Covenant at the renewal meal of the Mosaic Covenant to emphasize the continuity, the connectedness between the two Covenants. The New Covenant is built on the Mosaic Covenant, which is built on the Abrahamic Covenant, which is built on a Noahide Covenant. See, they don't nullify each other. They build on each other. They improve, in a sense, on each other.

That continuity, as you may know, has been lost in the church for the past 1700+ years because the church is not keeping the Passover or the covenantal times that were given to us. But praise God, in our days, this is changing. The fact that there are Messianic synagogues, and the fact that they have Messianic Passover Seders and Shabbat services on Saturdays are indications, but also the fact that many pastors and many Christians are very interested in this right now indicates this change. It's all over the internet. There's all kinds of ways to learn more about the Jewish roots because so many people are interested.

I felt led by the Spirit to go through the core of the New Covenant and look at its promises and its conditions. I love to do this at a Seder, but there's so much to do there that it's hard to fit it all in. But it is so important and appropriate that people know what the New Covenant is really all about.

So we're going to look at what Yeshua said and did at His last Passover Seder, and we're going to look at it in a lot of detail. It's so important because this is the core of the Covenant that He made with you and me. We all need to be periodically reminded of its promises and its conditions. It needs to be renewed in our minds and hearts. So we're going to start with the promises and then we'll get to the conditions. We will end with looking at the Renewal Ceremony of the Lord's Supper to seal it all in our hearts.

So rather than go through them the way they're structured in the chapters as He spoke these things, I rearranged them by subject. Okay? So we're going to go through a lot of verses here. Actually, each verse that we're going to look at could be a complete sermon by itself, but we're just going to look at each one briefly. I think the Spirit's intent is just to renew them in our minds.

Your part as we go through them is to receive these promises and then let them speak to your heart. Actually what you should do is, as you see each Scripture, you should read it aloud because I think you get a little more out of it when you hear them. Read them as if the LORD were speaking to you as He gives you these promises.

Understand that God is able to fulfill these promises. He doesn't make promises that He can't keep. So these are promises that you can hang your hat on because He's going to do these things.

Also understand that receiving His promises is conditional on being one of His disciples. That means very simply trusting in His atoning sacrifice to pay for your sin and making Him LORD or Boss or Director of your life. So if you've done that, then these are promises to you, individually, directly.

If you haven't, you can do that right now. Just declare to the Lord yourself that you want to make Him LORD. Repent for your sin and thank Him for taking your sin and for forgiving you because you repented in the Name of Yeshua.

So we're going to move through these relatively quickly. The first one was given after Yeshua washed His disciples feet. He said these words to them. Go ahead and read them out loud. Put your heart into it.

> John 13:14-17 *Now if I, the Lord and Rabbi, have washed your feet, you also should wash each other's feet. 15 For I have set you an example, so that you may do as I have done to you. ... 17 If you know these things, you will be blessed if you do them.*

So here's the promise. You will receive Yeshua's blessing for following not just His words, but also His example. In washing their feet, He was serving them. So you will be blessed by following His example of serving others. So receive that.

> John 17:24 *Father, I want those you have given me to be with me where I am; so that they may see my glory, which you have given me because you loved me before the creation of the world.*

This is interesting because this promise is in the form of a prayer from Yeshua to the Father. I consider that a promise because I believe all of His prayers get answered. So here's the promise. You will someday be with Yeshua in Heaven and see His Glory. Just receive that.

> John 14:2 *In my Father's house are many places to live. If there weren't, I would have told you; because I am going there to prepare a place for you.*

The promise is this. Someday you will live in a home prepared for you by Yeshua. He will be the architect and the builder, so, it will be amazing! And it will satisfy your very deepest heart's desire because He knows everything about you.

> John 14:3 *Since I am going and preparing a place for you, I will return to take you with me; so that where I am, you may be also.*

He's going to come back. You're not going to have to find your way there. He is going to come back and take you with Him to that place.

> John 14:12 *Yes, indeed! I tell you that whoever trusts in me will also do the works I do! Indeed, he*

will do greater ones, because I am going to the Father.

Now let's just stop on this one because I think many people, including myself at times, have unbelief about this one. This is a huge promise! Right? So let's just receive it. You will do greater works than Yeshua. *Lord, we don't know how You are going to do that in us, but that's Your promise. You really promised that.* Whoever trusts in Yeshua. Do you trust in Him? You will do greater works than Yeshua Himself did, if you trust in Him and allow Him to work through you.

> John 14:13-14 *In fact, whatever you ask for in my name, I will do; so that the Father may be glorified in the Son. 14 If you ask me for something in my name, I will do it.*

Here's the promise: you're prayers in Yeshua's Name will be answered. However, there is a condition on this one. Do you see the condition? They must be glorifying to the Father. The prayers that glorify the Father will be answered.

> John 15:7 *If you remain united with me, and my words with you, then ask whatever you want, and it will happen for you.*

This is another amazing promise. Your prayers will be answered. But again, it's conditional. What is the condition? Remaining in Him. Abiding in Yeshua. That means worshiping Him, His Words living in you, being in His presence, hearing from Him. If that's your lifestyle, you will begin to pray prayers that He can answer. That's how I understand this. Your prayers will be aligned with His will, and He'll begin to answer those prayers.

> John 14:15-16 *If you love me, you will keep my commands; 16 and I will ask the Father, and he will give you another comforting Counselor like me, the Spirit of Truth, to be with you forever.*

So this is the promise of the Ruakh, the Holy Spirit. Notice it says that He will comfort you and counsel you forever. He will comfort you and guide you. The way I understand this is He will be like a legal counselor, helping us to understand God's Torah, God's Law, His instructions, and how we are to follow them. He will guide us with His counsel. But also here, there are two conditions. Do you see them? *Love Me and keep My commands.*

Here is another one about the Ruakh. Read it with confidence.

> John14:26 *But the Counselor, the Ruach HaKodesh, whom the Father will send in my name, will teach you **everything**; that is, he will remind you of **everything** I have said to you.*

Whoo! This is a promise that the Holy Spirit will reveal to you understanding of all that Yeshua has said. Now what all has Yeshua said? Well, the Words in red, some people would think, right? Is that what you think? You know it's a trick question, right? He's the Living Word! He wrote it! It's the whole Word! He will bring understanding and remembrance of His Words—His whole Word to us!!

Here's one more on the Holy Spirit.

> John16:13 *However, when the Spirit of Truth comes, he will guide you into all the truth; for he will not speak on his own initiative but will say only what he hears. He will also announce to you the events of the future.*

Wow! The Holy Spirit will reveal Truth. There's a difference between giving understanding and showing you what is Truth, because what if you hear somebody speaking or you read somebody else's writing and you understand it, is that Truth? Does it line up with Biblical Truth? That's the job of the Ruakh, the Holy Spirit, to reveal that to you. And He will reveal the future to us!

Remember, read it loud and clear.

> John14:21 *Whoever has my commands and keeps them is the one who loves me, and the one who loves me will be loved by my Father, and I will love him and reveal myself to him.*

Amazing! You are loved! You are *already* loved. This is not a "will be." You are already loved by the Father and by Yeshua and He will reveal Himself to you. You will get to know Him as a being, as the Lord. You will know Him intimately. And again, this one has conditions. Do you see what they are? *Has My commands and keeps them.* Those are the conditions.

> John 15:9 *Just as my Father has loved me, I too have loved you; so stay in my love.*

Now, this is amazing. You just have to grasp this. Yeshua is saying here that you are loved by Yeshua as the Father loves Him. Do you see that? *As my Father has loved me, I too have loved you.* Can you receive that? How much does the Father love Yeshua? That's how much Yeshua loves you! That's amazing! How could anyone love someone more than that?! 17:23 says almost the same thing, but with just a little twist of difference. Read it aloud the way Yeshua might have prayed it.

> John 17:23 *I united with them and you with me, so that they may be completely one, and the world thus realize that you sent me, and that you have loved them just as you have loved me.*

Do you see the difference between this one and the last one? The other one was saying, Yeshua loves you as the Father loves Him. This is saying, the Father loves you as He loves Yeshua. How could there be any greater love than that?! Right? How much does He love Yeshua? Whoo! It's His Son. It's Himself! Are you sitting there, stunned?! He does!! He loves you this way! Receive it! Believe it!

> John 17:26 *I made your name known to them, and I will continue to make it known; so that the love with which you have loved me may be in them, and I myself may be united with them.*

Now what's the promise here? I believe the promise here is that the Father's love by which He loved Yeshua, will be **in you** in the sense that then it can pour out to other people. So that you can have that love in you, so that you can love others.

> John 13:35 *Everyone will know that you are my talmidim* [or disciples] [Come on, you're getting a little weak. Read it out loud with gusto.] *by the fact that you have love for each other.*

So, here's a promise. If we show love to our brothers and sisters here, the world will be able to recognize that we are the disciples of Messiah because they will have never seen love like that before. That's an awesome promise, too.

> John 14:7 *Because you have known me, you will also know my Father; from now on, you do know him—in fact, you have seen him.*

So here we have the promise of not just knowing Yeshua, but knowing the Father.

> John 14:23 *Yeshua answered him, "If someone loves me, he will keep my word; and my Father will love him, and we will come to him and make our home with him.*

So, this is the promise of the indwelling. This is the promise of the Father and Yeshua, of course, in the form of the Spirit dwelling, living in you and in me, in all who will trust in Him. And of course, there's a condition. It's a repeat. Love Yeshua and keep His Word. He has given this condition a couple of times already.

> John 15:5 *I am the vine and you are the branches. Those who stay united with me, and I with them, are the ones who bear much fruit; because apart from me you can't do a thing.*

Awesome promise! You will bear much fruit. Condition? Abiding in Yeshua, spending time with Him, listening to Him, following in His Ways, listening for His voice, spending time in prayer, never being apart from Him.

> John 15:11 *I have said this to you so that my joy may be in you, and your joy be complete.*

Wonderful! And no conditions. You will have complete joy—the joy that Yeshua has.

Remember, use your voice to read it.

> John 14:27 *What I am leaving with you is shalom [peace]—I am giving you my shalom. I don't give the way the world gives. Don't let yourselves be upset or frightened.*

You will have Yeshua's shalom; not the world's shalom that's dependent on circumstances, but Yeshua's shalom. And *shalom* in Hebrew, by the way, means more than just *peace*. It means *prosperity,* it's *health*, it's *well-being*, it's *fulfillment*. It's all those things. You will have that shalom in you. And the condition—see the condition? Don't give in to fear. Don't let yourself be upset or frightened.

> John 17:22 *The glory which you have given to me, I have given to them; so that they may be one, just as we are one*

So this is promising unity among the brethren, and Yeshua's glory. And remember we learned that the glory of God is His Goodness. So He's saying that you will have My Goodness. And that's why we can be in unity, because we need His Goodness in us. We need to have that inner moral purity to be able to have that unity with our brothers and sisters.

> John 15:16 *You did not choose me, I chose you; and I have commissioned you to go and bear fruit, fruit that will last; so that whatever you ask from the Father in my name he may give you.*

Whoo! This is a promise of being chosen and commissioned. You have already been chosen and commissioned for what? To bear fruit! And when you are in the process of bearing fruit, if you're praying prayers that lead to bearing fruit, they will be answered! They *will* be answered!

> John 17:15 *I don't ask you to take them out of the world, but to protect them from the Evil One.*

We have the promise of protection from ha-satan.

> John 17:17 *Set them apart for holiness by means of the truth—your word is truth.*

RENEWING THE NEW

We have the promise of being set apart for the Lord—separated unto Him.

So, those are some of the promises. Here are some of the conditions. Let's just read these together, too.

> John 14:1 *Don't let yourselves be disturbed. Trust in God and trust in me.*

Again, don't give in to worry and anxiety. Trust in the Father and in Yeshua.

> John 15:12-13 *This is my command: that you keep on loving each other just as I have loved you. 13 No one has greater love than a person who lays down his life for his friends.*

This is a pretty heavy command. We are to love one another as He loves us. And we know that He gave His Life for us. So the implication is clear. Right? We must be to be willing to lay down our lives for each other.

Then we have commemorations or ceremonies. Here's the footwashing ceremony again.

> John 13:14 *Now if I, the Lord and Rabbi, have washed your feet, you also should wash each other's feet. 15 For I have set you an example, so that you may do as I have done to you.*

We should be eager to serve each other because of this command.

So, whew! It has come to the ceremonial meal. Let's read about it here. You don't have to read it aloud. This is the Covenant meal, the Renewal Meal of that Covenant for which we just read all the promises and conditions.

> Matthew 26:26-28 *While they were eating, Yeshua took a piece of* matzah, *made the* b'rakhah *[the blessing], broke it, gave it to the* talmidim *[the disciples] and said, "Take! Eat! This is my body!" 27 Also he took a cup of wine, made the* b'rakhah, *and gave it to them, saying, "All of you, drink from it! 28 For this is my blood, which ratifies the New*

Covenant, my blood shed on behalf of many, so that they may have their sins forgiven.

So this is the instruction for the Covenant Meal. There is the promise at the end of it of having our sins forgiven. We call this the *S'udat Adonai* or The Lord's Supper. It is just like the elders eating before the Lord. It's just like the commandments for the Passover. It's eating and drinking as a commemoration of the Covenant. Before we do this, I want to just end with one final reason for giving the New Covenant at a Passover Seder, at the Renewal Meal of the Mosaic Covenant. I believe that the most important reason is so that we would remember that God keeps His promises to Israel. That's what the Covenant Meal is about. And in remembering that God is keeping His promises to Israel, we have assurance that He will keep His promises in the New Covenant because how can we believe the promises of the New Covenant, if we don't see Him keeping His promises to Israel? That's why we renew both Covenants at the Passover Seder.

Now I want you to look over the promises as they are listed below and pray to receive those promises into your heart.

Prayer:

So Father, I pray that as we look at these Words, our faith will grow. You are a God of Words, and You are a God that keeps Your Word. You are a God that is not silent. You are a God that spoke to Your people and fulfilled what You said. I pray Lord that as we read these Words, they would sink into our hearts and we would receive them and believe them. In Yeshua's Name.

Promise of blessing for following Yeshua's example of serving
Promise of being with Yeshua in heaven and seeing His glory
Promise that someday I will live in a home prepared for me by Yeshua in Heaven
Promise of Yeshua returning to get me and bring me there to be with Him
Promise that I will do greater works than Yeshua did
Promise that my prayers in Yeshua's Name will be answered

Promise the Ruakh HaKodesh will be with me to comfort and counsel and teach me all Yeshua has said, the entire Bible, and reveal the Truth and the future to me
Promise that I am loved by the Father and Yeshua
Promise that Yeshua will reveal Himself to me
Promise of the Father's love by which He loves Yeshua being in me, so I can love others
Promise that I will know the Father
Promise that the Father and Yeshua will dwell in me
Promise that I will bear much fruit if I abide in Yeshua
Promise that I will have His joy, complete joy
Promise that I'll have Yeshua's shalom, peace, not dependent on circumstances
Promise that I will have Yeshua's glory—His Goodness
Promise that I am chosen and commissioned by Yeshua to bear fruit
Promise that my prayers will be answered to enable me to bear fruit
Promise that I will be protected by the Father from ha-satan
Promise that I am set apart by the Father for holiness
Promise of having my sins forgiven
This is all in addition to God's other promises of healing, deliverance, power over ha-satan, wisdom, etc.

Conditions:
I must trust in my Heavenly Father and Yeshua.
I must keep Yeshua's commandments—which include the Torah since He wrote it.
I must abide in Yeshua—have discipline to read, pray, worship, be in His presence.
I must love Yeshua.
I must love others as He has loved me, laying down His Life for me.
I must not give in to worry or anxiety.

So, Father, we just thank You for these incredible promises. We've spoken them to ourselves. We've read them to ourselves.

We've heard them today. We pray, Father, that they would be real to us. We also thank You, Father, for explaining to us the conditions. We ask that we would be able to fulfill those conditions of keeping Your commandments, trusting in You, loving You, abiding in You, and not giving in to fear or worry. We thank You. We thank You.

Now let's go further and seal these Covenant promises by taking Communion together, you and me. Right now. Please go get your grape juice or wine and Matzah (or bread if you are reading this before Passover and have no Matzah yet). I will wait. Now go ahead and pour the wine or juice into your goblet or glass.

Taking Communion

Alright. Let's take communion. Lift up your Matzah, and say the blessing for bread with me:

"Barukh Ata Adonai Elohenu Melekh HaOlam. Ha-motzi lekhem min ha-aretz. Blessed art Thou O Lord Our God, King of the Universe who brings forth bread from the earth."

Yeshua took the bread, blessed it and broke it and said, *"This is my body which is broken for you. Do this in remembrance of me."*

Now, break a good size piece off your Matzah and lift it up as we pray.

Lord, we thank You that You took the Matzah, said the blessing over it, and broke it, and said, *"This is my body which is given for you. Do this in remembrance of me."* We thank You for Your body that the broken Matzah represents. We thank You that Your body on that Cross is an entrance way through the veil, into Your Kingdom, into the presence of God where we receive all these amazing promises.

I thank You for allowing Your body to be broken to make all these promises available to me. Thank You.

Take and eat.

Now lift up your cup.
Say the blessing for wine with me:

"*Barukh Ata Adonai Elohenu Melekh HaOlam. Boreh pri hagafen.* Blessed art Thou O Lord Our God, King of the Universe who creates the fruit of the vine."

He blessed and gave thanks for the fruit of the vine and said *"This cup is the New Covenant in My Blood"*

Keep your cup lifted up as we pray:

Heavenly Father, we thank You for what we see in this Passover cup, that You poured out Your Blood to redeem us. You bought us back when we had been sold. We sold ourselves into slavery to sin and ha-satan where there were only curses—no blessed promises, and You bought us back by the most precious substance that has existed in the universe—the Blood of the Son of God. We thank You for Your Blood and we thank You for giving us this "symbolic tradition" to do in remembrance of You, that we might remember Your Blood that was poured out for us, and remember all the promises Your Blood secured for us.

Thank You for going through that horrific suffering in order to make this Covenant of promises with me. I will never be able to thank You enough.

Take and drink. This is the Blood of the New Covenant.

[In the next chapter, we will study in more depth this cup of Communion—the Cup of Redemption—the Third Cup—along with all the other cups of the Passover meal.]

CHAPTER 19
THE CUPS OF THE COVENANT

One of the main focuses of the Seder Meal is the four cups, the Covenant renewal drinks of the Mosaic covenant, two before dinner, and two after. In Israel there's a fifth cup—the cup of the land. I realized recently that there should be a sixth cup. I will explain that later.

I always explain the four Cups at our Community Seder, but I can't go into depth as much as I would like to there, so I am going to explain all the wonderful, deep significance here.

We're going to look at the cups of the Covenant and we're going to see that they are like guide posts or labels or instructions for our walk with the Lord, for our walk from bondage to freedom.

We learned in the last two chapters that in the Bible whenever a covenant was made, it was almost always sealed by the people eating and drinking together. So when God makes His Covenants, He gives meals for making that Covenant and then for renewing it. So, the four cups that we drink during Passover

---

* Photo: Blessing the wine. Yemenite Habani family celebrating the Passover Seder at their new home in Tel Aviv, 1946, Wikimedia, public domain.

Seder, known as the Cups of the Covenant, are part of the Covenant renewal ceremony that renews the Mosaic Covenant.

In Exodus 6, God promises the Israelites what He was about to do.

> Exodus 6:6 *"Therefore, say to the people of Isra'el: 'I am ADONAI. I will bring you out from under the yoke of the Egyptians. I will free you from being slaves to them, and I will redeem you with an outstretched arm and with mighty acts of judgment. 7 I will take you as my own people, and I will be your God. Then you will know that I am ADONAI your God, who freed you from the forced labor of the Egyptians. 8 I will bring you into the land which I swore to give to Avraham, Yitz'chak and Ya'akov - I will give it to you as your inheritance. I am ADONAI.'"*

There are six promises here. They are represented in the four cups. But what I saw in studying this is that they also represent six steps in each of our walks with the Lord, from the bondage of this world to freedom in the Spirit. So that's what we're going to talk about here.

The First Cup

The first cup is called the Cup of Sanctification. It is a memorial of God's promise in that first verse: *"I will bring you out from under the yokes* [The Hebrew word *sfilot* is plural.] *of the Egyptians"*

The word there for *"I will bring you out"* is *hoh-tzeh-ti – bring you out, separate you from,* and we would understand it as *sanctify you,* meaning, I will separate you from Egypt and separate you to Me. Sanctification is separating you to God. So that's what God is promising, that He will bring them out and to Himself.

So how does this apply to us today? None of us are slaves in Egypt. The traditional book that we follow for the Seder called the Haggadah says that Egypt represents the sinful world we live in, and that we have become part of Egypt because we have participated in this world. This is talking about all of us coming out of Egypt. Yeshua talks about this.

> John 8:34 *Yeshua answered them, "Yes, indeed! I tell you that everyone who practices sin is a slave of sin.*

God promises in the verse in Exodus to separate us from the power that this world has over us due to our sin and the bondages that ha-satan has put on us. Yeshua prayed to the Father for His followers to be sanctified, set apart.

> John 17:17 *Set them apart [sanctify them] for holiness by means of the truth—your word is truth.*

So here He tells us what the means of sanctification is. Do you see it? It is His Word. The Word is what takes us out of Egypt and brings us into the Kingdom of God. It is the first step of our spiritual growth. A verse in Romans that is a very familiar verse tells us this.

> Romans 10:17 *So trust [faith] comes from what is heard, and what is heard comes through a word proclaimed about the Messiah.*

When a person hears God's Words about the Messiah and puts their trust in Him and His sacrifice, they are brought out from this world and set apart for God. This happened to me, and I hope it has happened to you. I actually didn't hear the Word proclaimed, I *read* the Word from two good Jewish boys, Mattityahu and Yochanan. Do you know who they are? They are Matthew and John. And I received the Word, and obeyed it. I repented of my sin, and put my trust in Yeshua and His sacrifice on the Cross, and committed my life to following Him.

I can still go back to that moment in time as if it was yesterday. I knew instantaneously that it was the most important moment in my life. I knew I was entering into a new life. And like Yeshua said, it was like being born all over again. I was no longer a part of this world or of Egypt. I was set apart for the Lord. My sins had been forgiven.

I was right with God, and I knew that He loved me. I knew I could hear from Him, and serving Him became my number one priority. That wasn't hard because the rewards of this world, they just sort of faded away. They were vain. They were empty. They had lost their importance to me.

So that's what happened to me, and we're going to pray later about being brought out and set apart for God. But, I want to encourage you that when you take the Cup of Sanctification at a Seder this year, if you're still enslaved by any of the things of this world, realize that only God can bring you out, and use that first cup as a time of prayer to break off those things. If you're already set free, use that cup as a time of thanksgiving to God for bringing you out of Egypt.

The Second Cup

The second Cup of the Covenant is called the Cup of Deliverance. It is from the second phrase in verse 6.

> Exodus 6:6 ... *I will free you from being slaves to them*

When I first learned about the cups and I read this passage, I didn't understand it because it seemed like God was just repeating Himself. What difference is there between *bringing us out from under the yoke* and *freeing us*?

> Exodus 6:6 *I will bring you out from under the yoke of the Egyptians. I will free you from being slaves to them*

It didn't make much sense to me. But, you know, I've learned that whenever it seems like the Bible is repeating itself, but is a little bit different, there's an important meaning in it. The two words in Hebrew are very different. *Bring you out* in Hebrew is *Ho-tzeh-ti* and *free you from* is *Hee-tsal-ti*. They are two very different words.

Bring you out – Ho-tzeh-ti – separate you from –
   Cup of Sanctification
Free you from – Hee-tsal-ti – rid you of the bondage –
   Cup of Deliverance

So sanctification means to separate you out from your former slave masters to God. It's like escaping slavery, basically. But deliverance is what the second word is, and it means to remove the slave mentality. Think about this. Imagine that a slave escapes after being a slave all his life, but he's still wearing the distinctive clothing of a slave. Maybe he's even still got the shackles on his hands. Maybe he got them off his feet and ran, but he still has them on his hands. But more than that, the person who was a slave all their life, what's in their mind? There's the mentality of a slave. They've been abused. They've been mistreated. They've been crushed all their lives. They are broken people.

This is a huge theme in the Book of Exodus. The Israelites were separated from the Egyptians out in the desert, right? But they still needed deliverance from their old slave mentality. As you read through Exodus and through Numbers, you can see that the slave mentality brought destruction on the people over and over again.

When God brought them out of Egypt, they were afraid He wouldn't feed them. They were afraid He wouldn't give them water. Remember that? When Moses was away too long, they were afraid he had deserted them. Finally, when it was time to go up and take the Land, what happened? Remember? They were afraid to go and take it. God had parted the Red Sea and destroyed the Egyptian army. Still they thought, "He's not going to enable us to take the Land.

So what had to happen? That slave mentality amongst those people was so strong that, except for only two people—Joshua and Caleb, the entire generation that had been slaves had to die in the desert before the next generation that had never been slaves could take land. To me, what it seems like is that God could not re-train those people. That slave mentality was so strong that they were never going to become the warriors that they needed to be to go and take that Land. They simply could not stop thinking as slaves.

So what's the meaning of this to us today? When we are born from above, do we hang onto our slave mentality? This was my experience. When I was set apart for God, I was transferred into His Kingdom, but you know what? I brought along my suitcase. ☺ What was in my suitcase? Baggage. ☺ Lots of baggage.

What's some of the baggage people bring into the Kingdom of God? Well, some people bring addictions. I did. I was still smoking pot when I came into the Kingdom of God, and I didn't stop until several months later when the light went on.

People bring the baggage of hurts they've experienced, wounds that haven't healed, fears, obsessions, bitterness, anger, and broken hearts. Many people bring the baggage of low self esteem. They don't think much of themselves. They don't think God can use them.

Others bring the baggage of idolatry. They've got things that are really important to them—more important than God. Some bring the baggage of curses they've brought upon themselves or vows that they've made, or generational curses. Sometimes the baggage is actually self hatred. Another one I've seen is people bring a need to show the value they have. They always have to be looking good. They always have to perform so people will look up to them. Others have the need to always please people. All of those things.

That's what the cup of deliverance is all about. Yes, we are brought into the Kingdom of God, but we need to get rid of the baggage. We need deliverance from our slave mentality. Yeshua talks about this.

> *John 14:15 I no longer call you slaves, because a slave doesn't know what his master is about; but I have called you friends, because everything I have heard from my Father I have made known to you.*

When I first read that, I said, "Wow! He's taking away my slave mentality. He's making me a friend—a friend of God!" I still needed a lot of deliverance, and it was a process. Not only did I need to be set free from smoking pot, but I had practiced yoga for years. I needed to be set free from worshipping false gods.

Actually, those two things were relatively easy. The harder things were pride, needing to demonstrate to other people that I was good, so they would look up to me, and thinking I could do everything on my own.

Another thing that I had to be delivered from was that I had been wounded by rejection. I was a very shy person. I remember when a friend from high school re-contacted me and found out

I was a rabbi, he was shocked. He said, "You were the shyest guy in high school. How could you be a rabbi?" It was the Lord. He delivered me from that fear of being rejected, and also that need to demonstrate my self-worth all the time, to have people think highly of me.

Actually, I'm learning a couple of these things from reading Henry Wright's material. He's done a lot of work with Jewish people, and what he has discovered is that those last two are strongholds over the Jewish community: rejection because of all the persecution we have suffered, and the attitude of having to strive to achieve due to tradition. You've heard the stories about Jewish mothers that all of the children have to be doctors and lawyers. What's that about? The kids grow up with all this pressure to succeed, to become a professional, and it affects many people in a negative way.

We're going to pray later for deliverance from bondages. Again, when you take the Cup of Deliverance this year at a Seder, don't just take it as a cup. Take it as deliverance from that slave mentality, from the baggage, and from whatever else the Ruakh HaKodesh reveals that you are dragging behind you on wheels or carrying on your back in your backpack. And if you don't have any baggage, pray for your loved ones to be set free. There is probably someone you know that has some stuff they need deliverance from. Declare deliverance over them.

The Third Cup

The third cup in the Seder is called the Cup of Redemption. It is based on this verse.

> Exodus 6:6... I will redeem you with an outstretched arm and with mighty acts of judgment.

Those phrases are very important. The Hebrew word for *redeem* is *Gah-alti*. It means I will pay the ransom for you.

What exactly does redeem mean? We have a great example of it in our culture. When we go to the store and we buy a six-pack of pop, we have to pay an extra 5 cents per bottle. When we finish it, we bring it back to the machine and we redeem it.

But actually, we don't redeem them, the store redeems them. The original owner is buying them back from us for 5 cents. They are paying the redemption price.

This is how it worked in Egypt. The Israelites were God's people when they went down into Egypt. They were free people descended from Avraham, Yitz'chak, and Ya'akov. They were free people. But after many years, the Egyptians enslaved them and claimed legal ownership of them. Slavery was legal in that culture, so they were legally slaves.

Israelites needed to be redeemed because even when they had gotten out, they needed to be redeemed so that the Egyptian slave owners would no longer have any legal claim on them; so they couldn't come after them five years later and say, "I found you. You're coming back to Egypt. You're my slave." They had to be redeemed so they could not be dragged back into slavery. This is very important to understand about what redemption means.

In this verse, remember I said that there are several very important phrases in it. It says that God **stretched out His arm,** with mighty acts of judgment. What was that? That was the ten plagues and the destruction of the Egyptian army. What was the Egyptian army trying to do? They were trying to take them back. Even though they had let them go free, now, "No, no, no. You're legally my slave. I'm coming after you, and I'm going to bring you back."

This was accomplished in fulfillment of this prophecy that was given by Moses before any of this happened. How was the Egyptian army destroyed? Moses **stretched out his arm** with the staff over the Red Sea, and the waters came back on them. That was God's act of judgment that no, they're not going to get you back because they are all dead. The entire Egyptian army just got wiped out and you are now free people. He redeemed them and made them His people—free people.

How does redemption apply to us today?

> *John 8:34 Yeshua answered them, "Yes, indeed! I tell you that everyone who practices sin is a slave of sin.*

So because we've all sinned, or is it just me? Am I the only one who has sinned? Here's the thing to understand. Because we have sinned, ha-satan has a legal claim on us. So, we all need to be redeemed to have that legal claim negated.

At Yeshua's Last Passover Seder, He declared that this cup, the Cup of Redemption, would become the Cup of the New Covenant, ratified by His Blood, meaning sealed or signed by His Blood. That cup, the third cup, became the Cup of the Lord's Supper. Understand this amazing connection, that that cup of Communion is the renewal covenant drink of the New Covenant. He used the covenant drink of the Old Covenant to give us the covenant drink of the New Covenant.

Why did He choose the traditional Cup of Redemption? Why not the Cup of Sanctification or the Cup of Deliverance? I think it is because of all the cups, the Cup of Redemption most clearly describes His greatest work. What is His greatest work? Well, God is a God of justice. So every crime, every breaking of His Law requires that there be a fitting penalty. The penalty has to be paid. So whenever a law is broken, whoever broke it, ha-satan has a claim on that. You have to pay for that way in which you broke the law.

When the Temple was in operation, according to the Law that God set up in the Bible, there was a way to pay that penalty by sacrificing an animal. But we can't do that anymore because there's been no Temple for the almost 2000 years. And for some of the laws, if you broke them, the only penalty was death.

But God loves us so much that He made a way for all the penalties to be paid. He came to earth as a miracle working Jewish Torah teacher. That's what He was. He was named Yeshua, and He allowed Himself to be executed by evil men who envied Him. And Yeshua's sacrifice paid the penalty for all the sins past, present, and future of everyone who trusts in Him. We need to see that it was about more than just being forgiven. He suffered and died and paid the penalty not just so we can be forgiven, but also so that we can be redeemed, so that the enemy would not have any claim on us any longer.

In Egypt, remember that God redeemed Israel *with an outstretched arm and mighty acts of judgment,* the ten plagues and the destruction of the Egyptian army. Well, 1500 years later on a hill outside Jerusalem, Yeshua fulfilled this prophesy. He redeemed all who would put their trust in Him. It was such an incredible, prophetic thing because He did it **with two outstretched arms and with mighty acts of judgment.** He stretched out His arms and allowed Himself to be nailed to a Roman cross, and He suffered terribly and died. That was the stretching out of His arms.

But what about the mighty acts of judgment? Instead of sending the plagues on us and all of the human race who deserved them and still deserve them, here's what He did. He received what we deserved. He took all the judgments upon Himself. That's what paid the penalty so that there is no debt that the enemy can claim on us. He received upon Himself all the judgment and penalty due all people for all time for all their sins, thereby redeeming us by paying the penalty each of us owed. It is such a beautiful thing. Peter talks about this.

> 1 Peter 1:18-19 (NKJV) ... *you were not redeemed with corruptible things, like silver or gold, from your aimless conduct received by tradition from your fathers, 19 but with the precious blood of* [Messiah], *as of a lamb without blemish and without spot.*

This is to me such a beautiful picture of the goodness of God. This is the true glory of God. Rather than sending judgments on the people who deserve it, He takes the judgment on Himself so that we don't have to experience the punishment.

Yeshua declared the Cup of Redemption to be the Cup of renewal of the New Covenant. So when you get to that Cup of Redemption in the Passover Seder, that's what it is all about. You've been redeemed. The penalty has been paid, so nobody has any claim on you. You were bought by the sacrifice of the Lamb of God on the Cross.

But, there's another aspect to redemption that I want to point out.

Baggage

It speaks of a third step of spiritual freedom because there's another step to spiritual freedom in addition to that. Remember that redemption means our former slave owners—sin and ha-satan—have no legal right to drag us back into slavery because the price of our freedom has been paid by Yeshua. But there are things in our baggage that drag us back. Have you experienced that? What are the things in our baggage that give the enemy legal claim on us to drag us back into Egypt, into our past?

1. What if I made some kind of a vow before I came to the Lord and I never fulfilled it? Where does that stand legally? Ha-satan has a claim on it. I need to fulfill that vow. The promise of Redemption is that Yeshua's redemption can break the enemy's claim on that vow.

What's another thing in our baggage? Debts.

2. When we sin against someone in a way that harms them, we owe them a debt. Right? In Tanakh, restitution had to be made to fix the damage they did before the guilt offering could be brought. In other words, if you stole something from someone, you had to pay them back before your guilt offering could make you right with God. You couldn't just bring an offering and be forgiven. You had to make restitution first.

In the same way, we have to make it right in any way that we have hurt people. But there are some people that we've hurt that we can never make it right. Maybe they died. Or maybe they wouldn't receive it. Thankfully, Yeshua's redeeming sacrifice can negate that legal claim against us.

Here are a couple more pieces of baggage:

3. Guilt over wrongs we've done in the past gives ha-satan a legal right to torment us about them until we receive Yeshua's sacrifice as being for our guilt.

4. Idols we have kept have a legal right to drag us back to Egypt.

These are some of the things that we drag around in that baggage. This year, when you come to that Cup of Redemption, if ha-satan still has a claim on you, realize that the Blood of the Lamb and only the Blood of the Lamb can redeem you from ha-satan's legal claims on you. Take that cup and declare that through the Cross that legal right is broken because you have been redeemed. If you've already been redeemed, give thanks for that too as you take the cup. We will pray later about that also.

The Fourth Cup

The fourth cup represents this part of the verse:

> Exodus 6:7... *I will take you as my own people, and I will be your God.*

This cup, interestingly, is traditionally called the Cup of the Kingdom. This is because when God brought our forefathers out of Egypt and gave them the Mosaic Covenant, He set up His nation, which was His Kingdom at that time. He made us His own chosen people and He was our God.

So this cup speaks of the fourth step toward spiritual freedom. What is that? It is that our mentality, our minds have to be renewed so that we start seeing ourselves, each one of us, as God's possession, as God's people. We have to see ourselves as one of His children, and we have to see Him as our God. That sounds pretty simple. Right? You might think, "Oh, yes. I've done that." But let me make it a little clearer.

If I am God's possession, what about all that I own? Who owns it? God owns it. If we are God's possession, shouldn't we have faith that He will take care of us and provide for us and protect us? Shouldn't we trust that He'll train us for whatever He calls us to do, that He'll give us the rest that we need, and that He will be seeking the best for us? The challenge is, are there ways that we don't believe all that? Are there some chinks in our belief system that says, "Well, I really don't trust Him to provide such and such." Well, this is a time to get that straight.

And then the other thing is that God is our God, which means that we are not to have any other gods before Him. So this is a time to seek the Lord when we take this fourth cup to ask, "Is there anything in my life, Lord, that is more important than You? Do I do other things rather than spend time with You?"

Whoa, that's a tough one. It's a tough one for me, maybe for you, too. We need to be ready to lay anything down that has become more important than Him and His Kingdom. Even ministry itself, even serving God can become more important to us than God. Can you see what I am saying there? It is very important to understand that because I've seen many people who burn out because they work hard for God, but don't spend any time with Him. They're not receiving any refreshing because they're not seeking Him, they're only seeking to do things for Him.

So we're going to pray for that later for each of us.

As you take the fourth cup at the Seder this year pray for the Ruakh HaKodesh to reveal ways that you can come into the fullness of being one of God's people and Him being your God.

The Fifth Cup

Now we come to the fifth cup. Like I said, the fifth cup is generally not done in America, but it's done in Israel. The fifth cup is called the Cup of the Land. It's from verse 8.

> Exodus 6:8 *I will bring you into the land which I swore to give to Avraham, Yitz'chak and Ya'akov - I will give it to you as your inheritance. I am ADONAI.'"*

Some believe that this fifth cup was part of the Seder prior to the Diaspora, before the Jewish people were scattered in 135 CE. When the people had the Land, the fifth cup was part of the tradition, but then it stopped being part of the traditional Seder until 1948, when it was added back in. Someone was looking at it and said they should put the cup back in because they were back in the Land. The verse had been fulfilled again in the restoration of the state of Israel.

But, as I studied it this time, I saw that there are actually two parts to this promise, so I believe there should be a fifth and sixth cup. Maybe I will start a new tradition. ☺ The first part of that verse says this:

> Exodus 6:8a *I will bring you into the land...*

I started to think about that. This is the promise of taking the people who had just come out of Egypt and were at Mt. Sinai— of taking them from Mt. Sinai to the Promised Land. And, you know, that didn't happen right away. If you've read your Bible, how long did that take? It took 40 years! It took 40 years in the desert during which time the older generation died out.

But as I understand it, that younger generation was being trained so that they were able to take the Land. They were trained by God to be warriors during that time in the desert, so when it came time to take the Land, they would be able to do it. And what about the un-teachable members of that older generation? They just had to die out because they couldn't be trained. That's a word for all of us who are over thirty because we see that a lot. We need to be teachable. ☺

While they were in the wilderness, the younger, post-slavery generation really learned to trust and obey God, even to the point of risking of their lives, even to going up into places where they thought they would be defeated.

So I call this cup, rather than the Cup of the Land, the **Cup of Discipleship** because that's what this was really about. Those 40 years were years of training.

How does this apply to us? Well, I don't know about you, but I've gone through some deserts. Have you? Maybe you're in the desert right now. We all go through years in the wilderness. It is a training time, a disciping time, a time to fulfill God's call on our lives. It's a time for our old man, our flesh, to die, so our new man can go and take the Land.

So we're going to pray to be discipled a little bit later.

When you take the fifth cup at the Seder this year, if you do this new tradition and have a fifth cup, pray to be submitted to His discipleship, to grow and endure the trials, to be conformed to image of Yeshua.

The Sixth Cup

Finally, we have the rest of this verse.

Exodus 6:8b ...*I will give it to you as your inheritance.*

This I saw was the promise to Israel of taking possession of the Promised Land. But then I started thinking about that a little bit. Did they just walk up to the borders of the Land and it was theirs? No! There were seven years of warfare against enemies of God who they said made them look like grasshoppers. So it was a battle. They had to risk their lives, and they had to trust and obey God to achieve victory.

So the sixth cup. I call it the **Cup of Inheritance**.

How does this cup apply to us? Well God has a land He promises to us which we don't get if we don't fight for it. Did you know that? Did you know that you have a Promised Land? Some people think that's Heaven, but I have another interpretation. It's more than Heaven. What is that land God promises to give us? It's not just Heaven. Your Promised Land is all the things that God wants you to become and accomplish in your lifetime. Can you grasp that? That's your Promised Land. That's what you are supposed to take.

It's not just doing things. It's about who you are, about becoming who you are. It's about the Spirit being born in you. Your Promised Land is all that, and we're going to pray that you inherit the land; that you accomplish everything God has planned for you. That's my prayer and goal at this point in my life.

When it comes to the end of my life, I want to be able to say, "Lord, I did everything You wanted me to do. Nothing is missing." How about you? Wouldn't that be great? All to His Glory. They are all things that honor Him. I want to accomplish whatever He wants me to do.

So when you take this sixth cup, you can pray that you have courage and endurance for warfare to be able to take your Promised Land. I can tell you that it's not easy, and I'm sure you could tell me that it isn't easy. It's not easy to do the things God has called us to do. There can be lots of opposition on the outside, and there can be lots of opposition on the inside, too.

Get Rid of the Khametz Crumbs

When you first think about searching for all the khametz in your house, you first go to your bread box and your freezer, and you take out all the bread, but traditionally it's much more than that. Traditionally, you go into all the cupboards and you look for all the crumbs. You remove every crumb that might be in there from the past year from all the cupboards.

So what's that talking about spiritually? Those little crumbs, little sins, little foxes, they can mess the whole thing up. So this is about finding the little crumbs, the things that aren't obvious. It's easy to get rid of the obvious things because they're right there in your face, but it's those little attitudes that can have a big effect.

Somebody was telling me that they were realizing that they were an angry person, and that it affected everything about them. They just thought that was who they were. It was so much a part of them that they couldn't even see it. It was a hidden crumb. So I encourage you to clean out your spiritual house this year. Look for those little crumbs. Ask God to reveal them to you.

Let's pray.

Father, thank You for the Cups of the Covenant. We come before You right now, Father, and ask for sanctification. I pray that if this reader has not been set apart for You, Oh Lord, that this would be their moment to step across that line and to enter into Your Kingdom, and to repent for not following You and to begin a new life with You.

And, Father, for those of us who have entered in, we look behind us and we see that suitcase following us, full of the baggage that we have. And we often don't know how to get rid of it, Lord. So we pray for the moving of Your Ruakh to get rid of that baggage, to bring us deliverance. We also see the things that have happened before we came to You that have us bound in this life. Maybe it's relationships that we messed up. Maybe it's that we quit doing something, like school, that we shouldn't have because we were not following You. Maybe it's something that we committed ourselves to that we're bound to do now, but we need to get out of it because it's holding us back.

We thank You, Lord, that You redeemed us by the power of the Blood of the Lamb from all the things that the enemy holds on us. And Father, we pray that each of us would come into the fullness of the Cup of the Kingdom, that we would come to know that we are Your children and that You are our God, and that we would begin to live like that, with that knowledge every day.

And, Lord, we lift up the Cup of Discipleship, and we ask, Father, that You would have Your way in our life, to train us, and to prepare us for all that You have for us, and that we would have the courage to face what you have for us, Lord. And finally, Father, we lift up to You, the Cup of Inheritance. I pray that we would inherit the Land, that we would accomplish all that You want to be achieved in our lives before it's our time to leave, not only in what we do, but in who we are. And that You would do that by the power of Your Ruakh. In Yeshua's mighty Name. Amein.

> Cup of Sanctification - pray to be set apart for God
> Cup of Deliverance - pray for deliverance from bondages
> Cup of Redemption - pray to be redeemed by the blood of the Lamb
> Cup of the Kingdom - pray for each of us to be one of God's own people and for Him to be our God
> Cup of Discipleship - pray to be discipled
> Cup of Inheritance - pray to inherit the land

1st Cup Prayer: Sanctification

Let's pray

> Thank You for separating our forefathers, the Israelites, from the Egyptians, and separating them to You.
> Thank You that sanctification is part of the New Covenant.
> Here's the **promise** He wants each of us to receive.
> *"I will set you apart for Me as My child, by the truth of My Word"*
> We each receive Your promise today of being set apart for You.
> We covenant to walk in the fullness of this promise.

2nd Cup Prayer: Deliverance

> Thank You for delivering our forefathers the Israelites from the Egyptians, removing the bonds of slavery.
> Thank You that deliverance is part of the New Covenant
> Here's the **promise** He wants each of us to receive:

"I will deliver you from the bondages & baggage that is oppressing you, holding you back because you are no longer slaves but my friends"

We receive your promise tonight to take off our chains and our slave clothing.

Deliver us from the baggage, addictions, scars, fears, anger, bitterness, grief, low self esteem we have picked up in the world.

We receive Your promise to make us Your friend.

3rd Cup Prayer: Redemption

We covenant to walk in the fullness of these promises, those who find Yeshua, Whose body was broken so we can receive a Passover gift.

God has a gift He wants to give to all people. Not just those who find the Afikomen.

It's the gift of having our sins born away and of redemption, of having God's judgment <u>pass over</u> us.

We receive Your promise tonight that You have redeemed us by Your blood.

We covenant to walk in the fullness of this promise knowing sin and Satan have no legal claim on us.

May we receive and walk in the full power of that promise.

This is a memorial of the Passover Lamb sacrificed to cause the plague of death to pass over our forefathers' houses.

His act of redemption causes the plague of eternal death to Pass Over us, those who put their trust in it.

Here's His **promise** concerning the Cup of Redemption:

"I have redeemed you with the precious blood of Messiah, I have paid the price so sin & Satan has no legal claim against you"

4th Cup Prayer: The Kingdom

We are thankful you brought our forefathers out of Egypt and established Your nation, Your kingdom;

And that Your Kingdom is still prospering & growing in the hearts of Your followers.

We receive Your **renewal promise,**

"to provide all our needs as long as we are seeking first Your Kingdom."

Lord, may those of us who are searching to find the Kingdom of God find it.

May those of us who have found it establish it in our lives.

5th Cup Prayer: Discipleship

We thank You, Father that You are training us and discipling us to be ready to take the Land.

Help us to be submitted to Your discipleship; to grow and endure the trials; to be conformed to the image of Yeshua.

We receive Your **renewal promise,**

I will bring you into the land

6th Cup Prayer: Inheritance

We thank You, Father that you have given each one of us a Promised Land.

We pray that You will give us the courage to fight the fight needed to take possession of our Promised Land.

We pray that we will accomplish everything You have planned for us in our Promised Land.

We receive Your **renewal promise:**

I will give it to you as your inheritance.

CHAPTER 20
CHILDREN And Passover

One year, we had this wonderful testimony from Gina, a young mother in our congregation:

I had an awesome blessed week. This is turning out to be the most memorable Pesakh for me. I always wanted my children to come to Messiah on their own. I never wanted them to be coerced. I wanted the Holy Spirit to lead them.

So last night, we were doing our little Deuteronomy and our Exodus. We were putting on our shoes, girding up our loins and preparing for Passover, like cleaning out our khametz. We went through all our videos and said okay, does this video honor the Lord? (This is just for us. I don't want to put this on anyone else.) We got rid of lots of videos that we felt weren't of the Lord. We called it khametz. We said this one has witchcraft, so we're going to get rid of it, etc. And they were like tossing, "Yea, so does this one and this one." And I was thinking, "Wow, this is awesome."

So we got rid of a whole bunch of stuff. We cleaned out the house, all to prepare for Passover. And somehow we got talking about the Holy Spirit and about how to be in the Kingdom of God, we have to have the Holy Spirit living

---

* Photo: Musical Passover, 1960s. Found on a blog. No source given. Unable to find original or photographer.

CHAPTER 20

inside of us. And my daughter looked at me and she said, "Well, I want to be in His Kingdom. Help me, please." And I was getting ready to cry.

And my son said, "Yea, so do I!! How do you do that? How do you get into His Kingdom?"

I said, "You ask Jesus to save you. You trust Him as your Savior. You trust Yeshua, and then His Holy Spirit comes and lives inside you and leads you and guides you for the rest of your life."

And they were saying, "I want that! Pray with us!" And they were jumping up and down.

Now I've taught them the same thing every year. It's just this year that, you know, it's kind of like we've decided to be more obedient this year, like painfully obedient to God. And I'm watching the Lord really super bless us. So this is the most amazing Passover to me. So now I have two little babies that have taken the Holy Spirit in and they are loving Yeshua!

Let's pray

So, Father, we lift up all children who have turned their hearts to You. We pray that You will watch over them as they begin their walk with the Lord. And we pray that You would bless all the moms and dads who have been praying for their children and are continuing to pray. Help them to teach their children to walk in Your ways.

And we ask right now that You would speak to our hearts as we look into Your Word to see how we are supposed to teach and protect our children. Give us understanding in Yeshua's Name. Amen.

Parenting Children

Passover has a lot to do with children and family. So I felt the Spirit leading me to talk about children and parenting in this chapter.

> Exodus 12:26-27 *Now when it happens that your children ask you, 'What does this ceremony mean to you?' 27 You are to say, 'It is the sacrifice of Adonai's Passover, because He passed over the*

> houses of Bnei-Yisrael in Egypt, when He struck down the Egyptians, but spared our households.'

In this verse we see God's wisdom concerning how people learn. Part of the purpose for keeping the Seder forever was to provoke the children to ask questions about the meaning of it all. Just like Gina shared about her children, it was questions they got provoked to ask: "How do I get into the Kingdom?"

I believe the passing on of the Seder traditions to our children was one of the most significant factors in keeping the Jewish people together for the last 2000 years when they didn't have the Temple. It's an incredible accomplishment when you consider the loss of the Temple, the scattering of the people, and even the demeaning of this ceremony over the centuries.

> Exodus 12:22 You are to take a bundle of hyssop, dip it in the blood that is in the basin, and apply it to the crossbeam and two doorposts with the blood from the basin. None of you may go out the door of his house until morning.

You know that on Yom Kippur (the Day of Atonement), the sacrifices were made by the Cohen HaGadol for the whole nation. One person made the sacrifice for everyone. You didn't even have to be there for that sacrifice to cover you.

But the Passover sacrifice was very different. It was made by the head of each family at the Temple, and then brought home. But if you didn't live in Jerusalem, you had to stay in a place that residents were letting out for visitors.[53] That's what Yeshua was doing when He asked for the room. You had to find a place for your family to eat the meal. This requirement put a spiritual responsibility on the father. He had to lead the Seder which would provoke his children to curiosity. He had to create teachable moments for that family, leading to further instruction.

It also put a spiritual responsibility on the mother. She had to prepare the house and the meal, thus supporting the father in his teaching role.

---

53 Israel Ariel and Chaim Richman say in *Carta's Encyclopedia of the Holy Temple in Jerusalem* that halakhah did not allow Jerusalem residents to charge rent. So the visitors "paid" with leftover food and gifts. Co-published by The Temple Institute and Carta, Jerusalem, 2005, p. 247.

CHAPTER 20

We see this emphasis in the traditional Haggadah. At the heart of it the children get to ask the four questions. Do you see that? Just like right out of the verse. What is this all about? You can see God's understanding of how we learn right there. And the father tells the story in response to the four questions that the children ask. Then what happens? Covenant foods are eaten, fingers are dipped in wine, hands are washed. All these things make it more memorable so that the children will remember it.

This chapter is a message to parents and grandparents. The message is that in God's plan, each family is responsible to disciple their children, to bring them into His covenant and guide them in walking in it.

We see this theme in many other places in Scripture. Moses recorded very similar instructions concerning our responsibility to our children. Jewish people consider it so important that we recite it every single day. Do you know what Scripture it is?

> Deuteronomy 6:4-9 *"Hear O Israel, the Lord our God, the Lord is one. 5 Love Adonai your God with all your heart and with all your soul and with all your strength. 6 These words, which I am commanding you today, are to be on your heart.*
> *7 You are to teach them diligently to your children, and speak of them when you sit in your house, when you walk by the way, when you lie down and when you rise up. 8 Bind them as a sign on your hand, they are to be as frontlets between your eyes, 9 and write them on the doorposts of your house and on your gates.*

You are to teach them carefully. So this is the emphasis of the v'ahavta. Teach your children God's Words, sitting, standing, when you're traveling, at bedtime, upon awakening. What Words is he referring to? Immediately preceding this passage, two verses before, is the Shema: the Lord is One, and the v'ahavta: "you shall love the Lord your God" passage.

In the New Covenant, Yeshua commands us to go into all the world and make disciples, but our children are our first discipling responsibility. You know in our family, we fulfilled this command when our children were young as best we could. We read Bible verses and stories at night and prayed with them at bedtime. I think one of the most important things we did was we dealt with life in a spiritual way. We prayed. We repented when necessary. We did spiritual warfare with and for our kids. And as they grew, the Bible reading became our after dinner custom. We always encouraged them to ask questions and we had discussions. Our culture today pushes us as parents away from this responsibility. "Children are taught in schools." "Spiritual teaching? Oh, I send them to Shabbat school classes every week. That's where they learn."

But that's not God's way. God's way is that we would be responsible ourselves. The world is trying to push us away from that so His Word does not continue on. If you are a parent, you are probably like my wife and I were. It's one of your highest priorities, you're motivated to raise your children in the way of the Lord. Absolutely. I just want to encourage you today to invest yourselves in your kids. No matter how the world pulls at your time and your resources, your kids are your most important responsibility before God.

But I also want you to know this. It is so important. Your role is a spiritual one. We learned over and over, as we raised our children, that ha-satan attacks children. He attacks them big time. We had to stand against those spirits that were attacking our kids and we had to teach them to discern those spirits themselves and stand against them. I would say that the greatest gift that we had for those childrearing years was the gift of discerning of spirits. Really! Because I spent a lot of time yelling or trying to discipline my kids for things that turned out to be the influence of the enemy in their lives. And when I finally prayed about it and saw that and broke that, everything changed. Amazing. I studied and read books on deliverance to protect my children, and I recommend that you do that. Absolutely.

Then they became teens. You know that was hard. Childrearing when they were young was hard, but when they were teens, it was something beyond that. When the kids become teens, they have a very real and normal Godly need, which is to mature and run their own lives. And they are attacked by spirits

CHAPTER 20

just as much as little kids are attacked. Spirits of rejection, spirits of fear, spirits of lust. And it's a really delicate task of teen parenting to keep them from the foolishness in the decisions that they're prone to make that can lead to destruction, while maintaining that loving relationship so that they're talking to you and haven't shut you off. It's important to be able to do both of those things. And I've got to tell you, it's really, really hard.

So I want to encourage those of you with pre-teens and teens. One of the things that is very, very important to understand is that this is not something that you are supposed to hand off to the youth leaders, even though they are very capable. Their job is to help you raise your kids, not to raise them for you. I believe there is great value in youth ministry. I think when young people become teens, if they choose to be in a youth group, and if that experience is positive, here's what I see it doing. It will give them a desire for Godly fellowship for the rest of their lives. It will become built within them. "This is what I do. I need to be around people who believe like I do. I need their prayers. All of those good things will become habits of their lives. That's what I saw when I was a youth leader in the 1990s.

Let me tell you that the worst problems I had as a youth leader was not with the youth, but with parents who wouldn't make the effort to bring their children. I drove all over the city to pick up kids for our events. One time I offered the parents a great teaching video series about raising teens. They came to the first one and we had a great discussion. But then the next week when it came the time for the second video, no one showed up. It was so sad.

I encourage parents of young children to make the way for their kids to attend Shabbat school regularly. It is really hard for the Shabbat school teachers to teach with continuity if the kids aren't there every week. For parents of teens, I want to encourage you to come along side the youth leaders and support them. Help them with rides. Help them with refreshments. Help them with prayer. Help them with finances. They need your help. They're helping you.

And finally, I want to end with some word of revelation for fathers and husbands. And I want you to receive this even if you are separated or divorced or if your kids are grown up. And single moms, I want you to receive this, too, because many times you as a single mom, you have to serve in that role of a father as well as the role of a mother, even though it is very difficult. You still have to be there. One thing I suggest to you single mothers is if you can connect with a Godly, married couple who can help you through the rough times, it's a great help.

So here's the word of revelation. It's from a verse that many know really well.

> Ephesians 5:23 *because the husband is head of the wife, just as the Messiah, as head of the Messianic Community, is himself the one who keeps the body safe.*

Now many misunderstand this, thinking it assigns men dominant control. You don't have to admit that's how you understand it, but many people do. I didn't really understand what it meant here to be the head, until I was serving as the senior rabbi for several years—as the head of the congregation. What I learned was that if you're the head of any grouping of people—an organization, a congregation, or a family—here's the word. God will hold you accountable for everything that goes on in that organization or group or family. What I learned was that I may not be the cause of a problem in the congregation. I may not even be the one that has to deal with it. But I'm responsible before God to make sure that it's dealt with God's way.

According to that verse, Ephesians 5:23, God will hold the heads, the fathers, the husbands accountable and responsible for all that goes on in their family whether it's their fault or not. And I didn't understand that, really, until we had some things happen in my congregation that were not good, and I found that I couldn't say, "Hey, it wasn't my fault. They did it." I had to say, "It happened on my watch. I was in charge. I'm responsible for it." It was an eye opener to understand what it means to be the head, and to understand that it's not just for the role of leading a congregation, but every family has a head whom God will hold responsible.

So, fathers, we won't be able to excuse ourselves by saying, "My kids won't listen to me anymore." or "My wife has issues."

CHAPTER 20

God says, "If they won't listen to you, don't assume that I won't listen to you about that. How much time did you spend praying about the issues in your family?" That convicted me, big time. And I'm sure it's convicting you if you're a father.

I want to encourage parents and grandparents of pre-teens and teens to not give up on your kids, but continue to pray for them, not just by asking God to bless them, but by asking what are the spirits that have been assigned against them? What's causing them to struggle. Take authority and protect them in your prayer time. Do spiritual warfare for them.

As this came to me, I was asking the Lord, "Where in the Scriptures is there an example of taking this kind of authority?" I found it in the account of Abraham.

> *Genesis 18: 19 For I have made myself known to him so that he will command his sons and his household after him to keep the way of ADONAI by doing righteousness and justice, so that ADONAI may bring upon Abraham what He has spoken about him."*

Now this is really interesting because many people believe that God's promise to Abraham was unconditional. Right? But do you see what this is saying? It was conditional on Abraham training his children because if he didn't train his children, that promise of multiplication and blessing and the land, it would not have gone to his children. And what is really interesting is that Abraham is responsible for his children. But for later generations, we read that they messed up really bad, and God says, "I'm still going to honor my covenant for the sake of Abraham. Do you see that? So even though the later generations messed up, God honored His Covenant with Abraham because of Abraham's faithfulness.

So for the covenantal promises to be fulfilled, according to this verse, Abraham needed to raise his children in the way of Adonai. And if they didn't follow Adonai they wouldn't have been blessed and inherited the land.

God must have revealed His ways and His laws to Abraham personally since God's laws weren't written down yet at that time. God still held Abraham accountable and responsible to teach his children to keep the way of Adonai and to do what is right and just.

So I imagine that to fulfill this responsibility required more than reading them Bible stories at night and praying with them before they went to sleep. So later, I found a difficult situation that Abraham was facing, a decision that determined how the family would walk out God's Covenant. This passage gets to the heart of what I'm trying to communicate. I find it really difficult to communicate this sense of responsibility before God we as fathers are supposed to have.

In Genesis 17:19-21, we learn that Abraham had two wives, Sarah and Hagar, and he had a son by each wife. He loved both of those sons.

In that passage, God promises that Sarah's son, Yitz'chak (Isaac), would be the inheritor of the Covenant, the blessing, the multiplication, and the homeland. It would not go to Ishmael, his son by his second wife, Hagar. A moment of decision came when Ishmael's jealousy of his younger brother, Yitz'chak, surfaced. You know we can see similar problems of jealousy in our families, especially if it's a "yours, mine, and ours" family.

Look at what happened.

> Genesis 21:9-11 (CJB) *But Sarah saw the son of Hagar the Egyptian, whom Hagar had borne to Avraham, making fun of Yitz'chak; 10 so Sarah said to Avraham, "Throw this slave-girl out! And her son! I will not have this slave-girl's son as your heir along with my son Yitz'chak!" 11 Avraham became very distressed over this matter of his son.*

Why was Abraham distressed? It's pretty obvious. He loved both of these boys. Ishmael was a teenager by now. Yitz'chak was just being weaned. So what did he do in his distress? Well, if this was a soap opera on television, he would say, "Sarah, this is your fault! You gave her to me as a wife! Get over it! I love my son, Ishmael, so much, I'm not going to throw him out! Are you crazy?!!" Or he would have said, "Yes, dear. Whatever you say, dear."

CHAPTER 20

But he didn't. He saw as the head of this family, that what was happening was his responsibility before God, not Sarah's. So what did he do? He got before God. And God answered him.

> Genesis 21:12-13 (CJB) *But God said to Avraham, "Don't be distressed because of the boy and your slave-girl. Listen to everything Sarah says to you, because it is your descendants through Yitz'chak who will be counted. 13 But I will also make a nation from the son of the slave-girl, since he is descended from you."*

So he received direction from God how to deal with this very difficult situation, **and** the knowledge that Ishmael would survive. So Abraham trusted in what God told him and obeyed and sent Ishmael and Hagar away. That allowed the covenant to continue, because I believe if they had stayed, Ishmael probably would have killed Yitz'chak at some point.

So that's an example of what this means that husbands and fathers are responsible. Whatever struggles, whatever issues, whatever conflicts, whatever problems are going on in your family, whatever ways your wife or your children are not flourishing or are suffering or unhappy or are rebelling or are sick, guys, those things are our responsibility before God. (It got very quiet at this point when I gave this message to my congregation.) Ultimately, God will say, "How did you handle that?" "Did you come to Me about it?" That's really what His question is going to be. "Did you come to Me and say, 'How am I supposed to handle this?'"

So this understanding for fathers and husbands, it absolutely implies an ongoing relationship with the Lord. It means being on your knees before Him and seeking His face to know how to handle every situation that comes up, especially the difficult ones. I believe He will give you the strength and the discernment and the wisdom to deal with the enemies that attack your family.

It sounds difficult, but remember that because the responsibility is so great, the reward will also be great.

If you are not a parent, this is something that you should not be ignoring. You need to pray for parents. We need your prayers. Rather than tuning out about this, pray for us. It is a huge responsibility.

Let's Pray

Father, we thank You for Passover, for z'man kheyrutenu, the season of our freedom. Thank You for freeing our ancestors and giving them Your Covenant. Thank You for giving us the New Covenant and the renewal meal, and using the Seder to preserve our people for 3500 years. And we Thank You, Lord, that You've given us this understanding of how important it is to raise our children in Your ways. So I pray that You would just burn that into hearts right now, Lord, to help us to teach our children to walk in Your ways and do what is right and just.

Prayer for fathers and husbands:

Father, I just thank You for these men, and I pray, Lord, that whatever level they have understood this, and to whatever way in which they have stepped up to that responsibility, that You would bring them to the fullness of understanding of what it means, because it's not just for our children, it's for our wives and our grown children, too. So I pray for these men to be able to step up to the responsibility of being the head. I pray against any lies, any false understandings of what it means to be the head, to be broken from their minds and removed from their hearts. Any lies about the ability to rule over others and make others serve us, I pray that You would just break that in our hearts and in our minds. I pray You would give us a healthy fear of having to face You concerning how we have fulfilled that responsibility of being the head. I pray that You would help us to see that it is impossible to fulfill that responsibility without being in intimate relationship with You, without being able to come to You for direction and have the faith and the power of Your Name. I come against any pride, any laziness, any selfishness, and any fear in these men. Break the power of those spirits to lie and deceive us, in the Name of Yeshua. Give them the discernment and the wisdom to stand against that attack on their children and wives.

I pray all this, Father, for each person, each man. In Yeshua's Name. Amein.

CHAPTER 20

Prayer for single moms

Thank You for these single moms, Lord, and the responsibility on them. I pray You would cause them to step up to this, because with You they can handle this responsibility, too. Give them the discernment and the wisdom to stand against that attack on their children.

Prayer for all of us,

We just uphold these who are heads. Teach us, Lord, to pray for them. We thank You, Lord, that this isn't just a one-sided thing, that You don't just lay this heavy responsibility upon us, that we have to walk around bent over with it, but Your Word says, Your yoke is easy and Your burden is light and You will bear it with us. We also thank You, Lord, that Your reward is great!!

[Just think of Abraham's reward that he raised his children this way and he saw them become like the sand of the seashore and he saw them take the Land.]

So we thank You, Father. We thank You for this Pesakh season. In Yeshua's Name. Amen.

BIBLIOGRAPHY

BOOKS

Ariel, Israel; and Richman, Chaim, Carta's Encyclopedia of the Holy Temple in Jerusalem, co-published by The Temple Institute and Carta, Jerusalem, Israel, 2005.

Appel, Rabbi James; Bernis, Rabbi Jonathan; and Levine, Rabbi David, Messianic Judaism Class Teacher Book, Olive Press Messianic and Christian Publisher, Lowville, NY, 2012, http://olivepresspublisher.com/messianic-judaism-class-teacher-book.html. Accessed Nov. 2018.

Sjogren, Steve, Conspiracy of Kindness: A Unique Approach to Sharing the Love of Jesus, Bethany House Publishers, Grand Rapids, Michigan, 1993.

PAMPHLET

Passover Haggadah, (Compliments of the Coffees of Maxwell House), Deluxe Edition Pamphlet – 1986

ARTICLES, WEBSITES

Chabad, Kitov, Eliyahu, "Shabbat HaGadol," Chabad.org, https://www.chabad.org/holidays/passover/pesach_cdo/aid/1692/jewish/Shabbat-Hagadol.htm. Accessed Nov. 2018.

Chabad, "War of the Egyptian Firstborn (1313 BCE)", Chabad.org, https://www.chabad.org/library/article_cdo/aid/117352/jewish/War-of-the-Egyptian-Firstborn.htm. Accessed Nov. 2018.

Chosen People Ministries, "The Origin of The Afikomen," ChosenPeopleMinistries.com, https://www.chosenpeople.com/site/the-origin-of-the-afikomen/. Accessed Nov. 2018.

Fisher, Kevin, "Revealing God's Treasure - Red Sea Crossing," https://www.youtube.com/watch?v=vaN2acVMGC8, Ark Discovery International, Inc., Sparta, Tenn., arkdiscovery.com, url: http://arkdiscovery.com/red_sea_crossing.htm, accessed Nov. 2018.

Jewish Encyclopedia, Executive Committee of the Editorial Board, Jacob Zallel Lauterbach, "PASSOVER SACRIFICE (Hebrew, "zebah Pesah"; lit. "sacrifice of exemption")," JewishEncyclopedia.com, http://www.jewishencyclopedia.com/articles/11934-passover-sacrifice Accessed Nov. 2018.

Sanders, April, "What Are Some of Ancient Egypt's Dessert Dishes," TheClassroom.com, https://classroom.synonym.com/ancient-egypts-dessert-dishes-15909.html. Accessed Nov. 2018.

Sumner, Paul, "HE WHO IS COMING: The Hidden Afikoman," HebrewStreams.org, http://www.hebrew-streams.org/works/judaism/afikoman.html. Accessed Nov. 2018.

Talmud, Midrash Tehilim 136:6 and Ancient Tanchuma Bo 18, according to Rabbi Ari Kahn, "Shabbat HaGadol," Eish.com, http://www.aish.com/tp/i/moha/48942426.html#5. (See footnote 5.) Accessed Nov. 2018.

"The Exodus Revealed," Questar Inc., Discovery Media Productions, https://www.youtube.com/watch?v=Lzb4ekyX1kc&list=PLDAetAbqQFkvaL9T3wGnv4Zj-cSV2GQEz

VIDEO

"Meet Rabbi Jim," About the Rabbi, Congregation Shema Yisrael, http://www.shemayisrael.org/about-the-rabbi Accessed Nov. 2018.

Appendix A

Passover Seder Notes

Rabbi Jim's congregation's Haggadah.
(See how to order it on the next page.)

EXPLANATION and LEDGER

What follows are my notes for doing our Passover Seder. They are basically in outline form.

These notes and the page numbers given in them go with our own *Messianic Passover Haggadah*. To order copies, email The Fig Tree at: thefigtree@frontier.com or call 585-484-7775.

[NOTE: This Seder is around 4 hours long. So children need to eat ahead of time.]

Ledger:

Headings are given bold like this with page numbers that go with our Haggadah

The notes of what I plan to say as I teach the guests are in this format.

Some notes are in bold to stand out.

[Notes in brackets are for me only, **not** to be read aloud.]

Directives: what I tell the guests or table hosts to do.

Blessings: the *Cantor* is to recite the blessings

Scriptures are written in italics.

(My notes for my prayers for the guests are in this font.)

Slides: My slides are numbered in my powerpoint. The numbers are given in this font for when they are to be shown.

NOTE: This powerpoint is nothing fancy. To receive it as a pdf, email me at rabbijim@frontiernet.net or go to olivepresspublisher.com where you can download it for a small fee. To receive my large print version of my notes, email me.

PASSOVER SEDER
WELCOME

[Let the guests read the Welcome on **page 1** themselves.]

We are a Messianic Jewish congregation,
a congregation of Jewish and non-Jewish or Gentile people who
believe Yeshua is the Jewish Messiah.
We are not all Jewish, but about half Gentile. Explain "Gentiles."

Yeshua is the Hebrew Name for Jesus

Prayer for blessing on our time and all we'll eat and drink

What is a Passover Seder?

Seder means order. It's the order for the evening.
Passover is one of the Moadim.
Appointed Times, Times God has appointed,
are to be kept forever.
They are appointed to carry out His purposes.
What is His agenda for us for today?

Slide 1

Exodus 12:14 (CJB) *"'This will be a day for you to remember and celebrate as a festival to ADONAI; from generation to generation you are to celebrate it by a perpetual regulation.*

"Commemorate this day" – Zee-kar-rone – a memorial,
an event that helps our memory, helps us remember.
Time of remembering God's deliverance of our forefathers, the Israelites:
Out the bondage of slavery in Egypt about 3500 years ago.

It's not just something to hear about or watch, it's participatory.

At our Seder we'll be eating, drinking, dipping, washing, singing,
dancing, crying, searching, receiving a gift

It's all done to make it fun for you to learn, so you'll have a stronger
memory of God's great deliverance.
We hope you participate with an enthusiastic spirit.
The more you put in,
the more memorable this memorial will be.

There's a deeper meaning to this Appointed Time than remembering
what God did.

The Seder is the **COVENANT RENEWAL MEAL** of Mosaic Covenant.
God's covenants are His "contract"
between He & human beings.

He **PROMISES** things & requires things in His Covenants.
The Mosaic or Sinai Covenant was the
agreement between God & Jewish people
that established Israel as a nation 3500 years ago.

Keeping the Passover was required for each person every year

It was a yearly renewal of the Covenant
In this covenant renewal meal, God restates His
COVENANTAL PROMISES to us

He does this for our sakes, to strengthen us to deal with
life's difficulties
Everyone here is struggling with something in their life.
Our ability to deal with these trials of life is dependent
on how much we trust God.

God wants each of you to receive His **COVENANT PROMISES**
to increase your faith to prepare you for the future.

Of course the Covenant is a conditional Covenant.
It is dependent on us doing our part – obeying Him.

There is also a periodic renewal meal of the
New Covenant (Brit Khadashah), called communion or
the Lord's Supper, in Hebrew: S'udat Adonai.
I will tie the two together as we go along.
Our Seder will follow the order of a traditional Seder.
But we will also do many things that are non-traditional.

The commandment to keep Pesakh was given to Jewish people.
But, we welcome those of you who are not Jewish
to participate in this covenant renewal.
Paul is speaking to non-Jewish followers of Yeshua:

Slide 2

Ephesians 3:6 … in union with the Messiah and through the Good News the Gentiles were to be joint <u>heirs</u>, a joint <u>body</u> and joint <u>sharers</u> with the Jews in what God has promised.

As joint heirs, a joint body and joint sharers in **GOD'S PROMISES,**
the **PROMISES** of this covenant are for you too.

We'll also be showing tonight how the New Covenant
– given by Yeshua –
builds on, rather than annuls, or ends the Mosaic Covenant.
I'm going to lead by stating God's **covenant promises**
of Mosaic & New Covenant
and praying for each of us to renew God's covenants
by receiving those **promises** for themselves personally.
I invite you to participate in those renewal prayers
with all your heart to receive all the power
He wants to impart to you tonight.
Or we invite you to enter into these covenants with the God of Israel
for the first time, if you've never done that before.
In showing how the two Covenants are related,
this verse is foundational:

Slide 3

Matthew 5:17 "Don't think that I have come to abolish the Torah or the Prophets. I have come not to abolish but to complete (fulfill)."

As we proceed I'll be pointing ways from Scripture in which
Messiah fulfilled the Law of Moses concerning Passover

We'll also see how He fulfilled traditions that developed
around those laws concerning Passover

Traditions are not in Scripture but are still practiced today in modern
Judaism and are recorded in ancient Jewish non-Biblical writings
such as the Talmud.

You have been provided with a Haggadah with the Hebrew
transliterations and English translations of the things
we'll be reciting in Hebrew.

CANDLE LIGHTING – Page 2

Lighting Candles to start holidays is an ancient Jewish tradition.
Passover, like most of the of the Holidays, is a Sabbath day
when fires are not to be kindled.
Festival candles are lit at sundown at the start of the day
and burn through the night
Lighting holiday candles is traditionally done by the woman of the house.
You will find some matches on each table.
One woman at each table should light the candles as Rabbitzen does.

Our Rabbitzen will light the Holiday candles at the head table.
Rabbitzen will sing the candle lighting prayer.
LIGHT THE CANDLES and sing the song. - Rabbitzen

Holiday *Blessing* - *Cantor* – page 2

INTRODUCTION – Page 3

Table Hosts read the introduction. – page 3

THE FOUR CUPS – Page 3

Today we will drink four cups

FILL YOUR CUPS, but don't drink.

Passover is kept by families (mishpokhah) in homes, around the table.
We attempt to create that family atmosphere around each table.
Table hosts are to lead around each table by reading and
explaining the things written in the Haggadah under "Table Host"
I'll tell you when and give you enough time.
Then I may say a few words or lead in a prayer for all.

Then our Cantor will lead us in Hebrew as we all recite the
traditional blessings together and read the English.

Covenants in the Bible are always sealed by eating and drinking.

The 4 cups during the Seder are known as the **Cups of the Covenant**.
Later we'll learn about the 3 foods of the Mosaic covenant
that also renew the covenant.

There are 2 cups before dinner and 2 cups following dinner.

FIRST CUP – the Cup of Sanctification – Page 3

Table Hosts explain the First Cup. – **Page 3**

The memorials are derived from Exodus 6:6-7 where God told the
Israelites what He was about to do.

Page 4

*Exodus 6:6-7 Therefore say to Bnei-Yisrael: I am Adonai, and I will
bring you out from under the burdens of the Egyptians. I will deliver
you from their bondage, and I will redeem you with an outstretched
arm and with great judgments. 7 I will take you to Myself as a people,
and I will be your God. You will know that I am Adonai your God, who
brought you out from under the burdens of the Egyptians.*

The 1st cup, **the Cup of Sanctification** is a memorial of the separation of the Israelites unto God *"I will bring you out from under the burdens (yoke) of the Egyptians."*
This is the first cup of the covenant.
As we drink it, understand that it is the means of Covenant renewal.

Slide 4

Exodus 6:6 (NIV)...*I will bring you out from under the yoke of the Egyptians*
Hoh-tzeh-ti – separate you from, sanctify you,
How does this apply to us today, we're not slaves in Egypt?
Egypt represents the sinful world we live in & have participated in.

Slide 5

John 8:34 Yeshua answered them, "Yes, indeed! I tell you that everyone who practices sin is a slave of sin."

God is promising to separate us from all other peoples,
and to separate us to Him as His chosen people,
to separate us from the power this world has over us due to our sin.

Slide 6

Yeshua prayed for His followers.
John 17:17 Set them apart (sanctify them) *for holiness by means of the truth—your word is truth.*

Let's pray - Thank You for separating our forefathers, the Israelites, from the Egyptians, separating them to you.
Thank You that sanctification is part of the New Covenant.

Here's the **promise** He wants each of us to receive, **"I will set you apart for Me as My child, by the truth of My Word."**

[Continue praying]: We pray that we do our part: regularly reading, studying, meditating on Your Word
We each receive Your **promise** tonight of being set apart for You.
We covenant to walk in the fullness of this **promise.** ¶

Please lift your cup as we give thanks. – **page 4**

Blessing over the First Cup, Hebrew and English – *Cantor* – page 4
FIRST CUP OF WINE - drink – **page 4**

KARPAS – Page 5

On each table is a Seder plate of ceremonial foods.
The foods are eaten as part of the Covenant renewal meal.
They are memorials to enrich our memory of the events of that time.

KARPAS is **not one of the renewal foods** but is traditional.

<u>Table Hosts, explain Karpas & distribute to each person at the table</u> – **Page 5**

We are using parsley. We dip it in the salt water.

Salt water symbolizes the TEARS OF SLAVERY of the children of YISRAEL because of the misery of being enslaved.
Remember that the **tears** from the children of Israel turned to JOY upon leaving their Bondage.
We'll eat the Karpas dipped in the salt water and think of being a slave and the tears it would cause.

*Let's pray – Lord we remember the tears of our forefather's slavery
And thank You for setting them free.*

KARPAS *Blessing* – *Cantor* – **page 5**

<u>Eat Karpas dipped in salt water & imagine the hardship of being slaves.</u>

YACHATZ – Page 6

YACHATZ **is a tradition performed at every Seder.**

I have here 3 matzahs in the Matzah Tosh (3-tiered matzah cover).
The matzahs are made in the traditional Jewish way.
Please look closely at the matzahs on your table.
Leaven is symbol for sin in Bible & matzahs are made without leaven.
Notice that they are striped, pierced, and kind of bruised looking.
Remember this for later.
I am removing the middle matzah, called the Afikomen.
I'm breaking it.
This broken piece of Matzah is saved for after the meal.
I'm wrapping the other broken half.

<u>Table hosts, please do what I just did. Take the middle matzah for your Afikomen. Break it in half. Wrap half of it in a linen napkin. Save it for later. Return the other half to the Seder plate.</u>

My wrapped piece will be hidden.
Later, after dinner, children 12 years old & under may search for it.
The one who finds it will receive a Passover gift.
Up until the destruction of the 2nd Temple in 70 CE, lamb was eaten.
Lamb is no longer eaten at a traditional Seder.
The Afikomen is now a memorial of Pesakh lamb.
Remember this for later.

Ha Lachmah Anya (The Bread of Affliction) – Page 6
The HaLachmah Anya is an invitation to participate in the Seder.

Sing Ha Lachmah Anya – *Cantor* – page 6

FILL YOUR CUPS FOR THE 2ND CUP, but don't drink it.– **page 7**

MA NISHTANAH the 4 Questions – Page 7
One of the goals of the Seder is to teach our young people our history.
It's part of our obligation under the Covenant.
Amazingly, 3 millennia later we are still telling the story.
For those not Jewish, remember if you're a Bible believer,
this is your spiritual history too.
Four questions are usually asked or sung by the youngest child who can read in the house. There are really 5 questions.
The English text of the questions is on **page 9**.
A child or children are going to sing now.
(This is usually planned ahead and the child has been practicing.)

or

[We'd like a different child to read each of the 5 questions,
starting with the youngest who is willing.
There's a prize for reading.]

Children read or sing the questions, – **pages 8 and 9**.

[Read the answers or have the table hosts read them.]

[READ THE ANSWERS AT YOUR TABLE, – **page 9**]

EXODUS STORY

Our forefather Jacob went to Egypt to survive a famine.
For over 400 years, God blessed Israelis, and multiplied them.
Egyptians began to fear them because of their great numbers.

Slide 7 - picture

Egyptians enslaved them. They continued to multiply.
Pharaoh ordered the murder of their innocent infant sons.
Moses was miraculously saved from being murdered.

Slide 8 - picture

Moses was raised by Pharaoh's daughter.
When he was 80 years old, the Israelites cried out to be rescued.

Slide 9 - picture
God spoke to Moses out of a burning bush.
God sent he & his brother Aaron to demand the release of the Israelites.
God gave them miraculous powers.
God Himself came with them to rescue the Israelis from Egypt.

Slide 10 - picture
Moses & Aaron demanded Pharaoh let the Israelites go,
but Pharaoh refused to let Israelites go.

Slide 11 - picture
Aaron's staff turned into serpent. Pharaoh still refused.
God sent judgments on Egypt - 10 plagues. He is a God of justice.
Ancient Egypt was a sinful nation.
The people worshipped many false gods.
Pharaoh was full of pride, considered himself to be a god.
Pharaoh had ordered the murder of innocent infant boys.
The plagues were meant to cause the Egyptians to repent.
But Pharaoh hardened his heart through 9 terrible plagues.
The 10th plague was the death of the firstborn sons.
This plague was a judgment fitting for Pharaoh's policy
of killing the Jewish infant boys.
The plague of the death of the firstborn sons came upon
all the land of Egypt

<u>Raise your hand if you are a firstborn son.</u>

All of you would have died in the plague.
God gave the Israelites instructions on how to survive this plague.

Slide 12

Exodus 12:3 (CJB) *Speak to all the assembly of Isra'el and say, "On the tenth day of this month, each man is to take a lamb or kid for his family, one per household – ...*

5 Your animal must be without defect, a male in its first year, and you may choose it from either the sheep or the goats.

6 You are to keep it until the fourteenth day of the month, and then the entire assembly of the community of Isra'el will slaughter it at dusk."

Slide 13 - picture of lambs
"Keep it" – *mishmeret* – *observe, a charge of yours, safeguard it, watch*
Observe it for defects for 4 days.

Messianic fulfillment – Yeshua entered Jerusalem the 10th day of month.
Churches celebrate it as Palm Sunday.
Over the next 4 days, scribes & Pharisees publicly questioned Him, trying to trip Him up in His words, looking for a defect.
We will talk about more Messianic fulfillments later.

Slide 14

Exodus 12:7 (CJB) They are to take some of the blood and smear it on the two sides and top of the door-frame at the entrance of the house in which they eat it.

Slide 15 - picture

Slide 16

8 That night, they are to eat the meat, roasted in the fire; they are to eat it with matzah and maror (bitter herbs).

Ancient covenants were made by eating and drinking together.
That night the sacrificed lamb was eaten as Passover covenant meal.

Slide 17

Exodus 12:12 (CJB) For that night, I will pass through the land of Egypt and kill all the firstborn in the land of Egypt, both men and animals; and I will execute judgment against all the gods of Egypt; I am ADONAI.

13 The blood will serve you as a sign marking the houses where you are; when I see the blood, I will pass over [Hebrew: pesakh] *you - when I strike the land of Egypt, the death blow will not strike you.*

We get the name Passover from this verse,
and the concept of being protected by the blood.

Slide 18

29 (CJB) At midnight ADONAI killed all the firstborn in the land of Egypt, from the firstborn of Pharaoh sitting on his throne to the firstborn of the prisoner in the dungeon, and all the firstborn of livestock.

30 Pharaoh got up in the night, he, all his servants and all the Egyptians; and there was horrendous wailing in Egypt; for there wasn't a single house without someone dead in it.

Slide 19 - picture

SEDER NOTES 349

Slide 20

Exodus 12:31 (CJB) *He (Pharaoh) summoned Moshe and Aharon by night and said, "Up and leave my people, both you and the people of Isra'el; and go, serve ADONAI as you said.*

32 Take both your flocks and your herds, as you said; and get out of here! But bless me, too."

Slide 21 - picture

Slide 22

Exodus 12:33 (CJB) *The Egyptians pressed to send the people out of the land quickly, because they said, "Otherwise we'll all be dead!"*

34 The people took their dough before it had become leavened and wrapped their kneading bowls in their clothes on their shoulders.

We eat matzah to remember this hasty departure.

Slide 23 - picture

Several million left Egypt guided by Lord in the form of the
Pillar of Cloud & Fire
Pharaoh changed his mind & led his army to trap Israelites at Red Sea.
God came as Pillar of cloud and fire and protected them.
Moses raised his rod over the Red Sea.
It divided for Israelites to cross.

Slide 24 - picture

Moses led the people through the Sea on dry ground.

Slide 25 - picture

You can see the pillar of fire protecting behind them.

Slide 26 - picture

Egyptians pursued, and the sea drowned them.

Slide 27 - picture

The Israelites went on to Mt. Sinai,
and received the 10 Commandments and the Law of Moses, the
Mosaic or Sinai Covent which establish us as God's people.

Slide 28 - picture

Moses sprinkled the blood of the Covenant on the people
and the altar and the scroll, etc.

Song, Slide 29-30   Horse and Rider song

Dance with us to the song they sang from Exodus 15: "Horse and Rider" – in the Haggadah.

TEN PLAGUES – Page 10

Table Hosts, explain the **Ten Plagues** dipping. – **page 10**

Slides 31-40 – pictures of the 10 Plagues

Reciting the Ten Plagues and dipping – *Cantor* – page 10

You're invited to dance the Hora with us to the song, "Da-yeh-nu" that says, "It Would Have Been Enough."

Song slide – Da-yeh-nu (Use your own slides)

THE SECOND CUP – Page 11

The second Cup of the Covenant is called **the Cup of Deliverance**

Slide 41

Exodus 6:6 (NIV)….*I will free you from being slaves to them.*

What's the difference between sanctification & deliverance?
Deliverance - *Hit-tsal-ti* - *free you, rid you of the bondage*
Sanctification - *Ho-tzeh-ti* – *bring you out, separate you from, bring you forth*
Sanctification – separating from slave masters, escaping from slavery
Deliverance - taking off the chains of slavery
Imagine a slave escaping but still having shackles on his wrists,
  or, the distinctive clothing of a slave,
  or the attitude of slaves, abused, broken people.
Even though Israelites were separated from Egyptians,
  they still needed deliverance from these things.
How does this apply to us today?
People come into the Kingdom of God with much baggage:
Addictions, wounds, fears, griefs, phobias, obsessions, bitterness,
  anger, broken hearts, low self esteem
They need deliverance from these things.

Slide 42

John 15:15 I no longer call you slaves, because a slave doesn't know what his master is about; but I have called you friends, because everything I have heard from my Father I have made known to you.

Yeshua removes our slave mentality.

Let's pray - thank You for delivering our forefathers the Israelites from the Egyptians, removing the bonds of slavery
Thank You that deliverance is part of the New Covenant

Here's the **promise** He wants each of us to receive
"I will deliver you from the bondages & baggage that is oppressing you, holding you back because you are no longer slaves but my friends"

*Continue praying: We receive Your **promise** tonight to take off our chains, and our slaves clothing*
Deliver us from the baggage, addictions, scars, fears, anger, bitterness, grief, low self esteem that we have picked up in the world.
*We receive Your **promise** to make us Your friend*
*We covenant to walk in the fullness of these **promises***

Blessing on the Second Cup – *Cantor* – page 11

<u>Drink the Second Cup.</u>

RACHATZ, a hand washing ceremony– Page 11

In Biblical times people wore sandals and walked on dirt roads.
Feet were constantly in need of washing.
I believe originally the Rachatz included a foot washing.
It was the role of the lowest servant.
Later, when people wore shoes in colder climates,
it became just a hand washing.

The New Covenant records that Yeshua washed His disciples' feet at the Last Supper
He didn't just come up with the idea of washing the disciples' feet.
He built upon the Rachatz ceremony,

<u>Table Hosts, explain the RACAHTZ, ceremonial hand washing.</u>
<u>– **Page 11**</u>

How can we wash each other's feet?
By serving each other even if it means doing a lowly task.
By serving each other by helping, praying for each, encouraging, exhorting, forgiving each other.

Slide 43

Matthew 20:26 Among you, it must not be like that. On the contrary, whoever among you wants to be a leader must become your servant, 27 and whoever wants to be first must be your slave!

Here's the **promise** He wants us to receive concerning the washing:

"He who is the greatest servant among you will be greatest in My eyes"

*Let's pray – Lord help us to serve each other according to Your example.
Teach us that true leadership is accomplished by serving each other.
We receive Your **promise** tonight that by serving each other,
we become greater in your eyes.
We covenant to walk in the fullness of this **promise***

Blessing over the washing – *Cantor* – page 12

Now, each of you has an opportunity to serve each other
by helping each other wash your hands.

<u>Washing: Please pass the towel and bowl around and pour for each other, and dry each other's hands.</u>

SEDER PLATE – Page 12

I call your attention back to the SEDER PLATE.
It has foods which teach us lessons through our sense of taste.

*The Matzah, unleavened bread is one of the foods
of the Covenant meal
It is specially important because it is to be eaten for the 7 days
of Feast of Unleavened Bread*

MOTZI (BRING FORTH) – Page 13

<u>Distribute upper Matzah and the half of middle Matzah not wrapped in the napkin to each person at your table.</u>

Page 13

Exodus 12:39 They had baked matzot cakes from the dough that they brought out of Egypt. It had no hametz (leaven), because they were thrust out of Egypt and could not delay, so they had not made provisions for themselves.

<u>Table Hosts explain the Motzi. – **Page 13**</u>

The matzah is a memorial of the coming out of Egypt in haste.
Matzah is also called: the Bread of Affliction.
It is the bread that acknowledges the suffering endured by the children
of Israel in Egypt
Note that it wasn't actually eaten while in slavery.
It was eaten on the day of deliverance.
So it is really the bread of freedom.

Leaven represents sin in the Bible.
Eating bread without leaven is symbolic of the Israelites
leaving behind the worldly ways of Egypt.
Of course, sin is something that still brings us into bondage today.
Here's the **promise** He wants us to receive concerning the matzah.

Slide 44

Romans 6:14 ***For sin will not have authority over you; because you are not under legalism but under grace.***

Let's pray: Lord we thank You for the unleavened Bread of Affliction which became the Bread of Freedom.
Help us to prevail in our ongoing struggle against sin.
*We receive Your **promise** tonight that "sin will not have authority over us"*
*We covenant to walk in the fullness of this **promise**.*

Blessing on bread – Ha Motzi Lekhem – *Cantor* – page 14
Special *Blessing* over the matzah – *Cantor* – page 14

Eat the Matzah.

PESAKH (Passover) Lamb – Page 15

The lamb is another of the foods of the Covenant.
In a traditional Jewish Seder today, lamb is not eaten.
Sacrificed lambs were eaten at Seders up until the destruction of the Temple in Jerusalem in 70 CE.
Sacrifices ended because Scripture commands that the sacrifices can only be made at the Temple.
Because the Passover lambs were to be sacrificed,
it was decided that lamb should not be eaten at Passover.
Traditionally the roasted shank bone of the lamb on the Seder Plate is a memorial of the Passover Lamb
We have chosen not to follow that tradition and do serve lamb in obedience to the command to eat lamb on Passover
We eat a small piece of lamb meat as a memorial
of the sacrificed Passover Lamb

Page 15

Exodus 12:13 The blood will be a sign for you on the houses where you are. When I see the blood, I will pass over you.

Please distribute a piece of lamb to each person at your table.

Table Hosts, explain the Pesakh. – **Page 15**

Lambs blood on the doorposts of the houses protected the Israelites from the plague of the death of the firstborn sons.

Blood on the doorposts was a sign of the Israelites' faith in our God, trusting His **promise** that it would protect them.

Through their faith and actions, they became covenant partners with God as He stretched forth His mighty arm to deliver them from Egypt.

Remember this lamb was kept in the household for 4 days.
Very playful, like any young animal, puppy or kitten.

Slide 45 – picture of lambs

It would have become a pet, beloved by the children.
Seders after the one in Egypt included the lamb & blood on doorposts.
If you were an observant Jew, you saw this ritual of the lamb every year.
You and your father selected the lamb, and observed it for defects.
Because the lambs had to be sacrificed,
and that could only be done at the Temple,
you traveled to Jerusalem where you stayed to prepare for your Seder.
You brought the lamb to Temple, and
watched priests slaughter it at the Temple with thousands of others.
You carried the slaughtered, dead lamb to where you were staying.
You must have carried the blood with you in a container.
You put blood on doorposts.

The prophet Isaiah said of Messiah:

Slide 46

Isaiah 53:7 (CJB)… Like a lamb led to be slaughtered, like a sheep silent before its shearers, he did not open his mouth.

8 … his being cut off from the land of the living for the crimes of my people…

Slide 47

John 1:29 .God's lamb! The one who is taking away the sin of the world!

Messianic fulfillment – Yeshua, God's lamb was precious, lovable, beloved by the people & most of all innocent as the Passover lambs.
Because everyone came to Jerusalem to keep the Passover,

so many lambs had to be sacrificed that they started just after noon, so they would all be done by sundown.

Slide 48

Luke 23:44 It was now about noon, and darkness covered the whole Land until three o'clock in the afternoon;…

46 Crying out with a loud voice, Yeshua said, "Father! Into your hands I commit my spirit." With these words he gave up his spirit.

So, in a precise Messianic fulfillment of prophesy, Yeshua died at the same time the Passover lambs were being sacrificed.

Here's the **promise** God wants us to receive concerning the lamb
Speaking of the Brit Khadashah, He said:

Slide 49

*Jeremiah 31:34 … **I will forgive their iniquity and remember their sins no more.***"

Let's pray: Lord we thank You for the unblemished, innocent lamb that was sacrificed to protect our forefathers from Your judgment.
We receive Your **promise** tonight, in which You said,
"I will forgive your iniquity and remember your sins no more."
We realize You were able to take our sins upon You
because You were an innocent man.
We covenant to walk in the fullness of this **promise**.

Slide 50 - picture of lambs

Lord help us to see the Messiah as an innocent lamb.

Blessing over lamb – *Cantor* – page 15

Eat lamb.

MAROR – Page 16

The third food of the Covenant is the bitter herbs or Maror.
The maror that we will use tonight is horseradish.

Table Hosts explain the Maror and distribute some with a piece of Matzah to everyone at your table. – **Page 16**

Maror represents the bitterness of the hard labor, the misery, and ruthlessness the Jewish people experienced in Egypt.
We eat it to remember the bitterness of slavery.
It's important to remember the reality of those years.
But we know we must not let bitterness rule our lives.

Slide 51

Hebrews 12:15 See to it that no one misses out on God's grace, that no root of bitterness springing up causes trouble and thus contaminates many,

Here's the **promise** He wants us to receive concerning the maror.
It's conditional.
"If you confess them to me, I'll remove every root of bitterness in your life"
*Let's pray – we remember the bitterness of the slavery in Egypt.
Lord, keep us from bitterness in our lives by helping us
to forgive those who have hurt us,
and to accept the difficulties we face in life.
We confess our bitterness for past hurts, present hurts, and future hurts to You.
We receive your **promise** tonight that You will remove our bitterness.
We covenant to walk in the fullness of this **promise**.*

Blessing over maror – *Cantor* – page 16

Eat Maror.

CHAROSET – Page 17

We put the charoset on a piece of matzah.
There's no traditional blessing for the charoset.

Table hosts, explain the charoset and distribute it. – **Page 17**

The charoset is a memorial of the MORTAR
used to build the cities of Egypt.
Charoset has a sweet taste that also reminds us of the sweetness of
freedom and of having a relationship with GOD.
It reminds us that through our relationship with the Lord,
even in times of bitterness, there is sweetness.

Eat Charoset.

Korach (Hillel Sandwich) – page 17

Table Hosts, read about Rabbi Hillel. – **page 17-18**

Shulchan Orech (Festival Table) (Meal) – page 18

[Let the guests read this on their own.]

Grace before the meal - *Rabbi*

EAT DINNER.

[Rabbi: Hide the Afikomen.]

FILL CUPS FOR THE 3ʳᴰ CUP. – **page 19**

TZAFUN (AFIKOMEN) – page 19

As you adults were schmoozing after dinner, your children have been looking for the Afikomen.

_____ has found it.

[Give gift to the finder.]

We thank all who worked on the Seder.

Now I want to share with you 2 examples of how Yeshua used the traditions that developed around instructions for Passover
We are about to partake of the Afikomen,
the matzah eaten after the meal.

Table Hosts, break the Afikomen and distribute it to the people at your table. – **page 19**

THE LAST SUPPER WAS A PASSOVER SEDER

Slide 52 (Verse 19 is on page 20.)

Luke 22:19 Also, taking a piece of matzah, he made the b'rakhah (blessing), *broke it, gave it to them and said, "This is my body, which is being given for you; do this in memory of me."*

20 *He did the same with the cup* **after the meal**, *saying, "This cup is the New Covenant* (Brit Khadashah), *ratified by my blood, which is being poured out for you.*

Notice it says He took both the cup and the Matzah **after the meal.**
**So, Yeshua was following Seder order,
and He built upon the Afikomen and the 3rd Cup**
to give His followers Lord's Supper or Communion.

Today at traditional Jewish Seders there is no lamb,
so the Afikomen is eaten after meal as a memorial of Passover lamb.

Listen to an incredible tradition that has developed around the Afikomen
This tradition is followed in the homes of all Jewish people.
Before the Seder, we placed 3 matzahs in the Matzah Tosh.
Earlier, in the Yachatz ceremony we removed the middle matzah.

We looked at it and saw that it was made without leaven,
was striped, pierced, and bruised looking.
We broke it and mine was hidden.
In the Tzafun ceremony a child found it and received a gift.
This tradition of the Afikomen actually paints a <u>detailed</u> picture
of the meaning of the life of Yeshua.

Slide 53

The Three Matzahs represent the Father, Son, & the Holy Spirit.
The Middle Matzah, which represents the Son, Yeshua,
is broken & hidden.
According to the Scriptures, He was without leaven
because He <u>never sinned,</u> 2 Cor. 5:21
He was <u>bruised</u> by being beaten, Isaiah 53:5
He was <u>striped</u> by being whipped, Isaiah 53:5
His body was <u>pierced</u> by nails & Roman soldier's spear John 19:34

Slide 54

His body was <u>broken</u> on the cross, 1 Cor. 11:24
His body was <u>wrapped in a linen cloth,</u> Matt. 27:59
His body was <u>hidden</u> in a tomb, Matt. 27:60
He rose from the dead and was <u>found</u> by His followers John 20
Those who found Him received a gift -
the gift of Eternal Life, Romans 6:23

What a clear picture the Afikomen tradition paints
of the life of Yeshua and the meaning of His coming.
This tradition points so clearly to Yeshua that some scholars
believe His early followers developed it.
The amazing part is that all Jewish people,
even those who don't believe in Yeshua still follow this custom.

It was this Afikomen that He broke and said
"Take eat, this is my Body broken for you."

The Afikomen is a double Covenant renewal food.
It's a memorial of the Passover Lamb that was sacrificed & eaten,
the Mosaic Covenant renewal food that can no longer be eaten,
and it's a memorial of Yeshua's broken and sacrificed body,
the renewal food of the New Covenant.

So, for believers in Yeshua, it's the bread of the Lord's Supper.

Whether you've put your trust in Yeshua's sacrifice or not,

we can <u>all</u> partake of the Afikomen together
as a memorial of the sacrificed Passover lamb,
which brought the Israelites deliverance from Egypt
and renews the Mosaic Covenant.

If you are thinking right now for the first time,
"I need the forgiveness Messiah obtained for us
by sacrificing His body,"
I invite you to partake of this Afikomen as the first act of obedience to Him
in remembrance of Yeshua's broken body,
and as your way of entering into the New Covenant.

Here's the **promise** concerning the Afikomen:

Slide 55

Exodus 15:26 (CJB) *He said, **"If you will listen intently to the voice of ADONAI your God, do what he considers right, pay attention to his commandments and observe his laws, I will not afflict you with any of the diseases I brought on the Egyptians; because I am ADONAI your healer."***

Its **promise** of healing is conditional on obedience.
Rabbi Sha'ul tells us in 1 Corinthians 11
that there is physical health in eating this spiritual Bread.
Physical healing is one of God's **promises** in both the
Mosaic & New Covenants.

<u>All who need physical healing please stand.</u>

[Pray for healing.]

<u>Hold up your Afikomen piece.</u>

Blessing on the matzah – *Cantor* – Ha Motzi Lekhem – page 20

*Let's pray. We receive Your **promise** tonight that You are Adonai our healer,
that by being obedient to You, we will be spared
from the diseases You bring on this world in judgment.
We covenant to walk in the fullness of this **promise**, trusting you for healing.*

This is a memorial of the Passover Lamb sacrificed
to cause the plague of death to pass over our forefather's. houses

This is the Body of the Messiah broken for you.

<u>Take and eat.</u> – **page 20**

Slides 56- 62 Sacrificed Lamb song

THE THIRD CUP – page 20

The Passover lamb's blood was applied to the wood
of the doorposts of the houses to cause God's mighty act of judgment
in the form of the death of the firstborn sons
to "pass over" the firstborn sons of Israel.
And the Cups of the Covenant are memorials of
the **BLOOD OF THE PASSOVER LAMB** on the doorposts.

The 3rd Cup is **the Cup of Redemption** based on:

Slide 63

Exodus 6:6 (CJB)... *I will <u>redeem you</u> with an <u>outstretched arm</u> and with <u>mighty acts of judgment</u>.*

The Israelites were God's people when they went down into Egypt.
They were free people, but Egyptians enslaved them, and owned them.
God stretched out His arm, with mighty acts of judgment.
He bought the Israelites back from those who owned them.
He redeemed them and made them His people, free people.
"Redeem you" - *ga'al-lih-tee* – can mean *to pay a ransom.*
The Israelites needed to be ransomed so the Egyptian slave masters
would no longer have claim on them,
so they couldn't track them down & drag them back into slavery.

The Cup of Redemption is a memorial of the great rescue of our
forefathers & the destruction of the Egyptian army,
which was trying to take them back into captivity.
All this was accomplished by Moses raising his arm over the waters.

This cup is a renewal of God's **promise** to ransom each of us.
We need ransoming because Satan has a legal claim on us
because we have all sinned.

At Yeshua's Last Passover Seder we read:

Slide 64

Luke 22:20 He did the same with the cup after the meal, saying, "This cup is the New Covenant (Brit Khadashah), *ratified by my blood, which is being poured out for you.*

The cup referred to in this verse, the cup after supper,
was this cup, the 3rd Cup, the Cup of Redemption.
So, He declared the Cup of Redemption <u>to be</u>
the Cup of the New Covenant
ratified by His blood, meaning sealed and signed by His blood.

When He gave this cup,
He was actually making a New Covenant with us.
It became the Cup of the Lord's Supper.
It is the renewal drink of the New Covenant
as Matzah, His broken Body, is the renewal meal of the New Covenant.

Why did He choose a Passover Seder to give us the New Covenant?

The Passover Seder is the renewal meal of the Mosaic Covenant.
So He gave a sense of the continuity between the 2 Covenants,
that the New Covenant does not replace or revoke,
but builds on the Mosaic Covenant.

Why did He choose this cup, the traditional Cup of Redemption to become the Cup of the New Covenant?

God is just – every punishment will be fitting for every crime.
The standard God will judge people on is His Law, His 10 commandments.
If we're honest, we'll all admit we've all broken His laws.
We're facing the prospect of being judged guilty, deserving of punishment.
What can we do to avoid this punishment?
When the Temple was in operation,
God's law required sacrifices of animals to pay the penalty.
But we can't make those sacrifices today because there's no Temple.
There's nothing **WE** can do to escape the punishment,
but **GOD** did make a way.
Yeshua died a sacrificial death.
His suffering paid the price for all the sin of all people for all time.
As He died on the cross, He said "It is finished" literally "Paid in full."
When you put your trust in Yeshua's sacrifice,
instead of what you can do,
the penalty will be paid for your sin.
His act of redemption causes the plague of eternal death to Pass Over
those who put their trust in Him.

In Egypt God redeemed Israel with an
"outstretched arm and mighty acts of judgment,"
which were the 10 plagues & the destruction of the Egyptian army.
1500 years later on a hill in Jerusalem, Yeshua fulfilled the prophesy
in Exodus 6:6 by redeeming all who would put their trust in Him.
He did it "with an outstretched arm & with mighty acts of judgment".
He came to Earth in the form of a man and stretched out His arm,
in fact both His arms,
allowing Himself to be nailed to a Roman cross, suffer terribly & die.

And instead of sending the judgment of plagues on Israel & human race,
   which we very much deserved and still deserve,
   He took the judgment that we should suffer upon Himself,
   receiving the judgment due all people for all time for all their sins,
   suffering & dying painfully even though He was an innocent man,
   thereby redeeming us by paying the penalty each of us owed.

Slide 65

1 Peter 1:18 ... you were not redeemed with corruptible things, like silver or gold, from your aimless conduct received by tradition from your fathers,
   19 but with the precious blood of Messiah, as of a lamb without blemish and without spot.

The just punishment for all those sins had to go somewhere,
   so He took it upon Himself.
This is the true glory of God – to take the judgment due us, on Himself
   As the Cup of Redemption is a memorial
   of the blood of the Passover Lambs on the doorposts,
   Yeshua made Cup of New Covenant a memorial of His blood,
   a renewal of His promise of redemption.
We saw earlier that the one who finds the Afikomen,
   the broken & hidden Matzah, receives a Passover gift.
In a striking parallel, those who find Yeshua whose body was also
   broken & hidden, also receive a Passover gift.
God has a gift He wants to give to all people,
   not just to those who find the Afikomen.
It's the gift of having our sins born away and of redemption,
   of having God's judgment <u>pass over</u> you.

Slide 66

John 5:24 Yes, indeed! I tell you that whoever hears what I am saying and trusts the one who sent me has eternal life—that is, he will not come up for judgment but has already crossed over from death to life!

To receive the Passover gift today, you must trust in what Yeshua did,
   sacrificing His life to redeem or ransom you.
And you must be obedient to what Yeshua says by repenting
   and making Him the Lord of your life.
Whether you believe in Yeshua or not,
we can <u>all</u> partake of the Cup of Redemption together as a memorial of
   the Redemption of the Jewish people from slavery in Egypt.

If you want to receive the Passover gift of personal redemption,
we invite you to drink this cup as the Cup of Redemption,
the memorial of the New Covenant in His blood
as a first step of faith and obedience.

For those who have already received that Passover gift of eternal life,
remember that Redemption means that our former slave owner – Satan
has no legal right to drag his former slave (you or I) back into slavery
because the price of our freedom has been paid by someone else.

Here's His **promise** concerning the Cup of Redemption:

"I have redeemed you with the precious blood of Messiah, I have paid the price so sin & Satan has no legal claim against you"

Please lift your cup as we give thanks. – **page 21**

Blessing on the Third Cup – *Cantor* – page 21

This is the Cup of Redemption, a memorial of the redemption
of the Jewish people from slavery in Egypt.
This is the Cup of the New Covenant in Yeshua's blood,
poured out for you for the forgiveness of sin.

*We receive Your **promise** tonight that You have redeemed us
by your blood
We covenant to walk in the fullness of this **promise**,
knowing sin & Satan have no legal claim on us.
This is a memorial of the Passover Lamb sacrificed
to cause the plague of death to pass over our forefather's houses.*

Take and drink. – **page 21**

Song [of your choice, using your own slides]

Slide 67

Matthew 10:32 "Whoever acknowledges me in the presence of others I will also acknowledge in the presence of my Father in heaven.

If you prayed to receive the Passover gift for the first time tonight,
tell someone about it.

ELIJAH'S CUP – page 21

I'm going to fill a special cup at the head table. It is Elijah's cup. Let's look at the next to the last verse of the Old Testament.

Slide 68

Malachi 4:5 (CJB) *Look, I will send to you Eliyahu the prophet before the coming of the great and terrible Day of ADONAI.*

That great and dreadful day of the Lord is usually interpreted as the coming of the Messiah.
Some people are waiting for the Messiah's first coming.
Messianic Jews & Christians are waiting for His second coming in which we also expect Elijah to have a part as one of witnesses.
So our seder includes a cup poured out for Elijah.
The door is opened to see if he has come yet.

[Someone] open the door and see if Elijah is out there.
Let's sing (or listen to solo of) Eliyahu HaNavi, – **page 21**

THE FOURTH CUP – page 22

Slide 69

Based on *Exodus 6:7* (CJB)… *I will take you as my people, and I will be your God.*

This cup is called **the Cup of the Kingdom**.
When God brought our forefathers out of Egypt & gave them the Mosaic Covenant, He set up His nation, His Kingdom.
He made us His own chosen people and became our God.
Here's His **promise** for this cup:

Slide 70

Yeshua said in *Matthew 6:33* **"But seek first the kingdom of God and His righteousness, and all these things shall be added to you."**

This **promise** is conditional on our seeking first His Kingdom, and following His will

Please lift your cup as we give thanks. – **page 22**

Blessing over the 4ᵗʰ cup – *Cantor* – page 23

Let's pray. We are thankful You brought our forefathers out of Egypt
and established Your nation, Your kingdom,
and that Your Kingdom is still prospering & growing in the hearts of Your followers.
We receive Your renewal **promise**
"to provide all our needs as long as we are seeking first Your Kingdom."
Lord may those who are searching to find the Kingdom of God find it.
May those of us who have found it seek to establish it in our lives.

Drink the 4<u>th</u> Cup.

Our Seder is now complete. We have completed the ancient journey.
We'll end with L'shanah Haba'ah – Next Year in Jerusalem.

Please all rise as we sing L'Shanah Haba'ah. Next Year in Jerusalem!

L'Shanah Haba'ah. Next Year in Jerusalem – **Page 23**

Appendix B

Yeshua's Last Seder Scripture Chart

YESHUA'S LAST SEDER CHART

Matthew 26	Mark 14
17 On the first day for matzah, the talmidim came to Yeshua and asked, "Where do you want us to prepare your Seder?" ...	12 On the first day for matzah, when they slaughtered the lamb for Pesach, Yeshua's talmidim asked him, "Where do you want us to go and prepare your Seder?" ...
20 When evening came, Yeshua reclined with the twelve talmidim; ...	17 When evening came, Yeshua arrived with the Twelve. 18 As they were reclining and eating, ...
26 While they were eating, Yeshua **took a piece of matzah**, made the b'rakhah (blessing), broke it, gave it to the talmidim and said, **"Take! Eat! This is my body!"**	22 While they were eating, Yeshua **took a piece of matzah,** made the b'rakhah (blessing), broke it, gave it to them and said, **"Take it! This is my body."**
27 Also he **took a cup of wine**, made the b'rakhah, and gave it to them, saying, "All of you, drink from it! 28 For **this is my blood**, which ratifies the New Covenant, my blood shed on behalf of many, so that they may have their sins forgiven.	23 Also he **took a cup of wine,** made the b'rakhah, and gave it to them; and they all drank. 24 He said to them, **"This is my blood,** which ratifies the New Covenant, my blood shed on behalf of many people.
29 I tell you, I will not drink this 'fruit of the vine' again until the day I drink new wine with you in my Father's Kingdom."	25 Yes! I tell you, I will not drink this 'fruit of the vine' again until the day I drink new wine in the Kingdom of God."
30 After singing the Hallel, they went out to the Mount of Olives.	26 After singing the Hallel, they went out to the Mount of Olives.

YESHUA'S LAST SEDER CHART

Luke 22

7 Then came the day of matzah, on which the Passover lamb had to be killed. 8 Yeshua sent Kefa and Yochanan, instructing them, "Go and prepare our Seder, so we can eat." 9 They asked him, "Where do you want us to prepare it?" ...

14 When the time came, Yeshua and the emissaries reclined at the table, and he 15 said to them, "I have really wanted so much to celebrate this Seder with you before I die! 16 For I tell you, it is certain that I will not celebrate it again until it is given its full meaning in the Kingdom of God."

17 Then, taking a cup of wine, he made the b'rakhah and said, "Take this and share it among yourselves. 18 For I tell you that from now on, I will not drink the `fruit of the vine' until the Kingdom of God comes."

19 Also, **taking a piece of matzah,** he made the b'rakhah (blessing), broke it, gave it to them and said, **"This is my body,** which is being given for you; do this in memory of me."

20 He did the same with **the cup after the meal,** saying, **"This cup is the New Covenant, ratified by my blood,** which is being poured out for you. ...

39 On leaving, Yeshua went as usual to the Mount of Olives; and the talmidim followed him.

John 13

1 It was just before the festival of Pesach, and Yeshua knew that the time had come for him to pass from this world to the Father. ...

2 They were at supper, ... 4 So he rose from the table, removed his outer garments and wrapped a towel around his waist. 5 Then he poured some water into a basin and began to wash the feet of the talmidim and wipe them off with the towel wrapped around him. ... , "If I don't wash you, you have no share with me." ... 12 After he had washed their feet, taken back his clothes and returned to the table, he said to them, ... 13 ...14 Now if I, the Lord and Rabbi, have washed your feet, you also should wash each other's feet.

I Corinthians 11
23 For what I received from the Lord... -

that the Lord Yeshua, on the night he was betrayed, **took bread**; 24 and after he had made the b'rakhah (blessing) he broke it and said, **"This is my body,** which is *[broken]* for you. Do this as a memorial to me";

25 likewise also **the cup after the meal,** saying, **"This cup is the New Covenant effected by my blood**; do this, as often as you drink it, as a memorial to me."

26 For as often as you eat this bread and drink the cup, you proclaim the death of the Lord, until he comes. 27 Therefore, whoever eats the Lord's bread or drinks the Lord's cup in an unworthy manner will be guilty of desecrating the body and blood of the Lord! 28 So let a person examine himself first, and then he may eat of the bread and drink from the cup;

John 18:1 (TLV)
When Yeshua had said these things, He went out with His disciples across the Kidron Valley, where there was a garden....

www.ingramcontent.com/pod-product-compliance
Lightning Source LLC
Chambersburg PA
CBHW050547160426
43199CB00015B/2567